IMAGES
of America

DUMAS

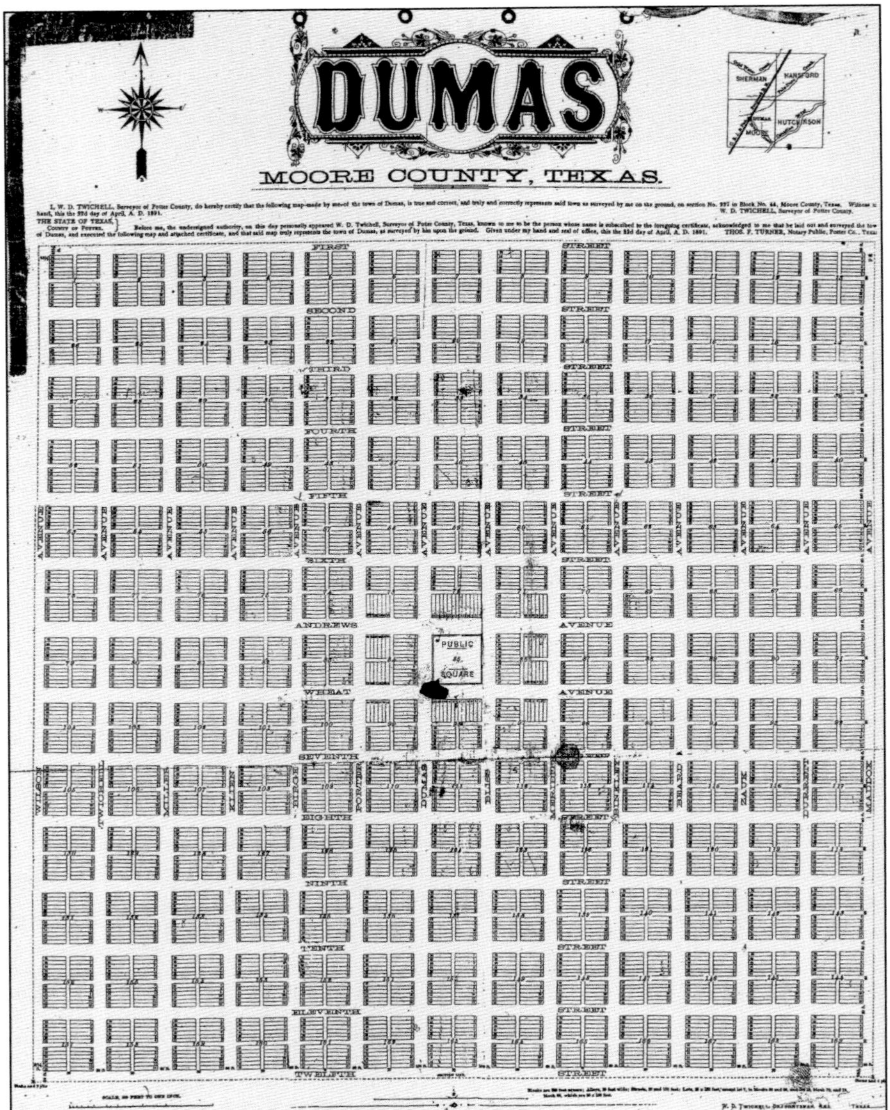

In 1891, Moore County was attached to Potter County for court procedures. The plat for Dumas, Texas, was filed at the courthouse in Amarillo. North-south streets were named for surveyors and shareholders in Panhandle Township Company. East-west streets were numbers and called avenues except for Second Street. The names of Wheat and Andrews Avenues interrupted the order by replacing Seventh and Eighth Streets. A barbed-wire fence soon enclosed the section that would become Dumas.

On the Cover: Standing on the porch of the newspaper office are, from left to right, Flo Brown, Katie Green, Gladys Bass, and Cara May McKee, editor of the *Moore County Pioneer*. The weekly newspaper was printed by Pioneer Publishing Company beginning in about 1909 and lasting until 1914. No other newspaper was published until 1927, when the first edition of the Moore County News was issued. That was the *Moore County News*. Since then, a newspaper has continually published biweekly editions. (Window on the Plains Museum archives.)

IMAGES
of America

DUMAS

Louise Carroll George

ARCADIA
PUBLISHING

ISBN 978-0-7385-7061-7

Published by Arcadia Publishing
Charleston, South Carolina

Printed in the United States of America

Library of Congress Control Number: 2008936536

For all general information contact Arcadia Publishing at:
Telephone 843-853-2070
Fax 843-853-0044
E-mail sales@arcadiapublishing.com
For customer service and orders:
Toll-Free 1-888-313-2665

Visit us on the Internet at www.arcadiapublishing.com

To Martha Crabb and Bert Clifton, friends and mentors

Contents

Acknowledgments

Since its beginning in 1976, Window on the Plains Museum has followed a path of growth and improvement. The board, staff, donors, and volunteers have made it into the best kind of place for research. I appreciate all their contributions. I also appreciate those who have preceded me in writing the history of our town.

I am truly grateful to everyone who donated photograph collections to the museum and to the board of directors for granting me permission to use them. Unless otherwise noted, the photographs in this book are from museum archives. For individuals who loaned me photographs from their collections, thank you. Gayle Stowers, Dale Pearson, and Carolyn Stallwitz, who made photographs for me, I appreciate you.

Sincerest thanks to Terri George, museum director, and Anna Reznik, summer intern. They cheerfully searched the archives with me to find photographs I needed.

For helping search in their archives, my thanks go to Warren Stricker, Panhandle Plains Museum Research Center at Canyon; Lisa Hanbury and Nick Olson, XIT museum at Dalhart; and to Ed Benz, Judy Mihm, and Lynn Hopkins, Hutchinson County Museum at Borger.

Thanks to members of the Moore County Historical Commission, advisors on many events taking place during their lifetimes in Moore County.

Special thanks to Martha Crabb, Glynda Pflug, and Bert and Marvin Clifton for reading and correcting content in this text. Your help and encouragement are deeply appreciated.

My thanks go to Kristie Kelly, my editor at Arcadia Publishing, for her kindness and patience.

INTRODUCTION

The town of Dumas began as a business venture when, in 1890, Louis Dumas of Sherman, Texas, decided to heed a strong urge telling him to go West and build a town. With several partners, he formed the Panhandle Townsite Company, which purchased a section of land, 640 acres, in unorganized Moore County where Dumas now stands. A surveyor platted the town and named the north-south streets after investors. The company drilled a water well on the town square and erected a combination office, post office, and general store. The second story, with no partitions, second floor that served as a hotel. Dumas moved his family to the new town and began raising cattle and promoting his newest project.

Moore County was organized in 1892 with 167 eligible voters—male residents and property owners age 21 or over—signing the petition. The required minimum was 150; however, county records reveal only 50 men met the requirements. Promoters of county organization scouted up all the cowboys, laborers, drifters, and perhaps a few local dogs to reach the magic number. Unfortunately, and surely purposefully, the petition failed to be entered in the records.

A two-story wooden courthouse with a cupola was built at a cost of $6,536 without a penny in the county coffers. The post office, a general store, and a corral served the few farmer-stockmen in the county. Cowboys from the big ranches, resenting intrusion into their domain, avoided Dumas except to shoot up a few signs.

The treeless plains of the Texas Panhandle can be beautiful when rain is abundant and vivid green grass sparkles with a profusion of colorful wildflowers. It can also be stark when howling winds flatten the dried grass. The area is famous, or perhaps infamous, for rapid and extreme weather changes. During winter, a lovely day can suddenly change when a massive, snow-laden cold front blows in from the north or a savage southwest wind bends the trees and fills the air with dust.

During the county organizational election in 1892, cowboys outnumbered farmer-stockmen and town residents, as Louis Dumas discovered when he lost the race for county judge to a cowboy. He was disappointed. He was also disappointed that the town failed to grow. A couple of years later, a severe blizzard killed most of his cattle. Dumas, deciding to cut his losses, moved back to Sherman.

During the first two decades of the new century, the permanence of Dumas was assured. Numerous businesses opened, including a bank, a barbershop, a blacksmith shop, and a meat market, plus a lumberyard, a cleaning shop, and a Ford garage. Telephone service began in 1905 when wires were strung along barbed-wire fences from a small exchange in neighboring Hartley County. Many dynamic young men who helped shape the town and the county for the next half century joined the few permanent residents: F. R. "Bob" Powell, Fred Makeig, W. J. Morton, J. C. "Jake" Phillips, Ezelle Fox, Noel McDade, and J. A. McMurry, to name a few.

The population of the town and the county grew slowly. Census records reported 561 persons in the county in 1910 and an increase of only 10 a decade later. Early in 1927, Dumas, with a population of 250, was a farming and ranching village 20 miles from a railroad. Nevertheless, the rumble of heavy machinery and the cursing of greasy roughnecks in neighboring panhandle counties did not go unheard in Moore County. On July 20, the boom that would sustain the county from that day until this began. Seven miles northeast of Dumas, an oil well rig began punching a hole in the ground. The rig's bit found natural gas deep in the earth.

Soon the county was alive with drilling rigs, turning Dumas into a boomtown. With the rigs came men and families, business activity and money. That same autumn, the Dumas Chamber of Commerce organized to secure a railroad and a highway to serve Dumas. During the next couple of years, North Plains Telephone Company began stringing wires on poles around the town and the county, West Texas Utilities began 24-hour electrical service, and bond elections passed to build a courthouse, to pave roads in the county, and to build a brick school with a gymnasium and an auditorium. The newly incorporated City of Dumas purchased a shiny red Seagraves 500-gallon fire truck.

The oil and gas boom in the Texas Panhandle spurred the Chicago, Rock Island, and Pacific and the Atchison, Topeka, and Santa Fe Railroads to build track to service the many new industrial plants utilizing the gas and oil. In March 1931, the Rock Island began laying track across the northern edge of Moore County, and on May 22, the first Santa Fe train puffed into town amid wild celebration. Dumas had changed from a village to a sizable town.

Louise George's images and text skillfully tell the story of Dumas as it grew and prospered through the decades.

—Martha L. Crabb
Archivist, Window on the Plains Museum

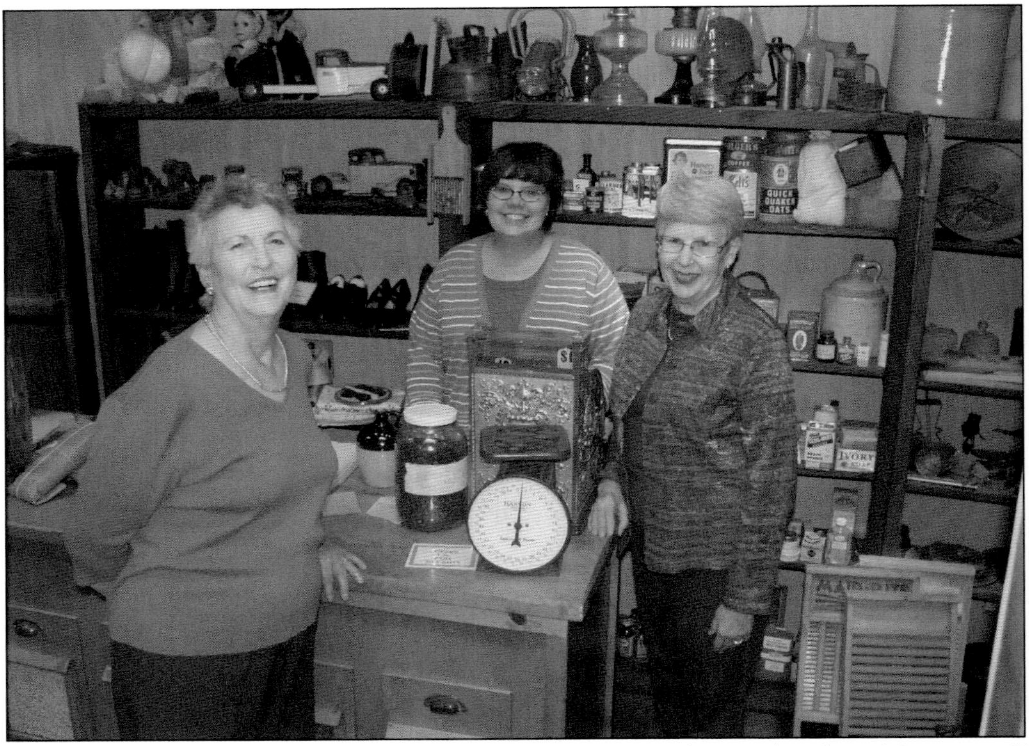

Author Louise Carroll George is on the left; with her are Window on the Plains Museum staff members Terri George (center), director, and Glynda Pflug, business manager. They are standing in the general store display in the museum.

One

The Texas Panhandle

Four classifications were given to the Native Americans who lived in the Texas Panhandle during four different time periods. The first, Paleo-Indians, arrived about 9000 BC. Big game hunters, they survived by hunting the huge bison and mammoth in the area. They and the large game were gone long before the 4000 BC arrival of the Meso Indians, who were hunters and gatherers. Neo-Indians were in the panhandle by about 1000 BC; hunters and farmers, they left more evidence of their presence than did nomadic tribes that followed. It is uncertain as to why they left, but some believe they were forced out by the Apache, the first of the historic Native Americans. Apache hunted small game, but buffalo was their mainstay. Their rule lasted until the early 1700s, when the Comanche took over the panhandle and much more.

The Comanche, superior in horsemanship and war making, took what they wanted. Their domain extended deep into the South Plains and into Kansas, Colorado, and New Mexico. In 1790, they formed an alliance with the Kiowa. Stories of their long-distance raids and depredations are well known.

In the 1870s, the panhandle became increasingly treacherous for traders, travelers, and buffalo hunters. The army was sent to conquer the Plains Indians. Within months, it was done. As they took the land and its bounty from others, it was taken from them. By 1875, they were forced onto reservations, and Fort Elliott, in Wheeler County, was established to keep them there.

Only a couple of hunters remained in the northern portion of the panhandle after the gory business of exterminating the buffalo was done. For a short time, the rest of the panhandle was quiet and still. In the 1938 "Special Anniversary Edition" of the *Amarillo Sunday News and Globe*, Laura V. Hamner described that period: "No homes . . . No people . . . Nothing but sky and grass . . . Sky rounding from sharp skyline to sharp skyline . . . Acres and oceans of grass."

Inevitably ranchers would be drawn to those acres and oceans of grass where there was open and free range. A new era had begun.

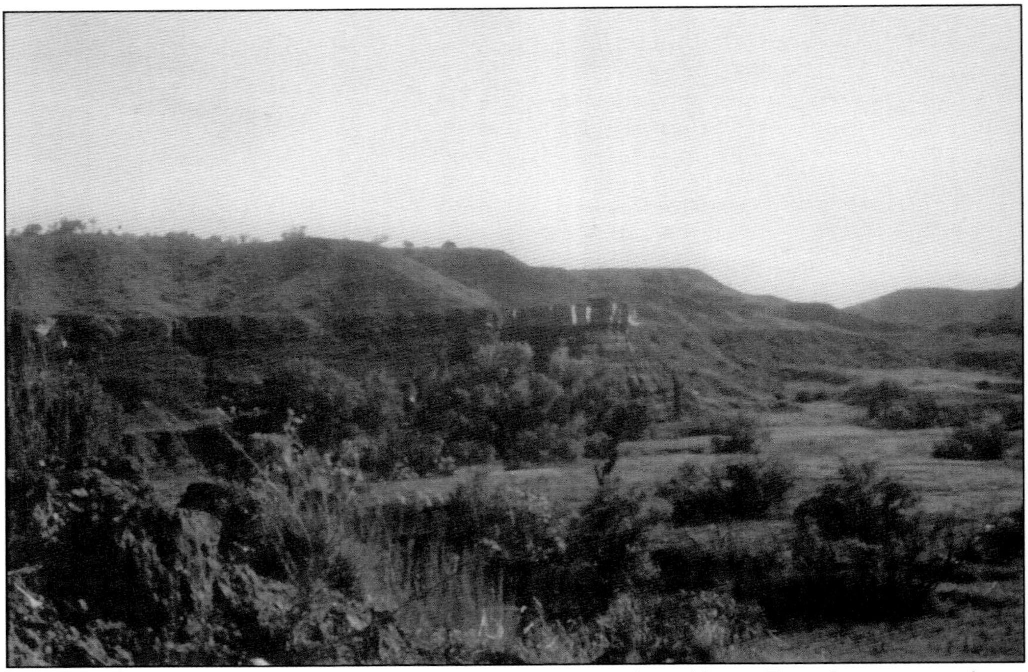

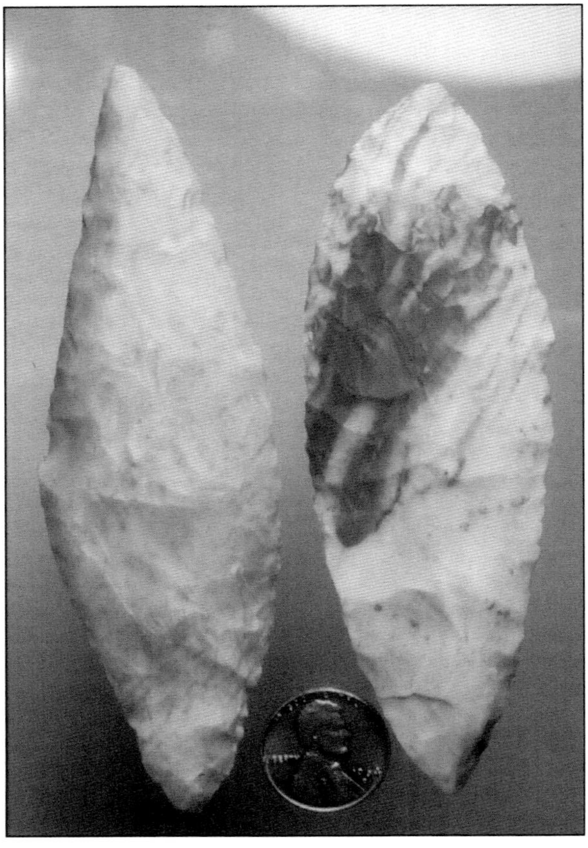

The Alibates Flint Quarries are the only national monument in Texas. Evidence shows that flint quarries near the Canadian River were mined as early as 11,000 years ago. Different cultures of Native Americans who lived along the Canadian river traded the flint with other tribes. It has been found in ancient sites throughout the Great Plains. The beautiful multi-colored flint is unlike any other flint in the world. Very hard, it was prized for making weapons and tools such as these knives from the Antelope Creek people culture. (Both, courtesy Martha Crabb.)

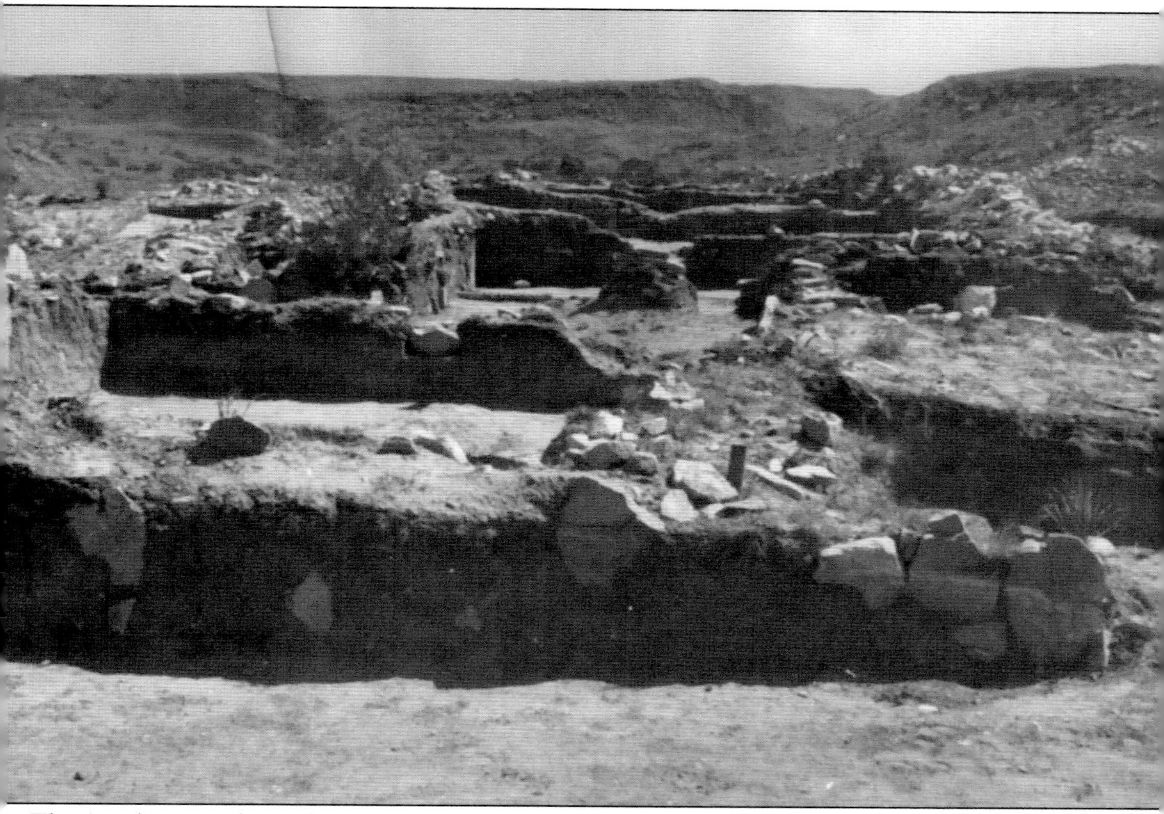

The Antelope Creek people were in the panhandle around the year 1200. They hunted plentiful game in the area, including bison, deer, and antelope. Their main weapon was the bow and arrow, as evidenced by the many arrow points found at excavation sites. Unlike the nomadic cultures that followed, their rock-slab homes were permanent residences. They built them along the Canadian River and its tributaries where they were assured a source of water. It appears that a central room was built, and one by one, other rooms were added. An excavation in the late 1930s discovered 26 such dwellings in one location. Though it is uncertain as to why the Antelope Creek people left, it is believed they were gone by 1541 when Coronado explored the area. (Courtesy Hutchinson County Museum.)

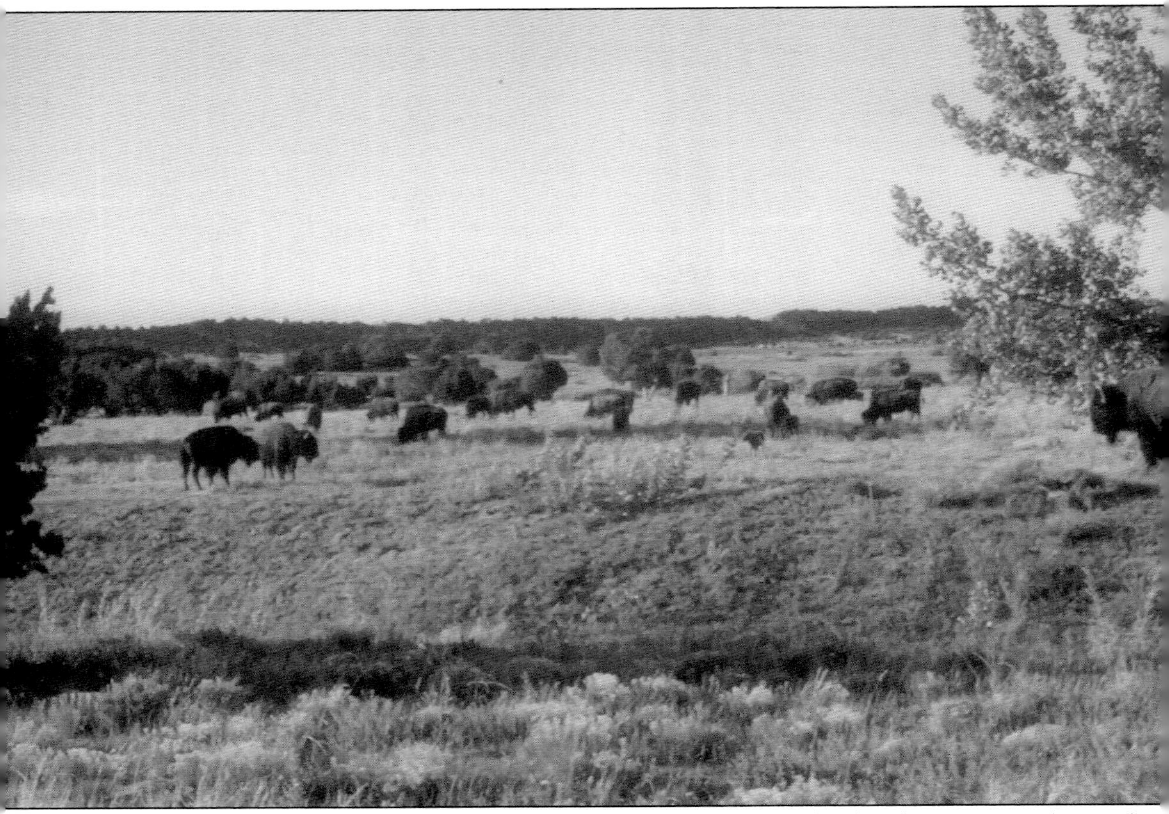

Enormous herds of buffalo once roamed the panhandle. Comanches lived in tepees and moved when the buffalo herds moved. When a buffalo was killed, the Native American men skinned it, then rested and feasted while women finished dressing the animal. They killed only what they needed and wasted little. Flesh that wasn't used immediately was dried into jerky. Sinew was used for bowstrings and thread; kidneys for canteens; bones, horns, and hoofs for cooking and eating utensils. The horns were also used to make bows and ceremonial headdresses. The hides were used to make teepees, blankets, clothing, and saddles. It is of little wonder that the sight of rotting carcasses left by buffalo hunters infuriated the Plains Indians. (Courtesy Martha Crabb.)

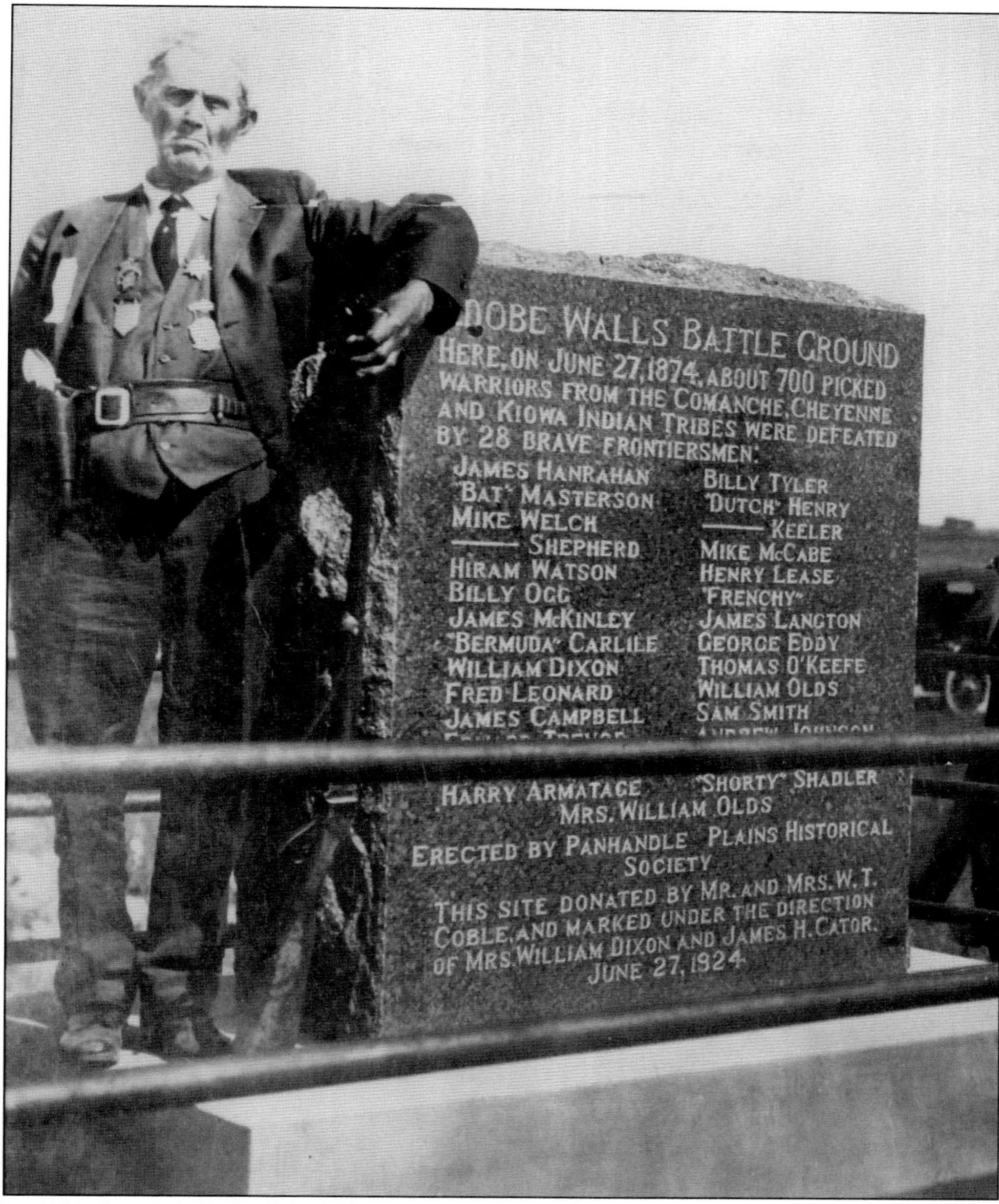

In 1874, demands for buffalo hides significantly increased profits for hunters. As the number of hunters increased in the panhandle, so did attacks on them. Four were killed within a short period of time. Taking heed of the warning, but unwilling to give up their lucrative occupation, hunters began to merge into larger groups. On June 24, one woman and about 20 men, including famous Bat Masterson, were at Adobe Walls trading post in Hutchinson County. They were ill prepared when Native Americans made a surprise attack, but their long-range rifles gave them an advantage, and their losses were minimal. Fifty years later, in 1924, a reunion and dedication was held at Adobe Walls. Andrew Johnson, one of the men at the battle, stands by the monument dedicated to those who participated in the battle, which signaled the beginning of the Red River War. (Courtesy Hutchinson County Museum.)

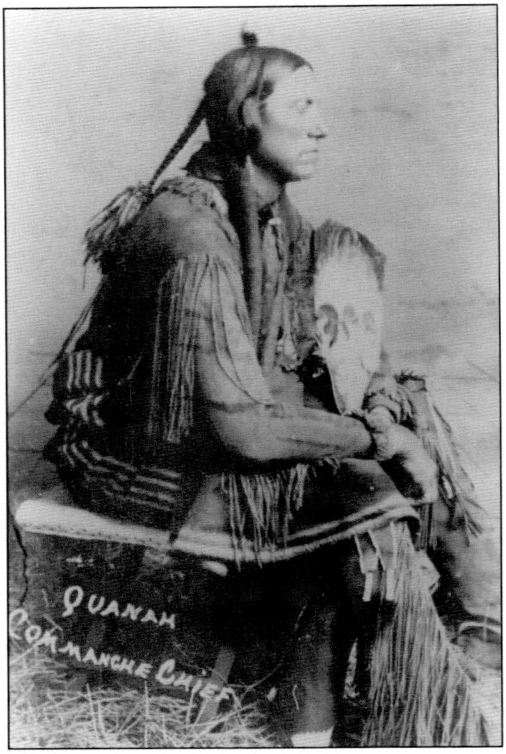

Quanah Parker, the son of white captive Cynthia Ann Parker, and medicine man Isa Tai led the attack at Adobe Walls. Prior to the battle, Isa Tai convinced the American Indian men that he had magic paint that would repel enemy bullets. When casualties proved the magic nonexistent, Quanah Parker became the sole leader of the Comanches in the panhandle. (Courtesy Hutchinson County Museum.)

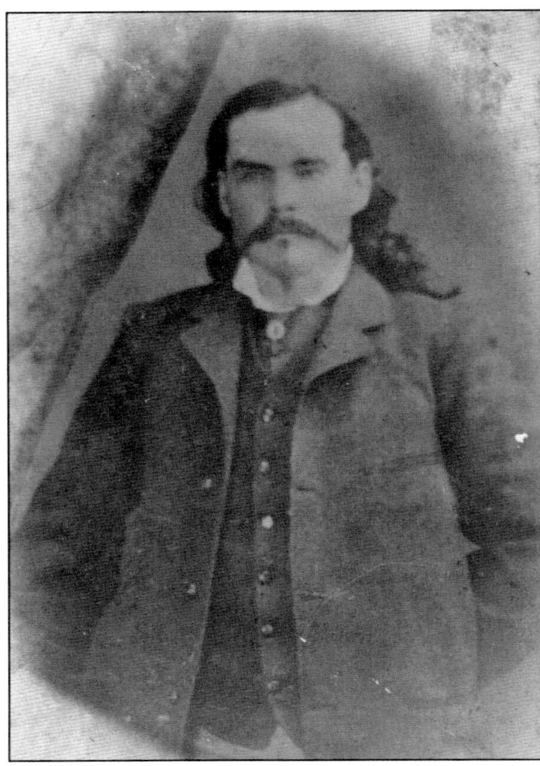

Buffalo hunter Billy Dixon was at Adobe Walls when it was attacked. His weapon was a Big 50 Sharps rifle. He is credited with using it to hit a Native American at a distance of 1,583 yards. Dixon is said to have claimed it was mostly luck. He soon gave up buffalo hunting and went to work as a scout for the army. (Courtesy Panhandle Plains Museum.)

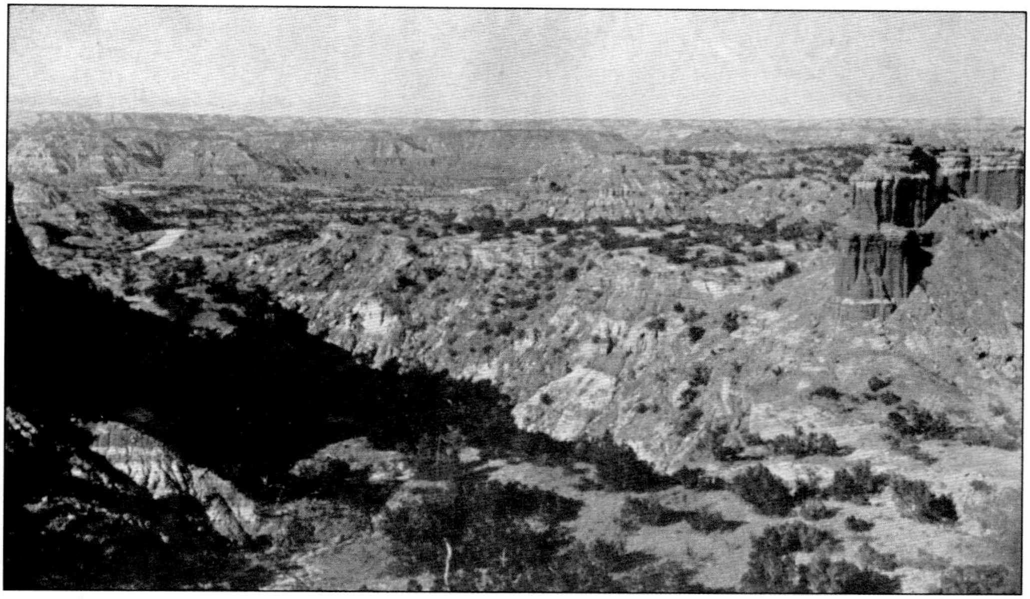

After the Battle at Adobe Walls, the army came to the panhandle to stop the conflict. A major battle during the Red River War took place in Palo Duro Canyon. For three years, Col. Ranald Slidell Mackenzie (right), commander of Fort Richardson near Jacksboro, had campaigned against marauding Kiowas and Comanches. In September 1874, Mackenzie learned of a large encampment in Palo Duro Canyon and marched his men to the location. Casualties were few because the Native Americans left camp and hid along the canyon walls. Mackenzie ordered destruction of their lodges and winter food supply. Over 1,000 horses were captured and destroyed. The Native Americans' future was bleak, and many reported to reservations. There were three more battles in the war but none as significant as Mackenzie's. (Both, courtesy Panhandle Plains Museum.)

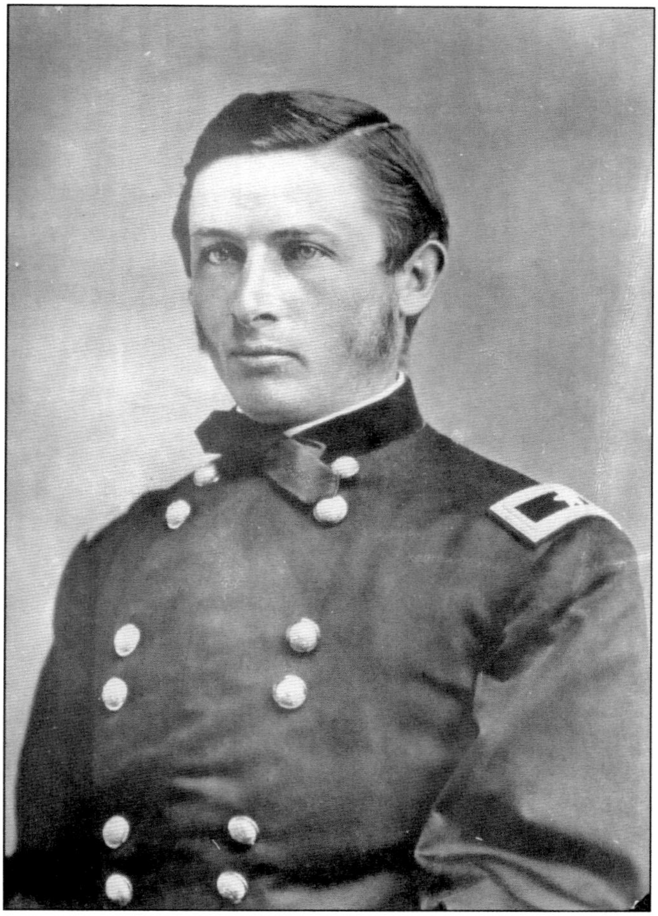

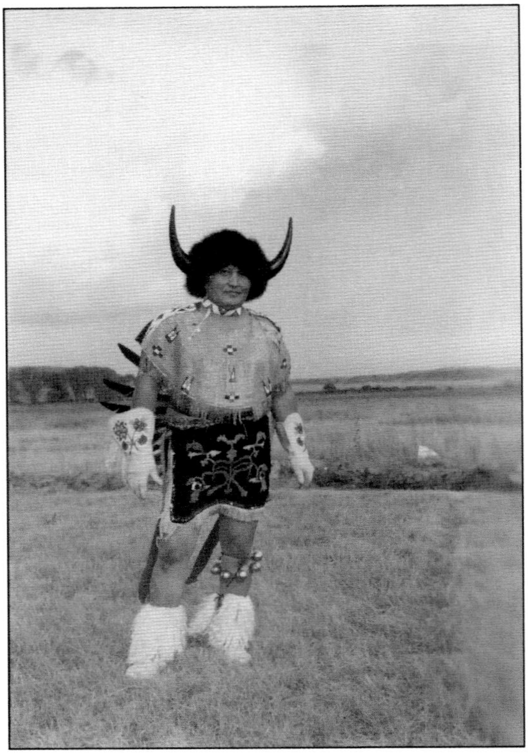

The Plains Indians were utterly defeated when the Red River War ended. They had no recourse but to surrender to life on a reservation. But their heritage was not forgotten. In 1941, the Plains Indians of a later generation gathered at Adobe Walls to dedicate their own monument to their ancestors at the battle. At left, Spencer Lalo Asa, Kiowa, poses in his dance costume complete with buffalo horns. He was a member of the Kiowa 5, a group of renowned artists. Below is George "Woosie" Wachitaker, Comanche, an artist, flute player, and dancer. These two men dedicated their lives to the preservation of the culture and heritage of their people. (Both, courtesy Hutchinson County Museum.)

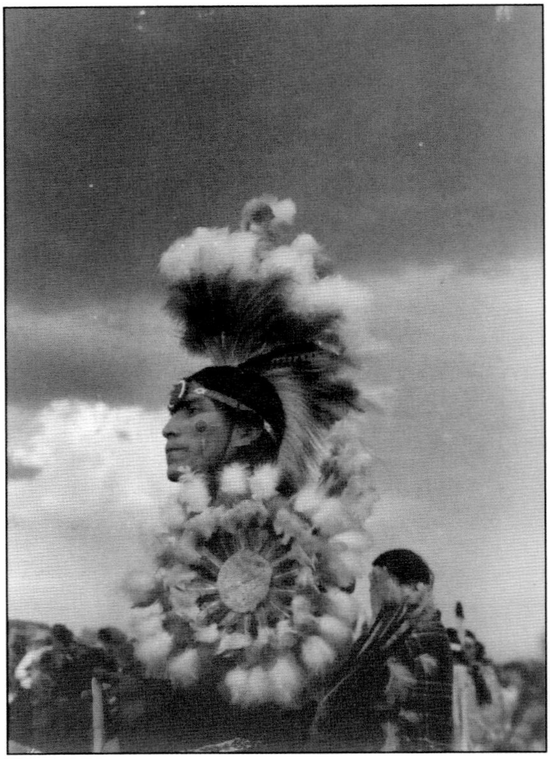

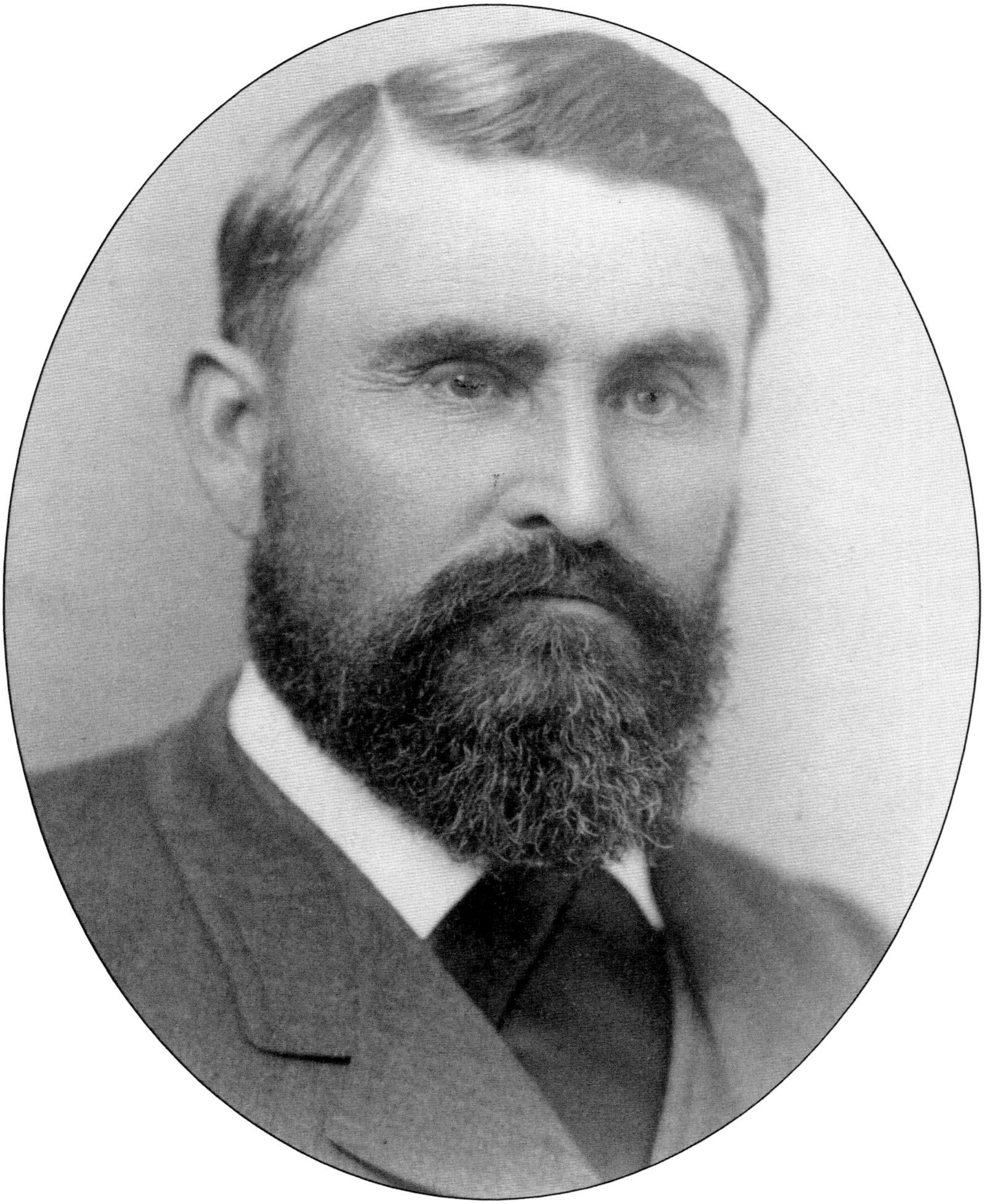

Charles Goodnight, born in Illinois, became a scout and guide for the Texas Rangers during the Civil War. He was not the first cattle rancher in the panhandle, but he was the first of his kind, amassing huge numbers in both land and cattle. In 1876, he drove his cattle to market in Kansas City but did not sell them at the low price he was offered. He drove them back to Texas and grazed them along the Canadian River in Oldham County. After sheep men arrived there, he agreed to leave, provided they agreed to stay out of Palo Duro Canyon where he planned to take his cattle. He established his first ranch there. Later he and partner John Adair bought 12,000 acres to start the famous JA Ranch. Under Goodnight's management, it expanded to 1,325,000 acres and 100,000 cattle. (Courtesy Panhandle Plains Museum.)

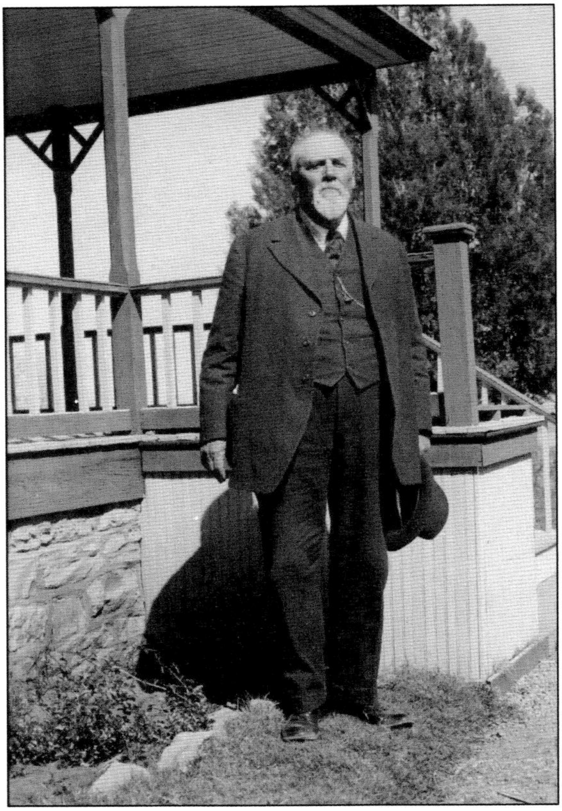

Thomas S. Bugbee organized several cattle drives from Texas to Kansas and Colorado. In 1876, Bugbee and his family lived in western Kansas among hostile Native Americans. With safety in mind, Bugbee moved his family to Hutchinson County and started ranching with 1,800 head of cattle. In 1881, the ranch and its 12,500 head of cattle sold for $350,000. (Courtesy Panhandle Plains Museum.)

The Bugbees lived in dugouts before building this rock home north of the Canadian River about 5 miles west of the site of the Adobe Walls Battle. Because they feared the return of the Native Americans, they built this home with walls 26 inches thick and two gun ports in every room. It was named Bugbee Fort. (Courtesy Hutchinson County Museum.)

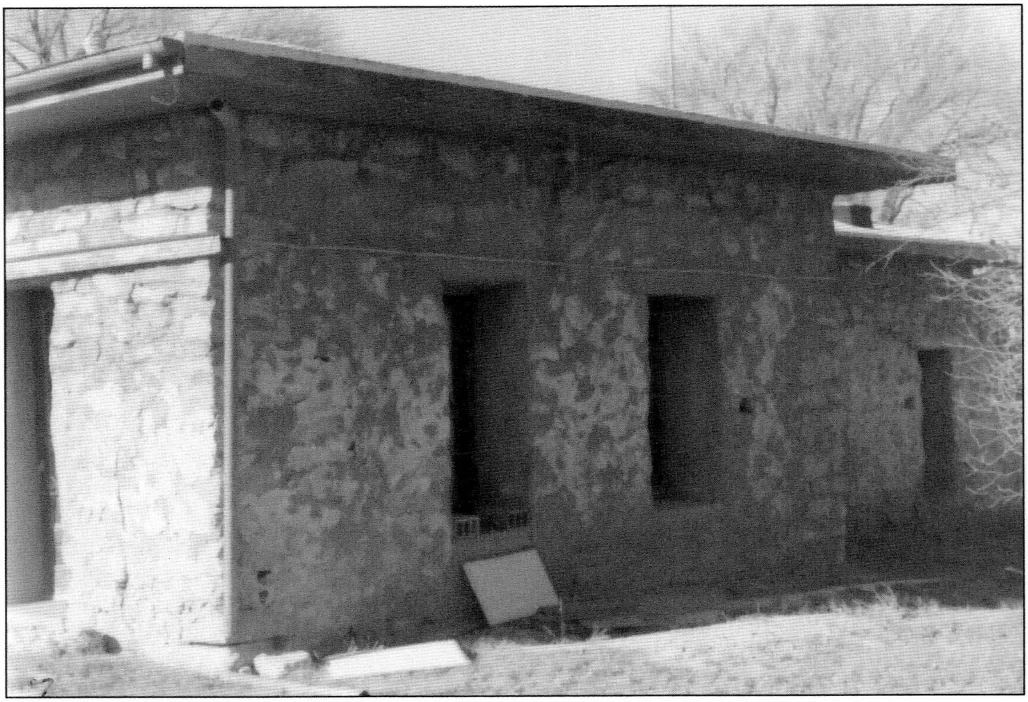

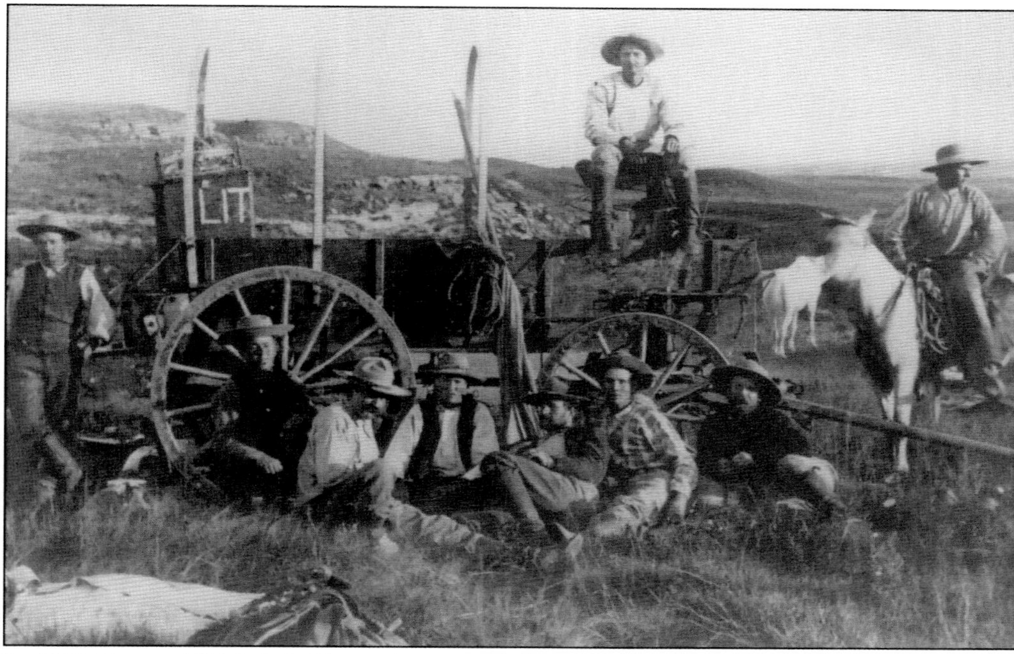

In 1877, George W. Littlefield's cattle pastured through the winter on grassland near Tascosa. The huge LIT Ranch started that summer. LIT cattle grazed on over 1,000 square miles of land in the panhandle for four years without a legitimate claim on the land being filed. When Littlefield left Texas, he sold 14,000 cattle to Prairie Cattle Company, found free grass in New Mexico, and began again.

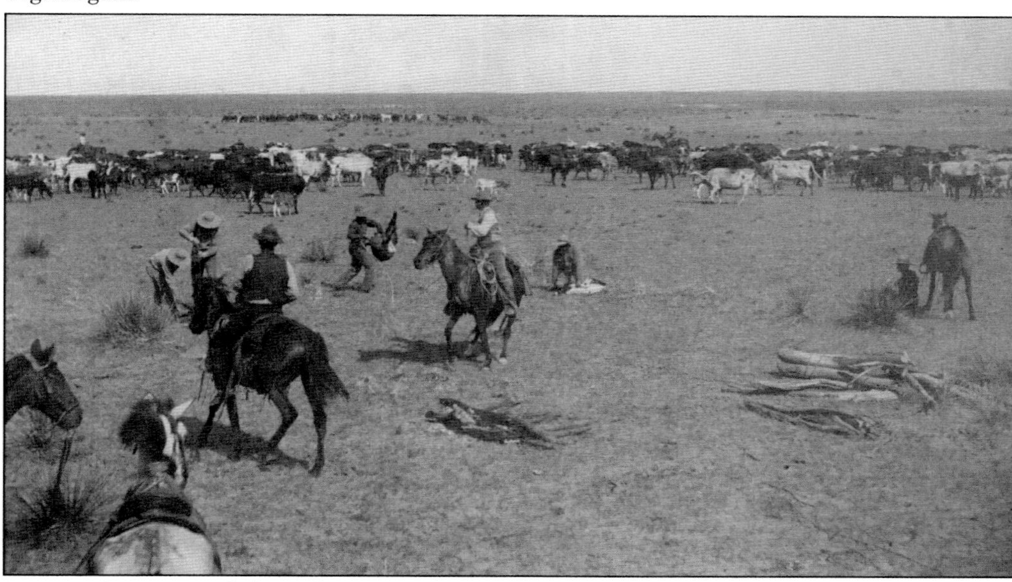

In 1884, the state traded 3 million acres of public land in northwest Texas to a group in exchange for building the state capitol in Austin. A group member went to England to solicit investors and raised $5 million in financing. Fences were built, and the first 2,500 cattle were pastured on the XIT in 1885. By 1888, there were 150,000 cattle and 150 cowboys to tend them. (Courtesy XIT Museum.)

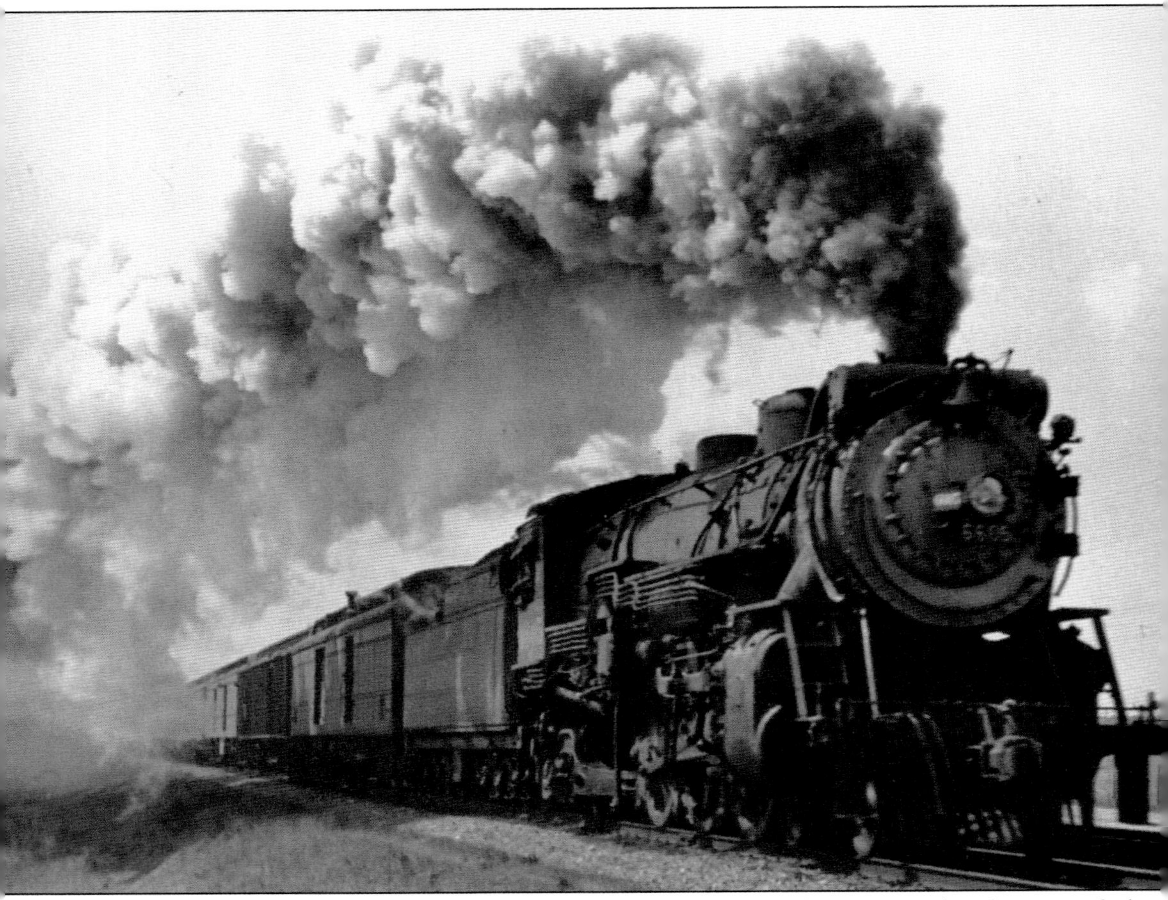

Other huge ranches were established and enjoyed prosperity for a time. They began to feel pressure when supply caught up with demand and cattle prices dropped. Blizzards, drought, and dust storms were also problems. Some of the big ranches had already broken up when settlers began to swarm into the panhandle and fence off their property. Free-range land disappeared. Construction of the railroads brought easier access to the land in the panhandle. The Denver and Fort Worth line was started in 1882. It entered the panhandle in the southeastern corner and exited the northwestern corner in 1888. In the next few years, other railroad lines would be crisscrossing the area and contributing their part to the settling of the panhandle. (Courtesy Panhandle Plains Museum.)

Two

The First 10 Years

When Texas was annexed in 1845, the U.S. government allowed the state to keep its public lands to pay off tremendous debts. Land in the panhandle and west Texas was given to railroad companies in exchange for building lines in eastern and southeastern Texas. Sections of land were arranged in a checkerboard pattern, with alternating sections designated as school lands or railroad lands.

Census takers recorded the population of Moore County as zero in 1880. That would change—but neither quickly nor easily. The cheap land was attractive, but it was two inventions that made it practical to risk one's future in the desert-like area: the windmill and the barbed-wire fence.

In 1890, Louis P. Dumas and other Sherman, Texas, businessmen formed the Panhandle Townsite Company. They planned to buy cheap railroad land in the panhandle, plat a town, and sell tracts. The next year, they bought a section of flat prairie land in Moore County that lay just to the north of a range of breaks and rolling hills.

Within months after the group purchased the land, they had it surveyed and platted, filed the plat in the neighboring Potter County courts, named the town and its streets, and built a land office building. Other individuals built a general store and a small building that would be used for a courthouse.

Dumas was a man of action, as evidenced by how soon the new town acquired its post office. Less than three weeks after the town was surveyed on April 22, Dumas filed the application. On June 27, the town was granted its post office.

Dumas's efforts to build the town were met with droughts, blizzards, prairie fires, and a plague of grasshoppers. Some settlers became discouraged and left. A recession in 1893 caused even more to leave; for a while, the little town struggled on.

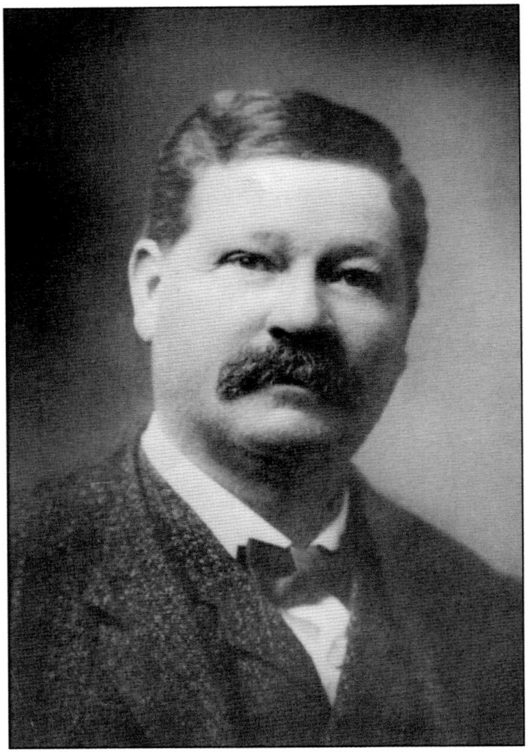

Louis P. Dumas was born on April 16, 1856, near Sherman, Texas. His father died when he was 19, and for a time, he stayed to help on the family farm. By 1890, he had married, moved onto his own farm, and achieved success in real estate. He became interested in land speculation, and in 1891, the energetic and ambitious Dumas left Sherman to go "build a town."

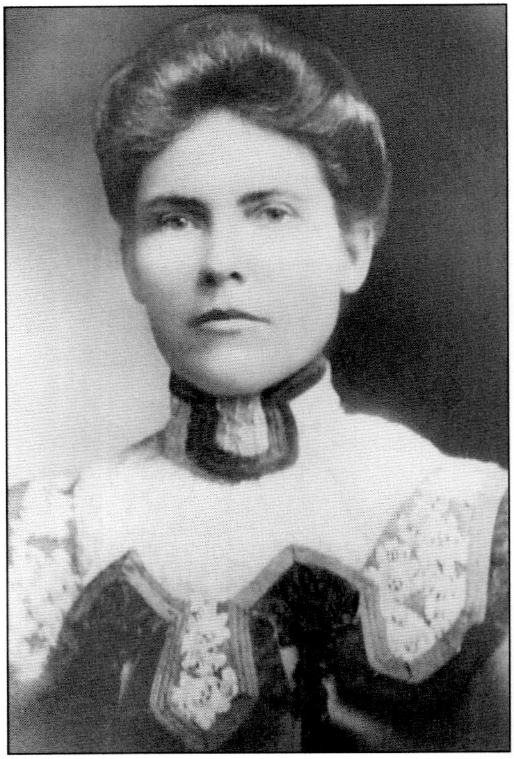

Florence Emberson married Louis Dumas in 1879. They had a daughter who died when she was five, and Florence was inconsolable, even after a son was born. When she and the baby joined Dumas, their home was a dugout. Later, in a letter to the Window on the Plains Museum, Florence's daughter wrote, "In the strangeness of her surroundings . . . she regained her invincible spirit, her courage and her faith."

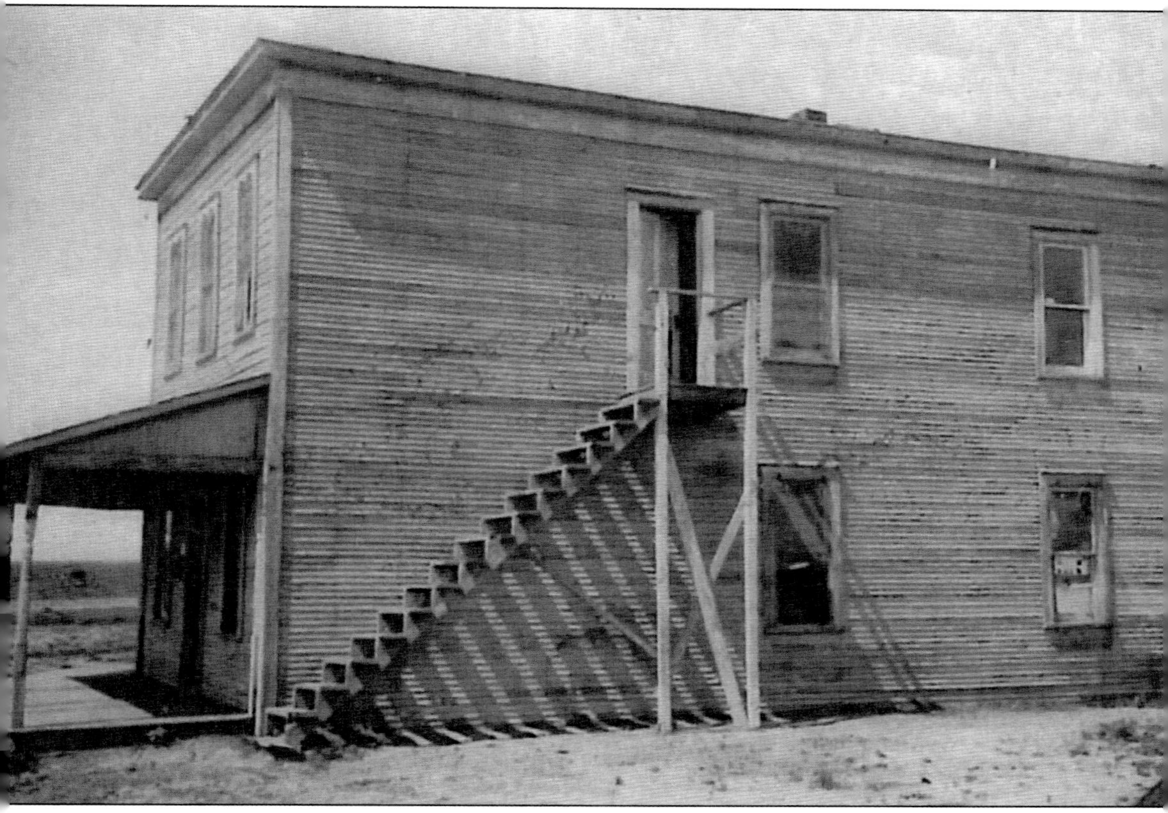

The first building in Dumas was a two-story building, much like the one in this illustration. No photograph is available of the first one, but its story has survived. It sat in the center of a section and for a time was surrounded by nothing but grass. The first floor housed the land office and a little later a general store and post office. The hotel was on the second floor. Known as the "bull pen," it was for men only, as there were no partitions, and guests slept on cots or bedrolls on the floor. Women had to seek shelter elsewhere. A couple from Van Alstyne, Jeremiah and Elizabeth Portman, was hired in late 1891 to run the hotel. When they arrived at the hotel, they found only a cowboy's bullet-riddled body. The town was completely deserted. The Portmans stayed for a while, but Elizabeth became ill, Jeremiah became discouraged, and they returned to Van Alstyne.

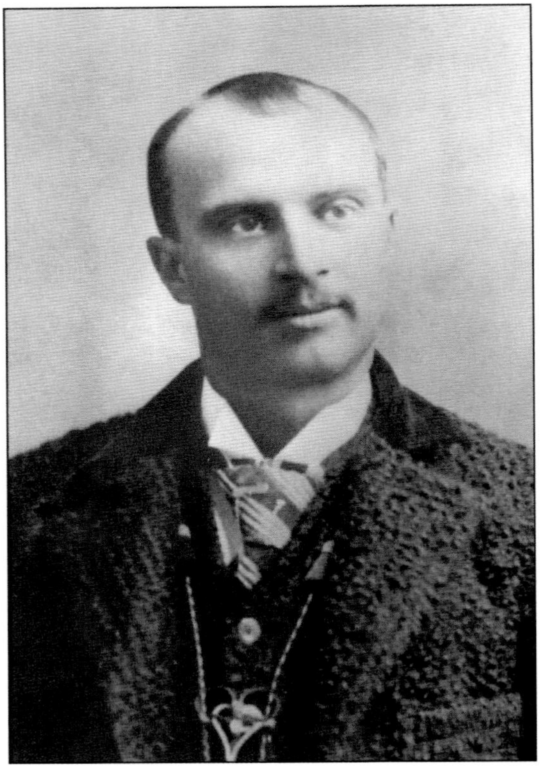

In 1892, Louis Trumble ran against Louis Dumas to become the county's first judge. Trumble was born in Canada, came to Texas as a child, and at 18 became a cowboy. According to one source, Dumas showed his disregard for his opponent by referring to him as a greasy windmill tender. But the 50 registered voters of Moore County preferred the cowboy and elected Trumble.

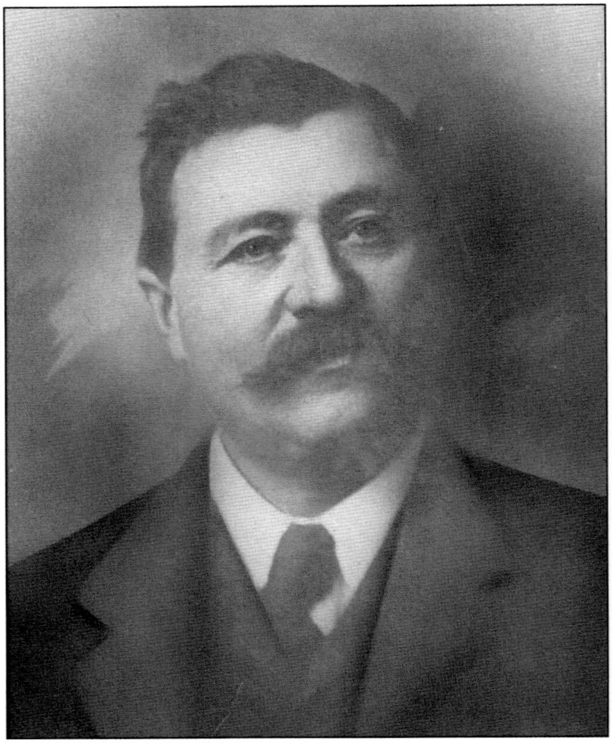

W. H. Lewis was elected as the first sheriff and tax collector of Moore County. Little is known about him, but his job must have been a challenge. Many of the settlers who came met defeat and quickly moved on. Large ranches had line camps scattered all around Dumas, but none of them had headquarters in Moore County.

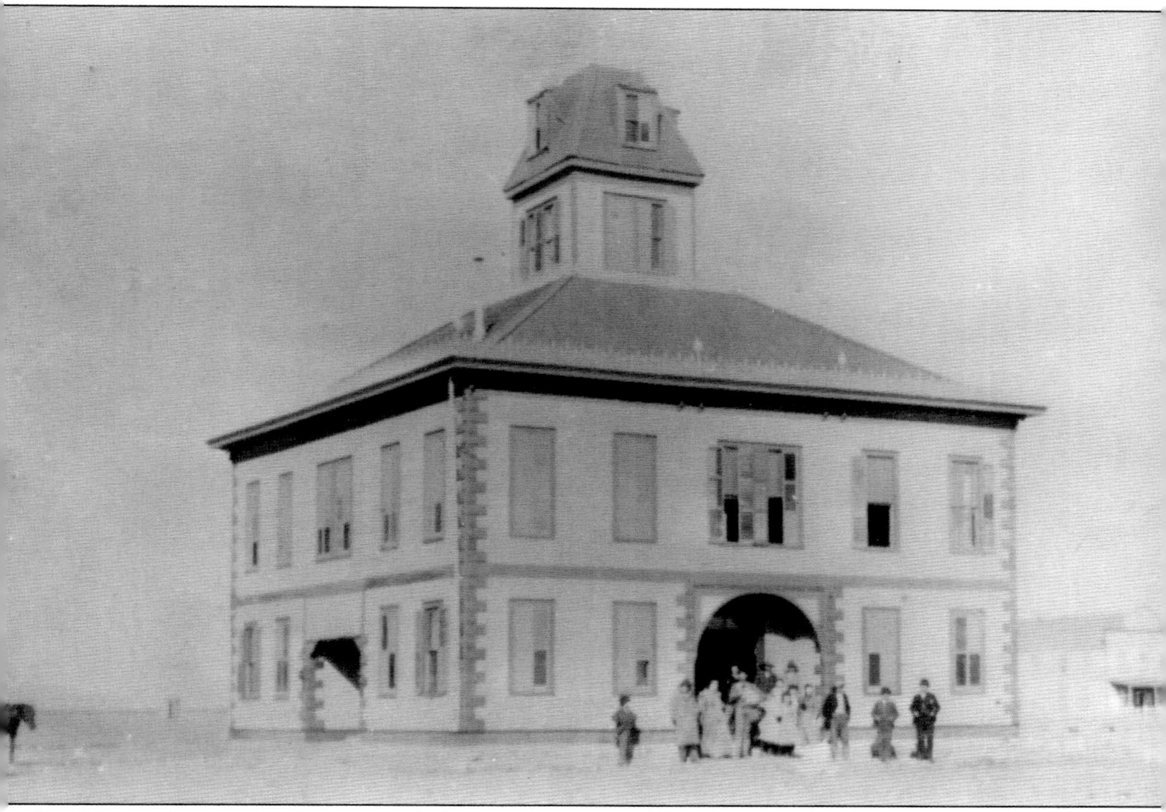

In 1892, county commissioners awarded a contract to J. R. Ryan for the construction of a two-story frame courthouse on the town square. It was completed in May 1893. The building, furniture, safes, and incidentals cost a total $6,536. The county also purchased the well that was drilled on the square by Panhandle Townsite Company. The well provided water until the late 1920s. Freighters and travelers were welcome to camp on the courthouse grounds, but there were rules. Horses could be watered at the water tank, but bathing was strictly prohibited. The second story of the courthouse was used by churches and organizations as a meeting place. It was also used as a dance hall and sometimes as a hotel. Albert Jones, an old cowboy, told a friend, "You didn't stay there unless you was desperate. The bedbugs was bigger than you."

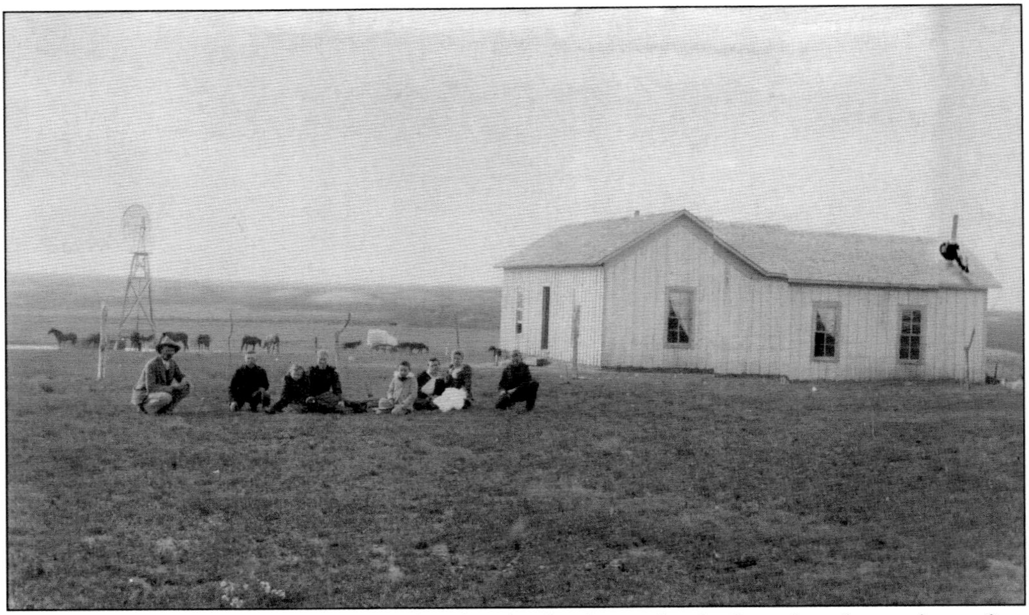

Families on small farms and ranches often lived miles from schools. Some hired a teacher to live with them and also took in one or more neighbor children during the week. The S. A. Bull family moved to Dumas in 1893 and had one of the earliest schools in the county. Here, S. A. and Mrs. Bull, students, and the teacher are outside the Bull home.

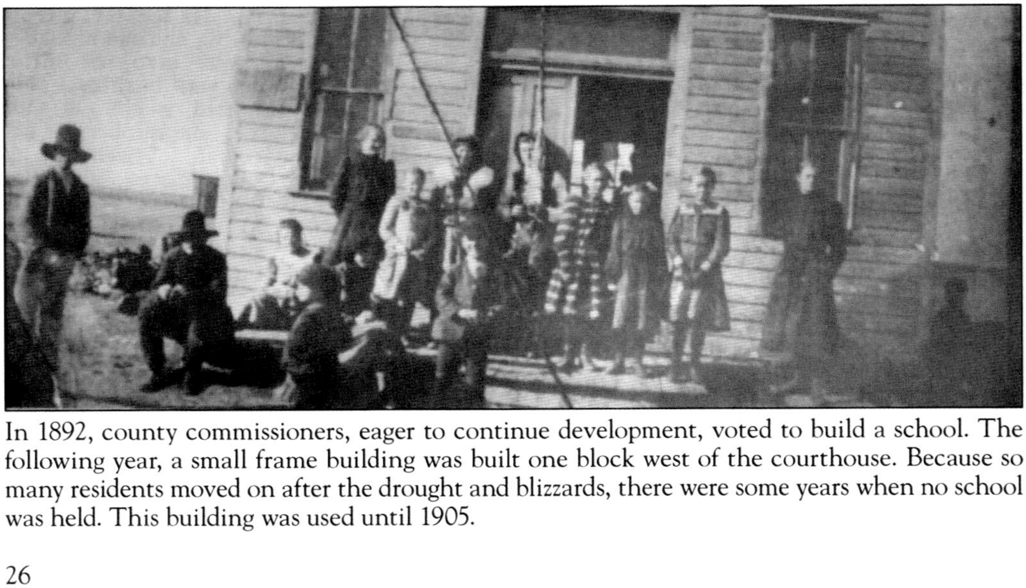

In 1892, county commissioners, eager to continue development, voted to build a school. The following year, a small frame building was built one block west of the courthouse. Because so many residents moved on after the drought and blizzards, there were some years when no school was held. This building was used until 1905.

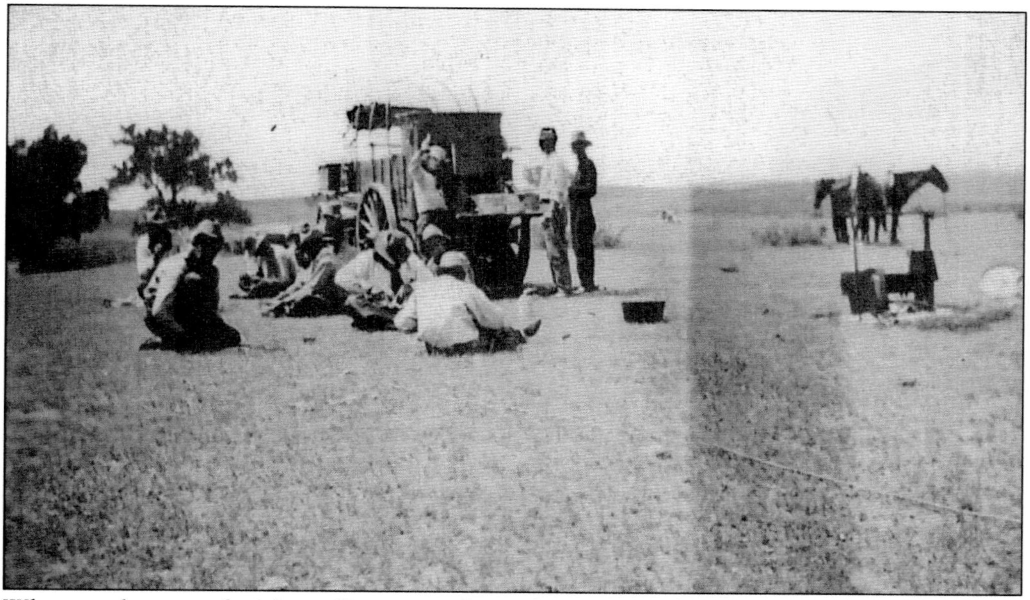

When payday came for Moore County cowboys, they were ready to go to town and have a little fun. The courthouse dance hall was a lively place at night. Since Dumas had no jail, a partier who got too rowdy was chained to a cottonwood tree near the well. If the offense was serious, he was taken to jail in Channing the next day.

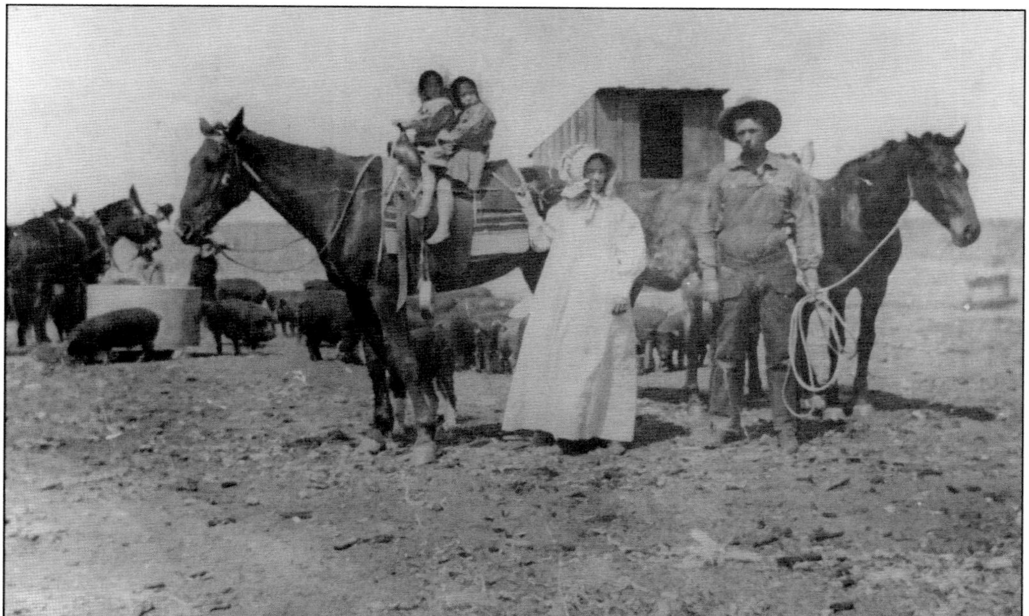

On the way to their new home in Moore County, settlers arrived by train in Channing and usually had to unload their livestock from a rented boxcar. There was no way to transport cash crops to market, and livestock production would provide their main source of income. The only grain crops grown were for feed until automobiles became available. (Courtesy Hutchinson County Museum.)

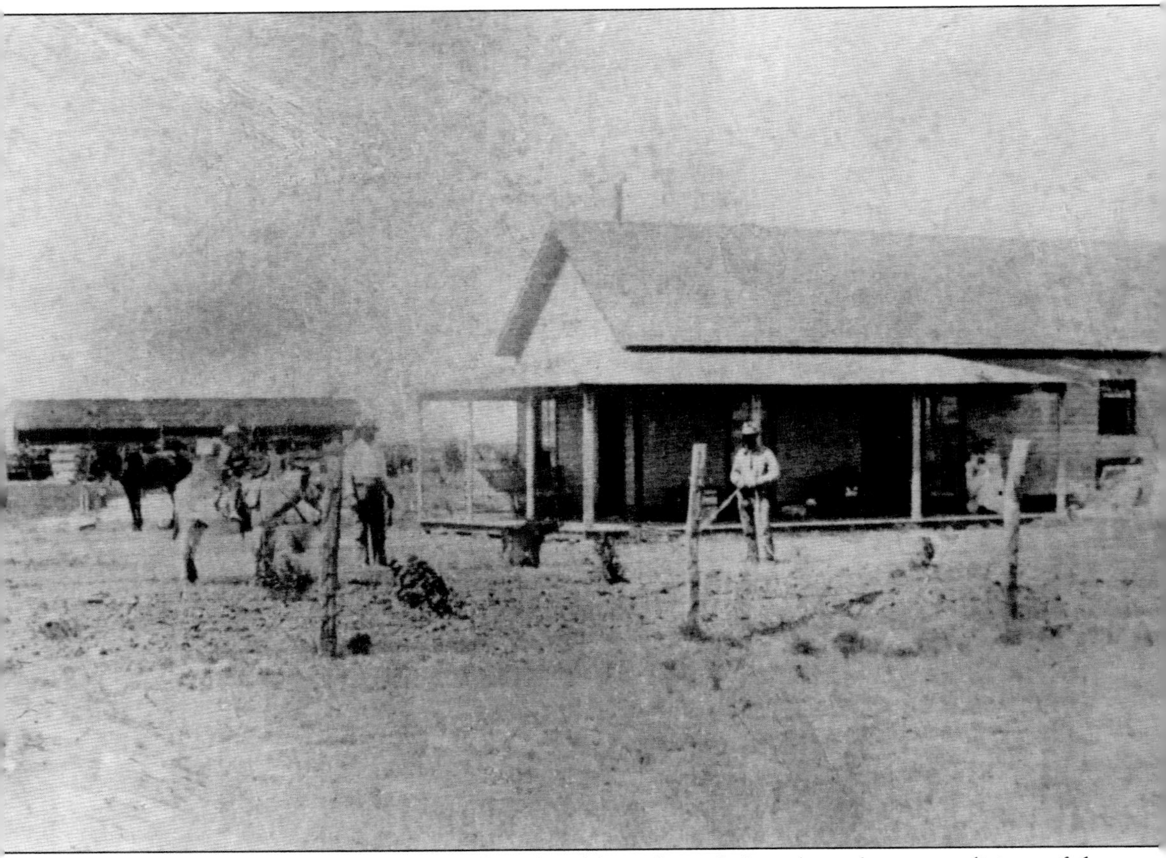

Louis Dumas persevered through droughts, blizzards, and the other adverse conditions of those first few years. By 1895, he had established a successful cattle-raising business, built this home for his family, and planted an orchard. In the photograph, his young son, Lamont, is mounted on the horse; Dumas stands nearby, and Florence is on the porch with their young son, Fred. Their good times would not last. A blizzard that winter, in 1895, took a tremendous toll. A letter written by his daughter, Mary, is on file at Window on the Plains Museum. She wrote, "Mama told me she could have walked on dead cattle in any direction as far as she could see." It was all too much for Dumas. Being a practical man, he quit Dumas and returned to Sherman County.

Three

A Farming and Ranching Village

When a Methodist minister arrived in Dumas in 1901, there was only one resident to hear his sermon. At least three times in the first 10 years of Dumas's existence, it became a ghost town. But the town would not die. Settlers who stayed were joined by a few others and then a few more. Merchants responded to the town's and ranches' growing needs, and the town survived.

In the early 1900s, there was still cheap land available in the area, and real estate companies were declaring the golden opportunities available in Moore County. In spite of their best efforts, the county population from 1900 to 1910 increased by only 352 persons. Evidently, word of the hardships spread as fast as agents' advertising. The next 10 years were even worse; only 10 people were added to the rolls.

The town grew slowly, with a new family moving in occasionally and a new business starting sporadically. A couple of general stores, a hotel, a bank, and an abstract office were started before 1910.

In *100 Moore Years*, Fred Squyres summed it up best when he wrote, "Agriculture in Moore County had its ups and downs from its earliest beginning in 1890 through the 1930's. Farmers made money one year and lost it the next year." Farmers who stuck it out tried to find new ways to supplement their income. The first wheat crop in Moore County was grown in 1900, but production of grain crops did not increase significantly until trucks and trains were available.

Area farmers profited from greater demands for hogs, cattle, wheat, and grain sorghum during World War I. The benefits were short-lived, however. Soaring prices resulted in overproduction, leading to a depression when the war was over. Once again, farmers in the area suffered extreme losses. Some would declare bankruptcy. Others barely escaped that fate and stayed to wait for a better year.

Dumas developed into a small, quiet town. It, too, waited for a better year.

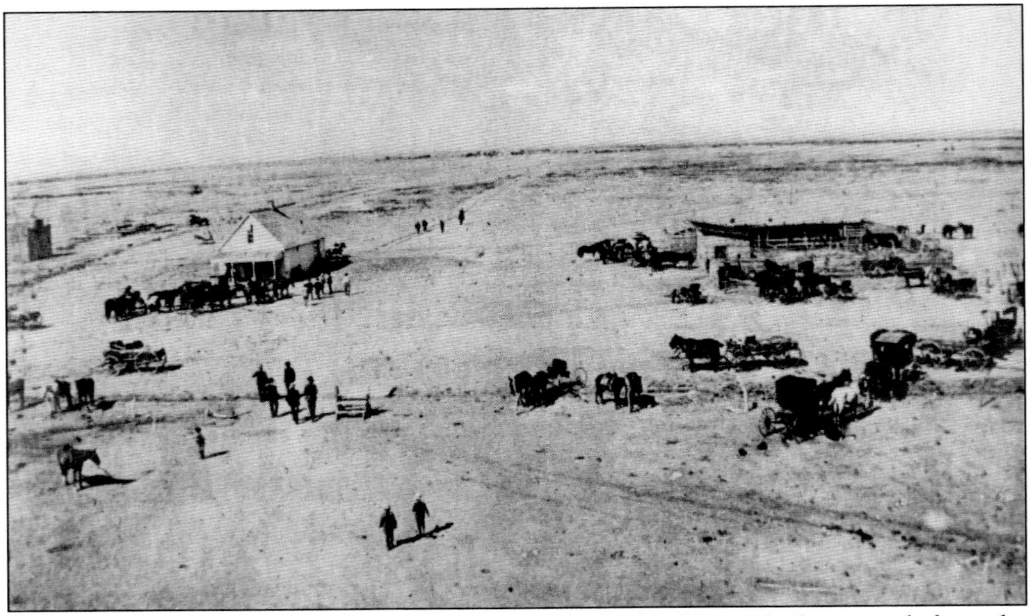

This photograph had the following notation on the back: "Dumas looking north from the courthouse, prior to 1904." The large building on the left is the general store. On the far left is the original land office/hotel/post office building. With so many buggies in town and most of the men wearing suits, there must have been something special happening.

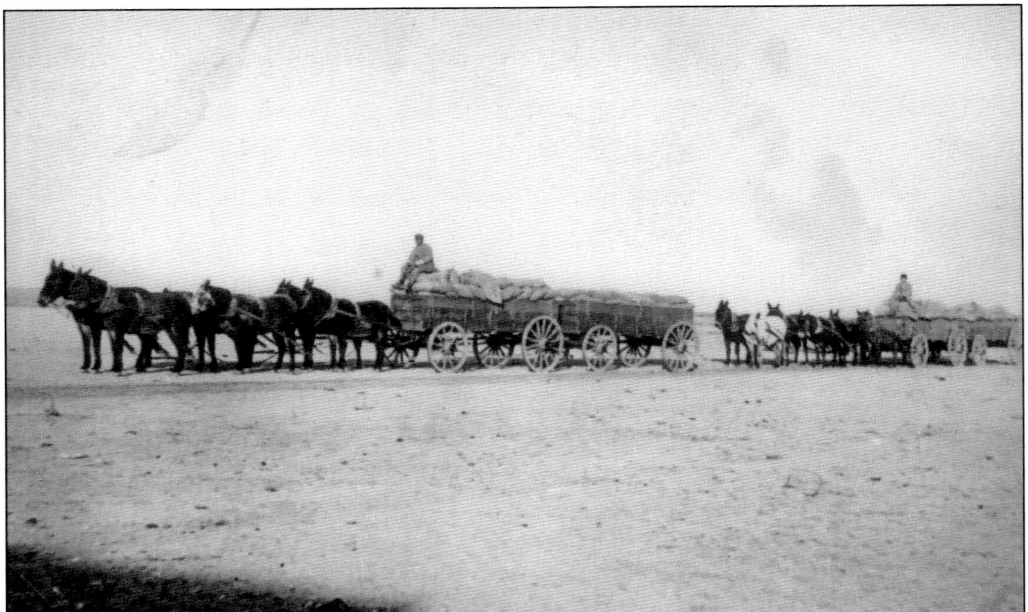

Since Dumas had no railroad and trucks were not yet available, freighting was an important occupation around the dawn of the 20th century. Most supplies were freighted from Channing or Dalhart. Will Jeter came to Dumas in 1897. Here he (on the left) and Jim Ball are shown on the flat plains west of Dumas with a load of feed.

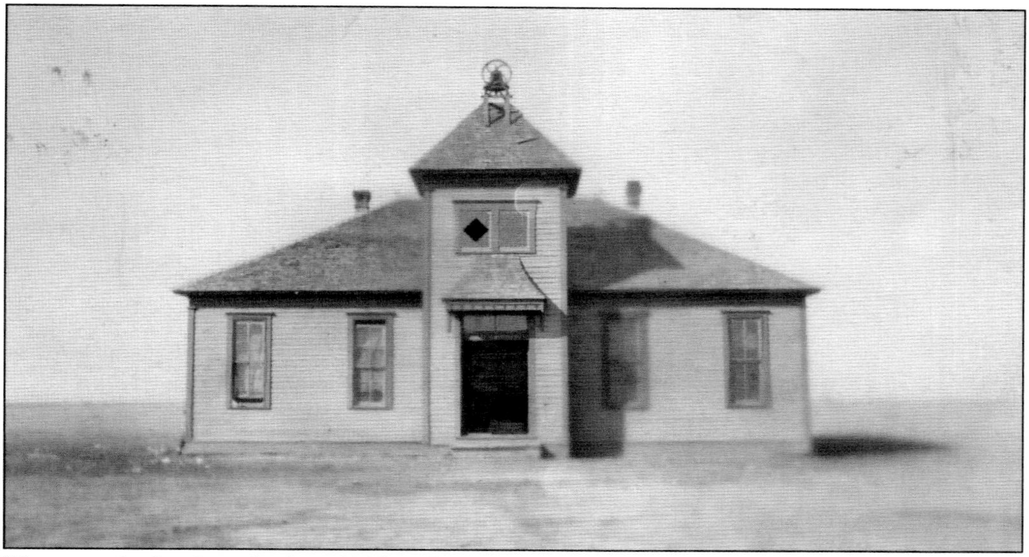

The second school was built in 1905 on Dumas Avenue and Second Street. The two-story frame building had a tower with a bell on top. After the building was completed, two teachers were hired. This photograph was dated 1912.

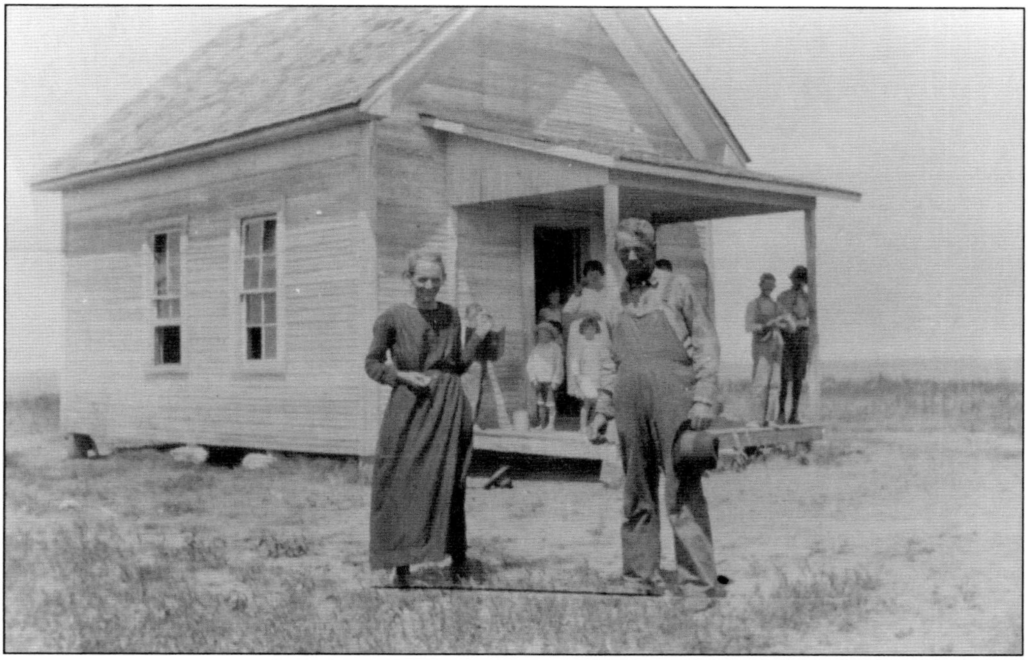

On farms and ranches, neighbors often banded together to build a school, and it was usually named for the person who furnished the land. This school in the Middlewell community, southwest of Dumas, was called Harbert School. Its only foundation was large stones. A longtime Dumas resident stated that when a family's children got too old for school or the family moved, the building was placed on a sled, taken to a new location, and given another name.

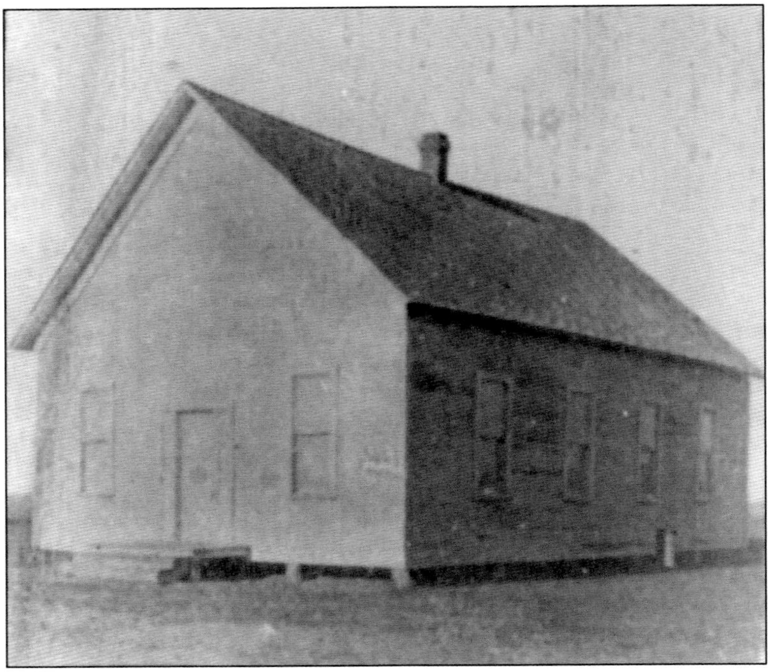

The R. A. McNabb family moved to Moore County in 1893. Within weeks, McNabb organized a Sunday school. First Baptist Church of Dumas was organized in July 1894 with 11 members. Like the town, it went through hard times. At one time, there were only two members: Mr. and Mrs. McNabb. The church held on and prospered after a time. Members built this church in 1915.

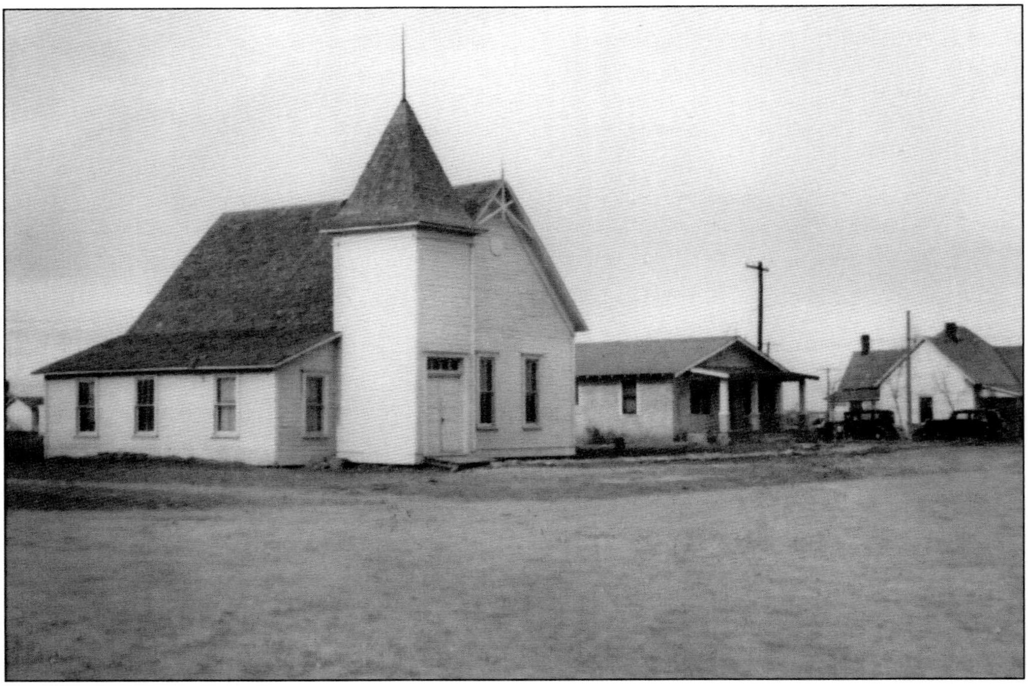

In February 1901, the Reverend W. C. McKeown, a Methodist minister, preached his first sermon in Moore County at Blue Creek School on the Trumble ranch. In March, he preached at the schoolhouse in Dumas, and in August, he organized a church, the Methodist Church, with seven members. In 1903, James Winford Hunt came to pastor the Dumas church and to oversee the construction of this building.

Alice Brown Burnett and husband, J. D., came to Dumas in 1901. He was a rancher and served as sheriff from 1908 to 1912. The couple had 11 children. The *Moore County Pioneer* carried a memorial tribute to Alice. It read, "Mrs. J. D. Burnett—Wife of Sheriff Burnett. She was loved by her boarders and was so patient at all times, a very unusual woman."

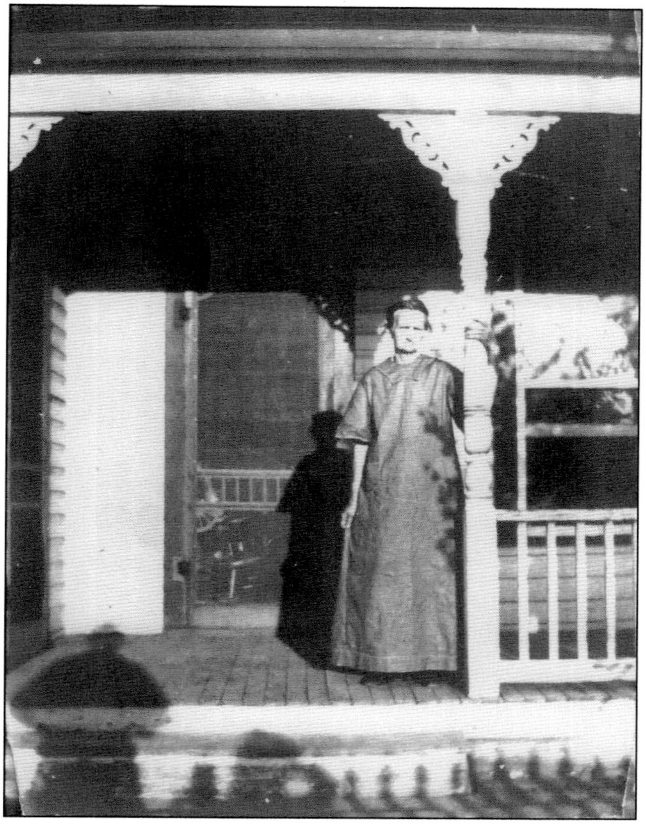

Martha Elizabeth and Ozy B. Burnett came from North Carolina to Hall County. Martha and two small sons went back while he improved the land. After returning two years later, she had six more children. In 1917, the family moved to Dumas. Martha worked hard caring for her family. A man once said about his grandmother, "Like most women back then, whatever it took, she done it." He could have been describing Martha.

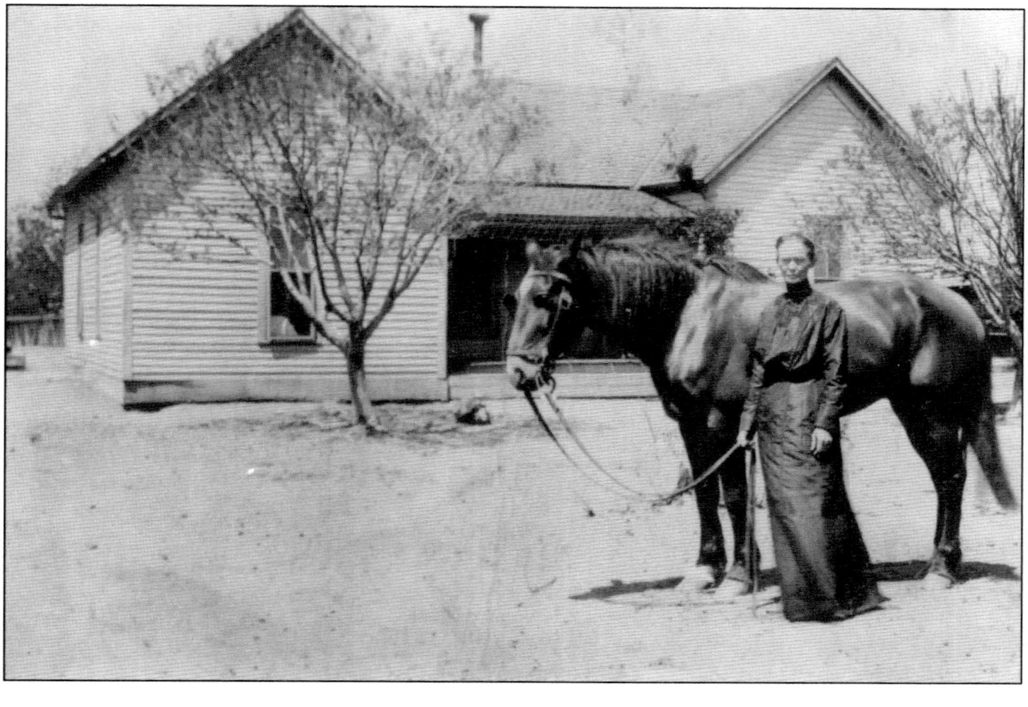

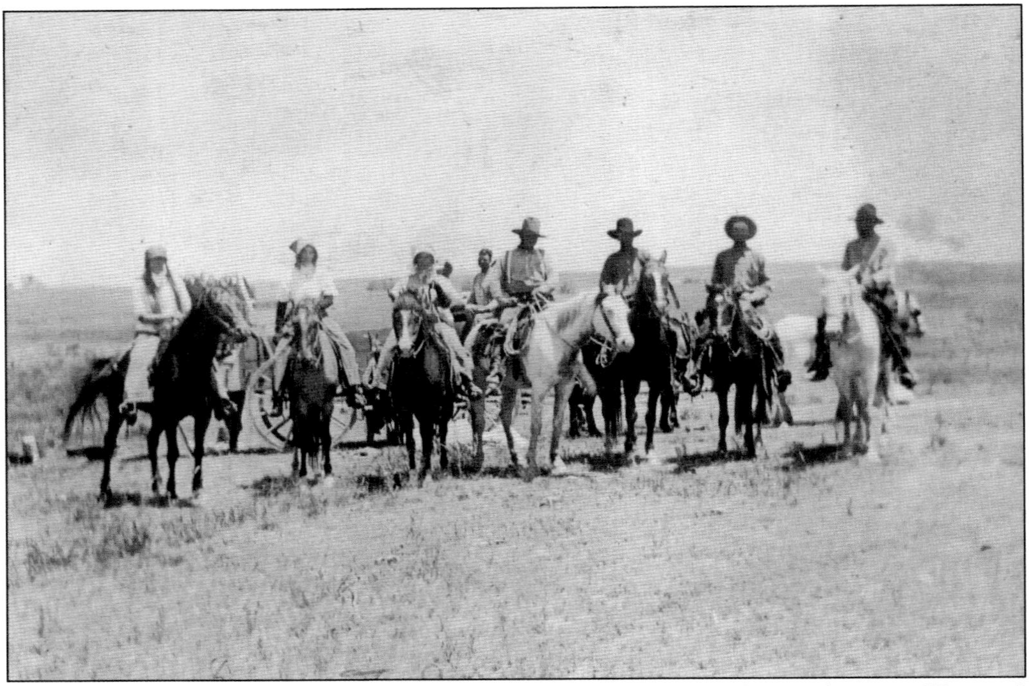

This 1912 photograph was labeled "Joe Record and help, Bar X ranch 16 miles east of Dumas." Joe is in the center on the light-colored horse. The three helpers on Joe's left should dispel any belief that ranch women were always in the home tending their domestic duties. Many of them "took a break" by crawling into a saddle to help work cattle. (Courtesy Lola Starkey.)

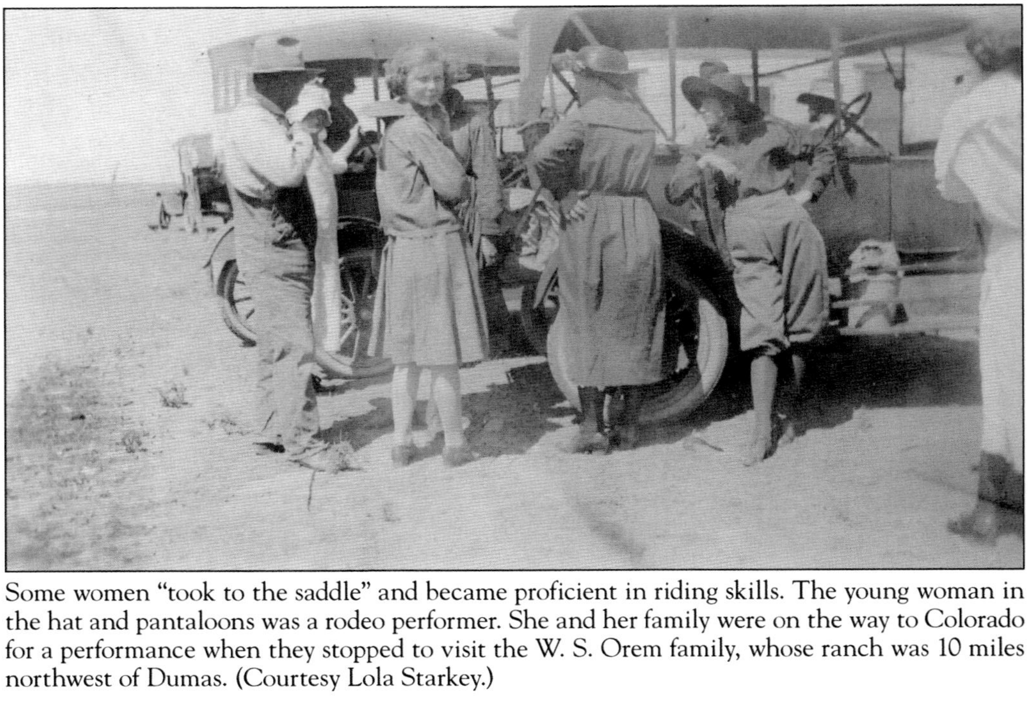

Some women "took to the saddle" and became proficient in riding skills. The young woman in the hat and pantaloons was a rodeo performer. She and her family were on the way to Colorado for a performance when they stopped to visit the W. S. Orem family, whose ranch was 10 miles northwest of Dumas. (Courtesy Lola Starkey.)

Obviously posing for pictures taken on the Tisdale place, northwest of Dumas, the cowboys in this photograph appear to be rolling cigarettes for a last smoke before climbing into the saddle for a long day's work. From left to right, they are Tot Byrd, Finis Jameson, Edgar Bryant, and Pete Byrd. (Courtesy Lola Starkey.)

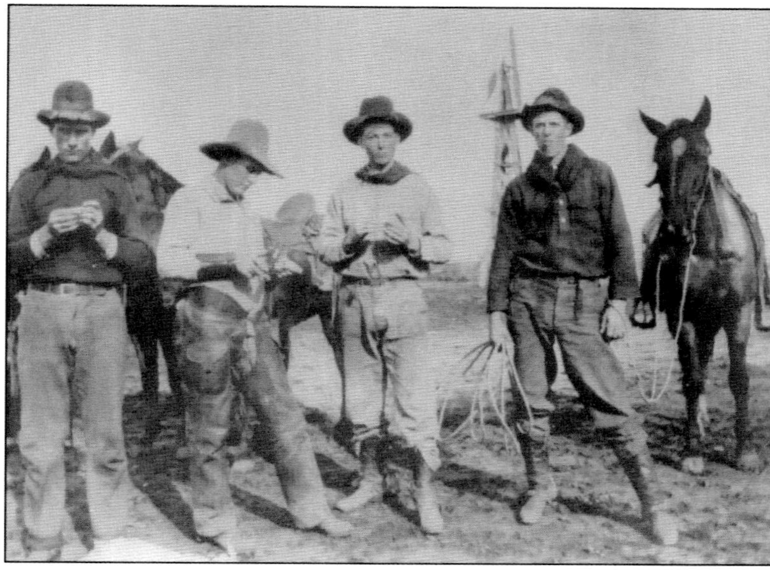

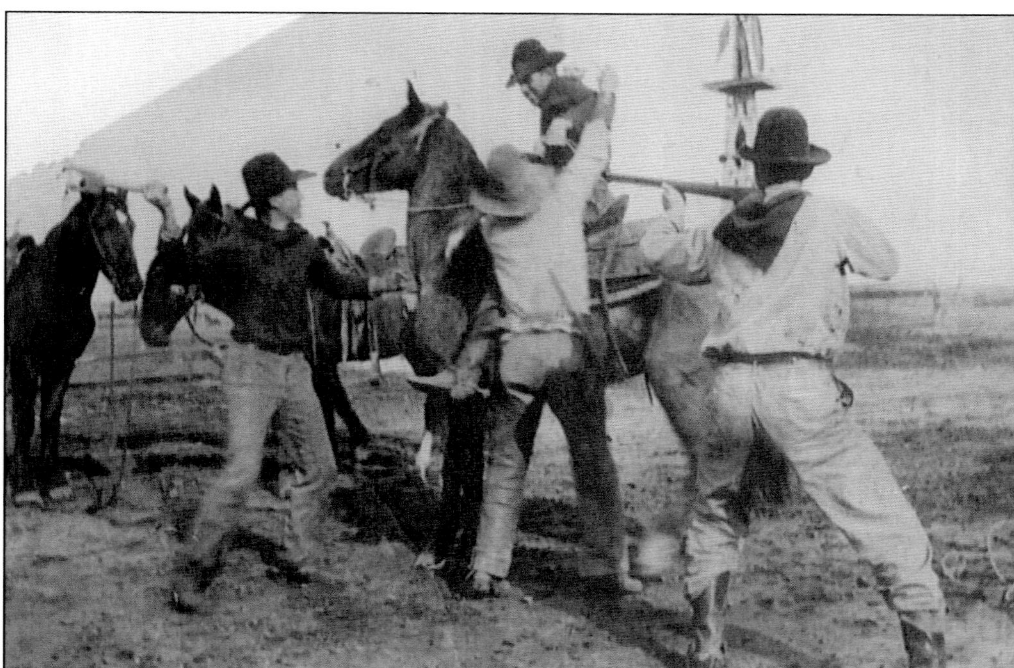

The same four cowboys are delayed from that day's work as they indulge in a bit of horseplay. (Courtesy Lola Starkey.)

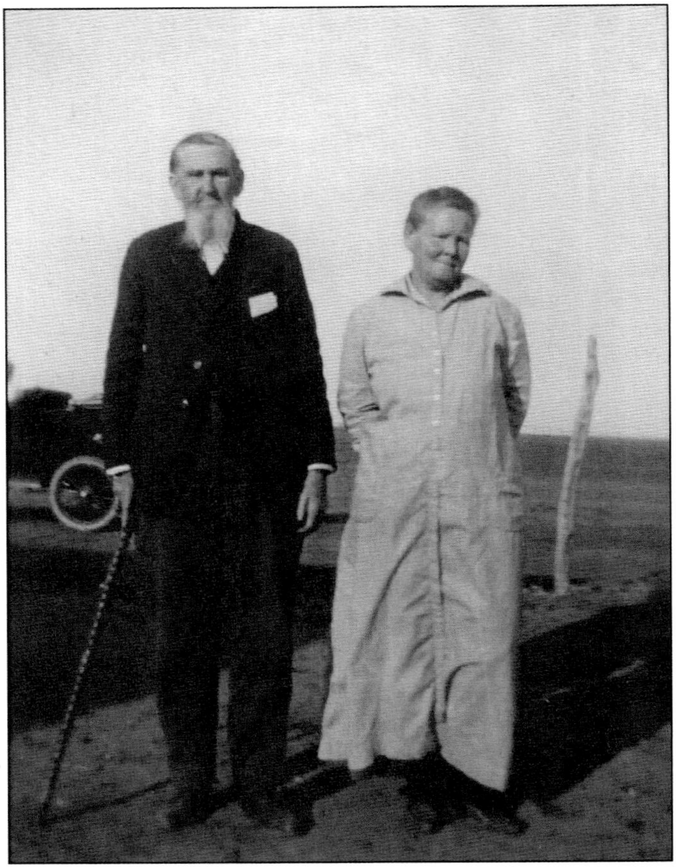

Dr. Samuel W. Anthony, a doctor in the Confederate army, was 76 when he came to Dumas in 1908. He set up an office, and his wife, Annie, became his assistant. An advertisement in the *Moore County Pioneer* read, "Dr. S.W. Anthony in General Practice / Call Answered Anywhere in the County / Day or Night / Office at the Courthouse."

If an illness wasn't too serious, a visit to Phillips and Sons store might help. Some medicines carried were syrup pepsin, colic medicine, castor oil, wood alcohol, and carbolic acid. Jacob Humble Phillips bought the store in 1904 from Arthur Neild, who established it in 1900. The Phillips family operated the store for almost 100 years.

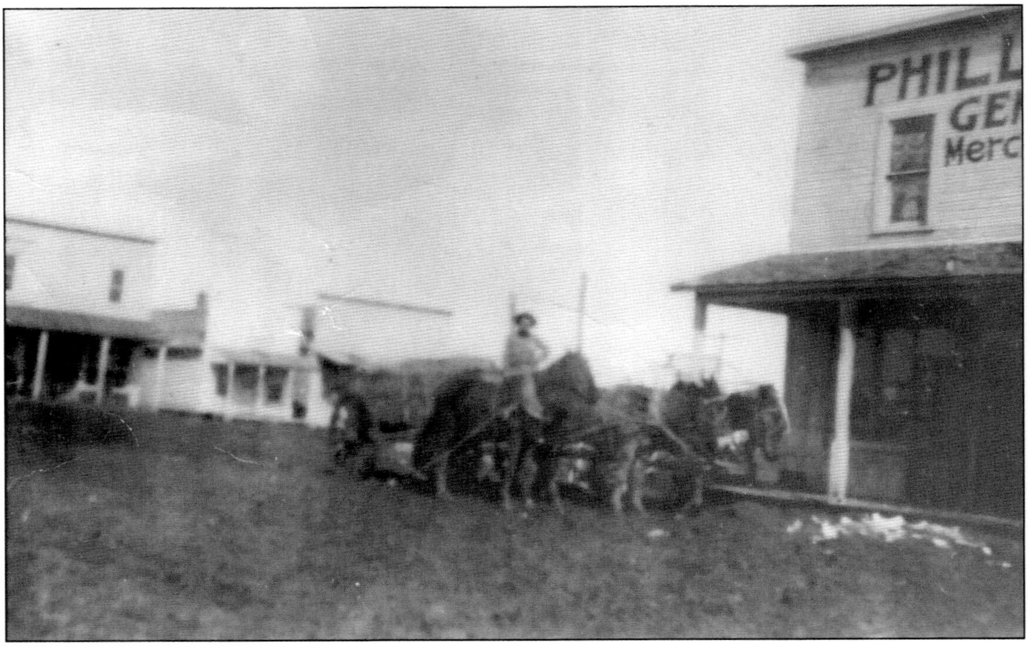

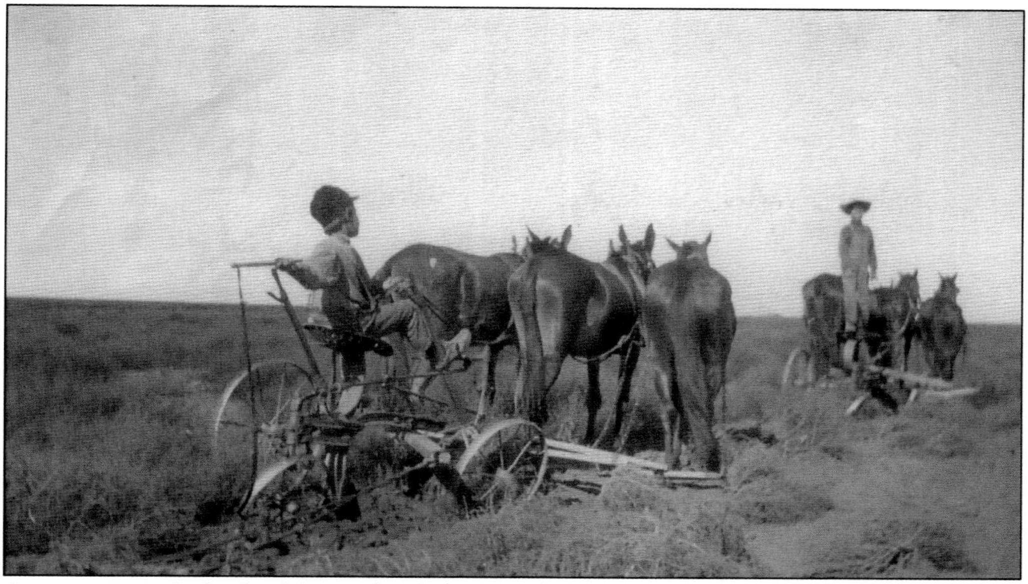

A notation on the back of this undated photograph reads, "Nail Boy and Wynn Boy on McKee farm, Dumas." The posture of the boy on the plow seems to indicate he's ready for a good day's work. He may not realize how very long the day will become before it's time to go to the house for supper.

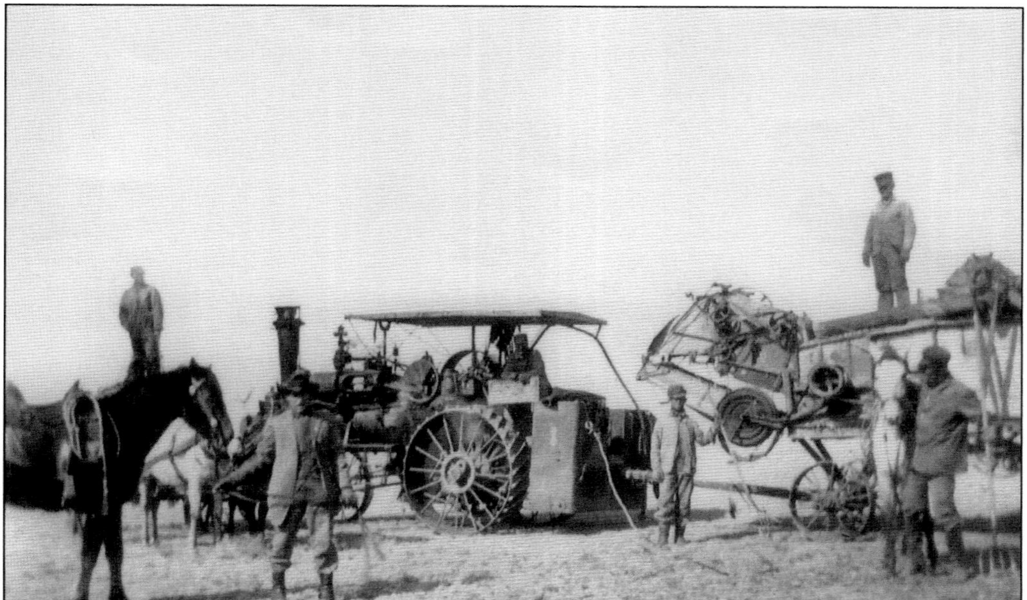

After a grain crop was harvested, it was put into shocks and left to dry. In the fall, a threshing crew moved from farm to farm to separate the grain from the chaff. Most farmers did not own a threshing machine but hired a crew that moved from farm to farm. This machine is said to have been owned by local farmer Louis E. Byrd.

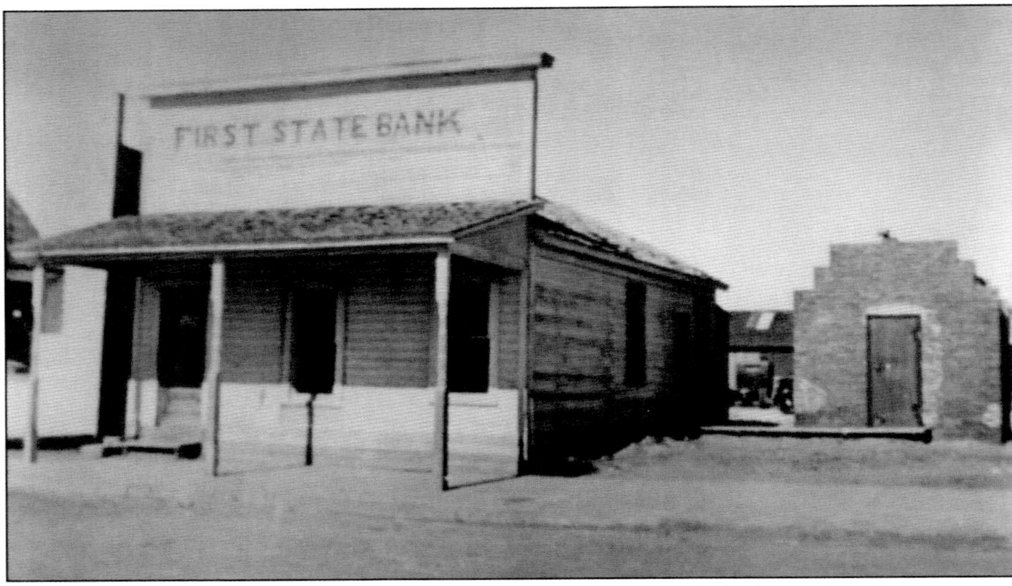

W. J. Morton opened the First State Bank in 1909 and ran it until the late 1920s. Because it was located in such a small place, the vault was built to the side and back of the building. In February 1910, the bank issued its financial report in the *Moore County Pioneer.* Listed as assets was the sum of $52,670.54 including overdrafts.

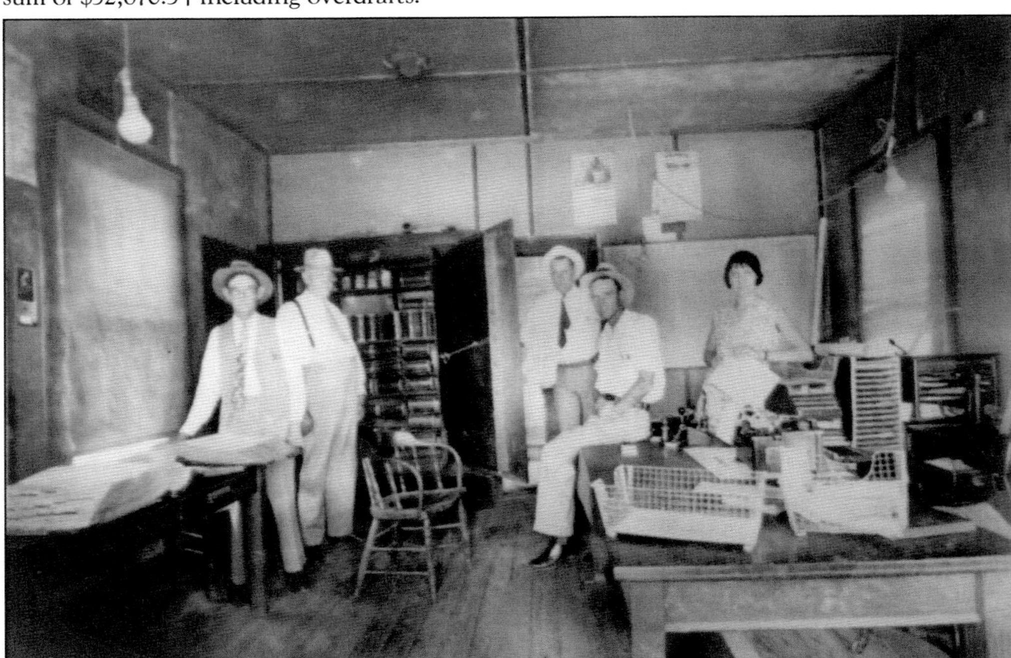

F. R. "Bob" Powell served two terms as Moore County clerk beginning in 1902. During that time, he indexed land records. Moore County's population of 209 in 1900 more than doubled in the following 10 years to 561. Powell saw the need for an abstract company to verify titles and began Powell Abstract in 1908. Family members were involved in its operation until 1988. Under different ownership, Powell Abstract is still doing business.

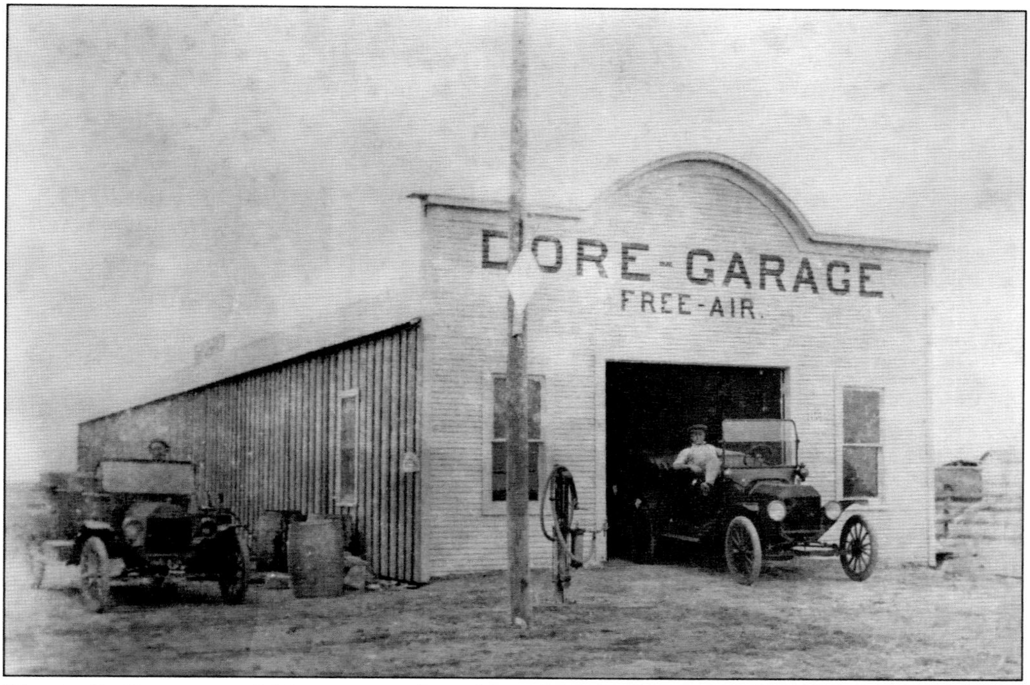

Charles L. Dore opened his garage and machine shop in about 1910. In addition to repairs, he carried all sorts of car accessories and supplies. He sold Goodyear tires and ran the Hupmobile service station. If he couldn't get the old car running, he could sell his clients a brand-new model Dort car for $700.

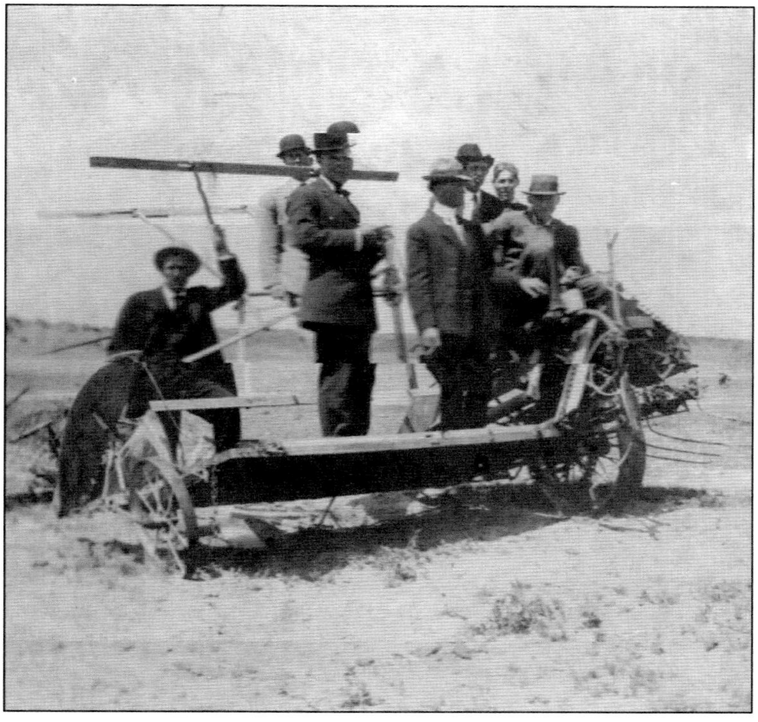

Noted on the back of this photograph was, "Charles Dore and land speculators." Little information is gained in that short description, but we know that civic groups in small towns, anxious to see their town prosper, often placed advertisements in distant city newspapers describing the wonderful benefits of their area.

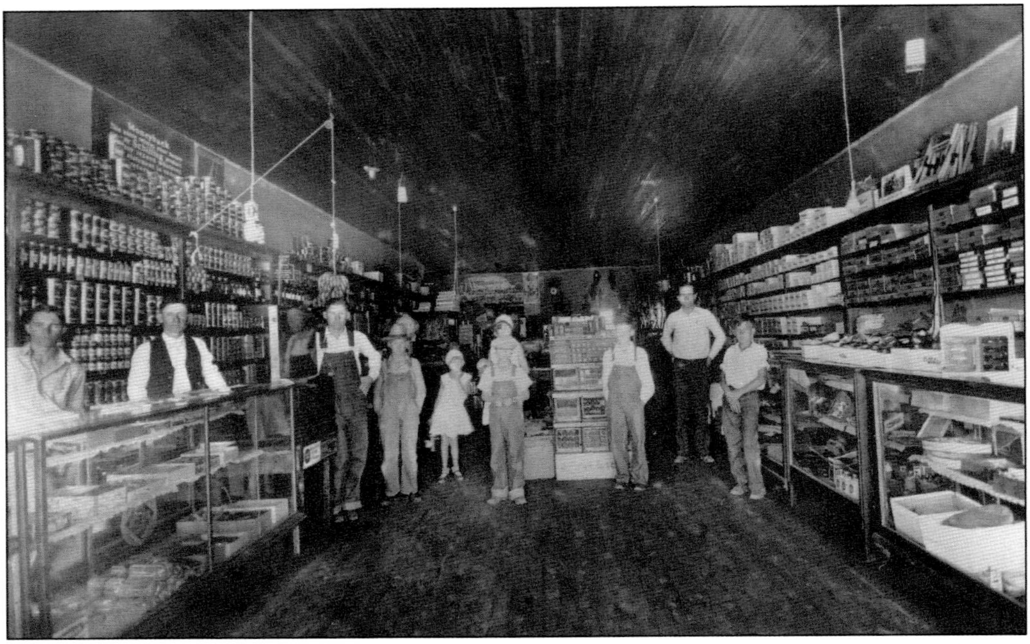

John V. Mills bought this general store in 1918 and operated it for 25 years. Like most general stores of that time period, he carried everything from overalls to ammunition in the store. After he sold his store, he was appointed city tax assessor/collector and served nearly 20 years in that office.

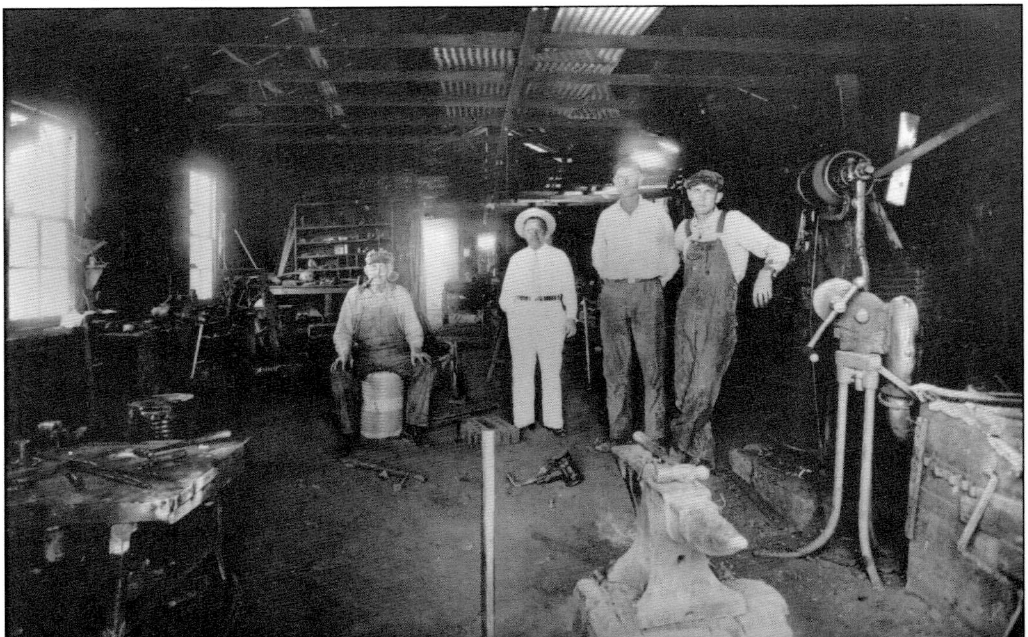

A. L. Anderson (seated) was born in Norway in 1856 and became a sailor at age 16. After many years at sea, he settled first in Bosque County, Texas. He came to Moore County in 1902. He bought the Dumas Blacksmith Shop in 1912 and operated it until his death in 1934. Old-timers tell that the first silent movies ever seen in Dumas were shown in his shop.

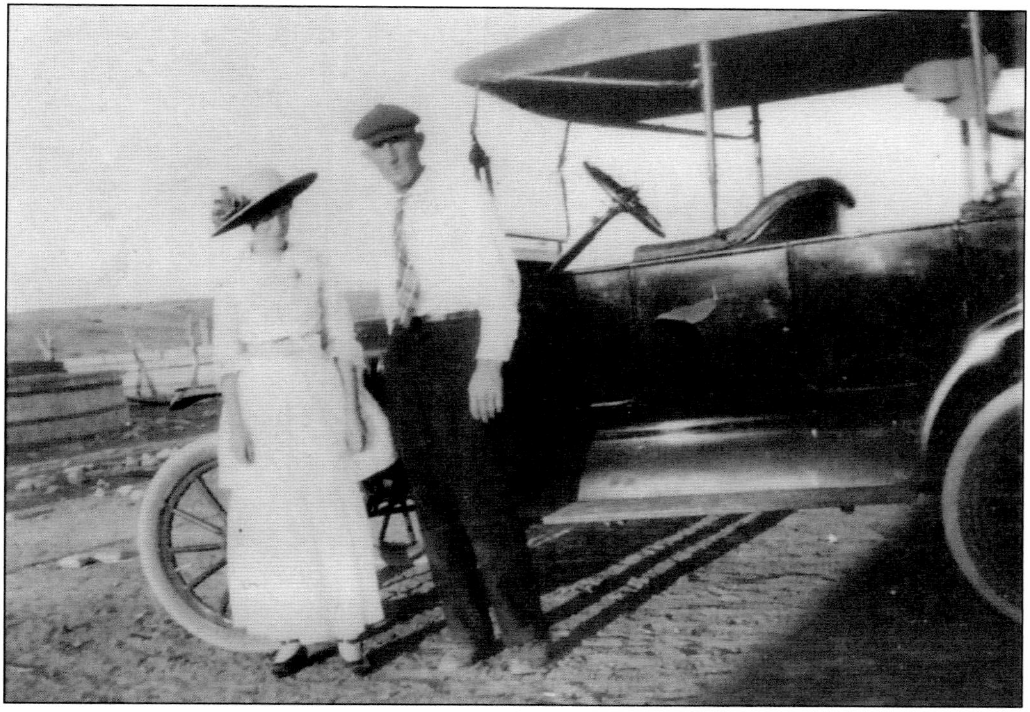

The first automobile in Moore County, a Reo, was registered in 1908. Only 12 more cars were registered during the next four years. Gradually two dealerships, the Ford and Willis-Overland, combined with garages, went into business. By the mid-1920s, it was common for families to own automobiles.

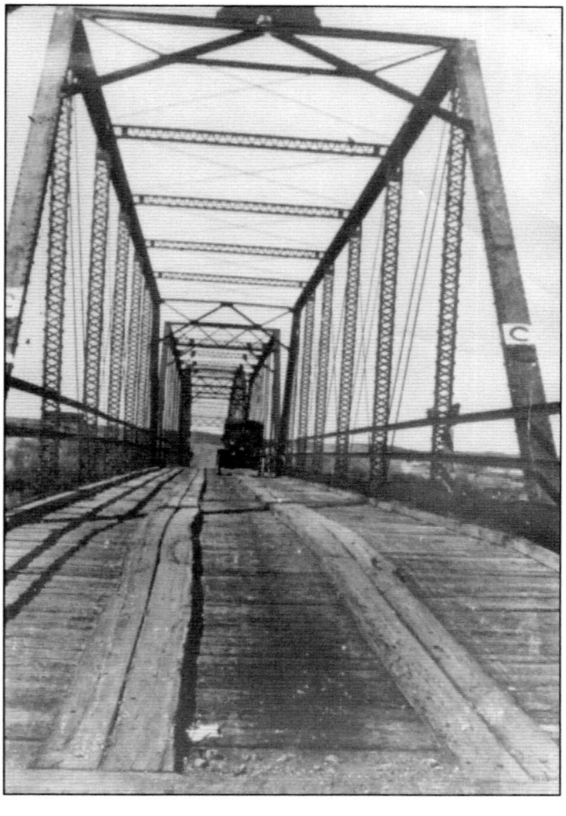

Over the years, crossing the Canadian River on the way to Amarillo presented different challenges. When Dumas was first settled, there was no bridge and it was necessary to ford the river. In 1907, a small, wooden, one-way bridge was built. It often washed out and had to be replaced. On this 1920s bridge, small vehicles had to straddle two rough timbers that were laid for larger vehicles.

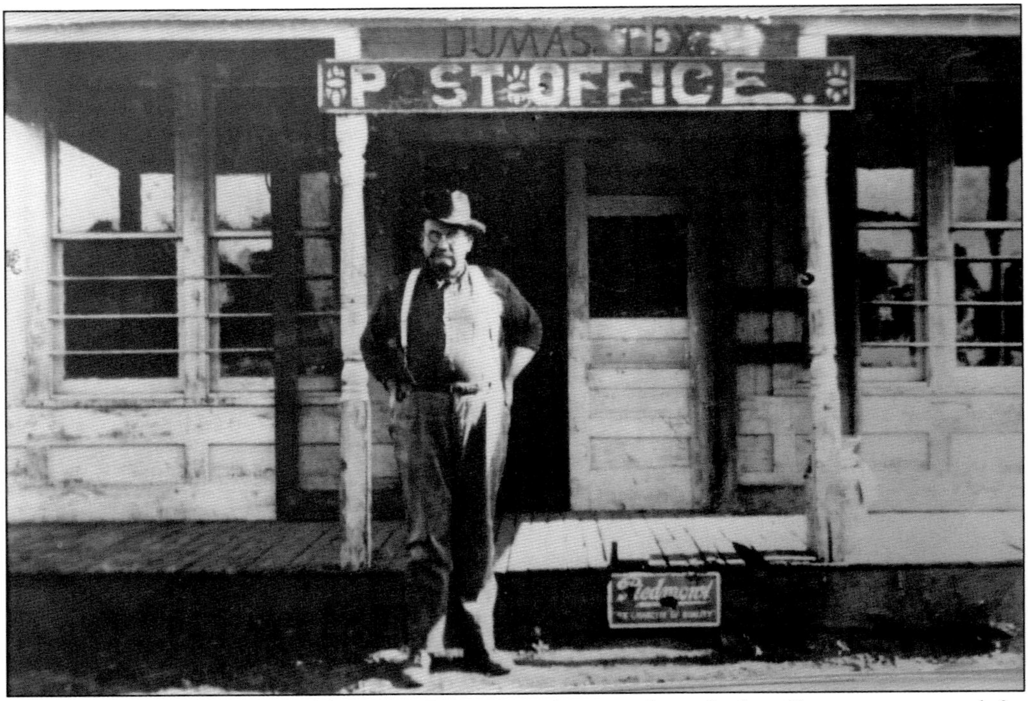

Wiley Fox had a colorful work history. He was a cowboy, ranch cook, sheriff, tax assessor, and, for a time, a successful cattleman. Between career changes, he was postmaster. He took the job in 1904 but worked only a short time before taking another job. He went back to work as postmaster in 1914. After leaving once more, he returned in 1921 to serve until he retired.

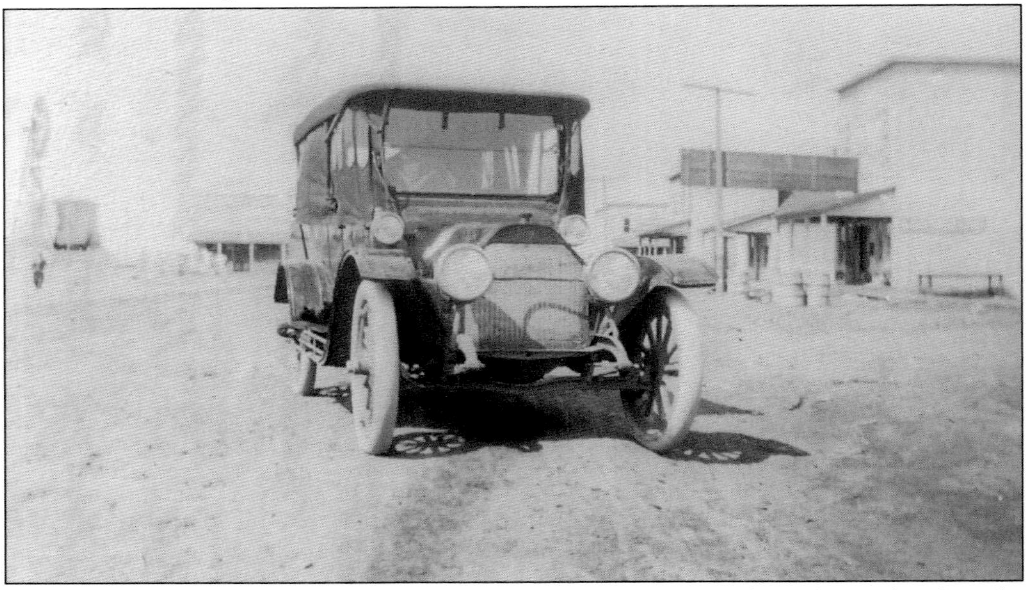

Until the railroad came, a carrier traveled 20 miles to Hartley to pick up the mail. When the town started, a horse and buggy made the trip three times weekly. When cars became available, the trip was made daily. In the 1930s, residents gathered at the post office at the same time each day to wait for this car to deliver the mail.

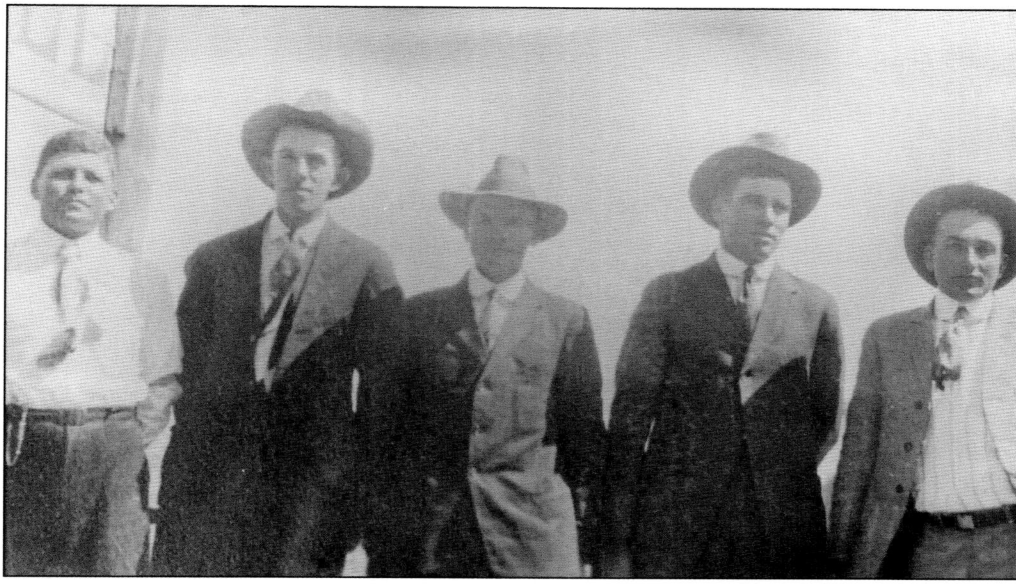

No accurate records were kept of the number of recruits in World War I, but at least 17 Moore County men served. Those in this group of departing inductees are, from left to right, unidentified, Sam McDade, Ray Bennett, Archie Stewart, and Henry Ham. According to one source, most of these men served in Germany. Jake Eiland was the only casualty recorded.

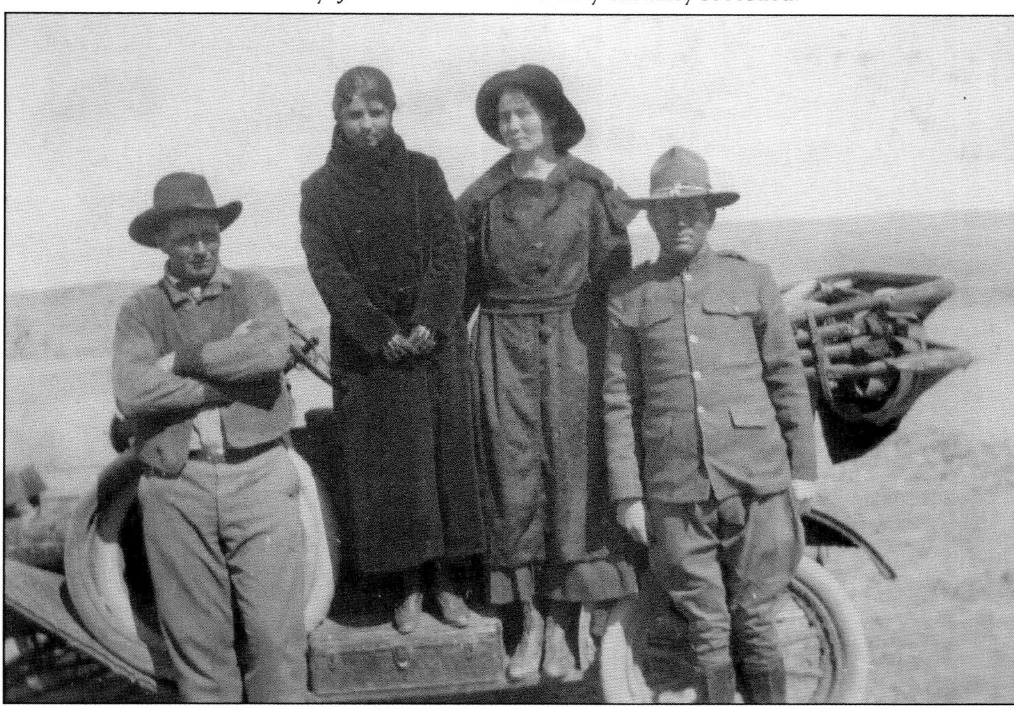

On the far right, Archie Stewart, one of the inductees, poses with friends Harry Record (left), an unidentified teacher (middle), and Maggie Record. Stewart worked on farms and ranches in Moore County before going into the army. After he was discharged from service, he married Maggie and went back to work on a ranch in east Moore County.

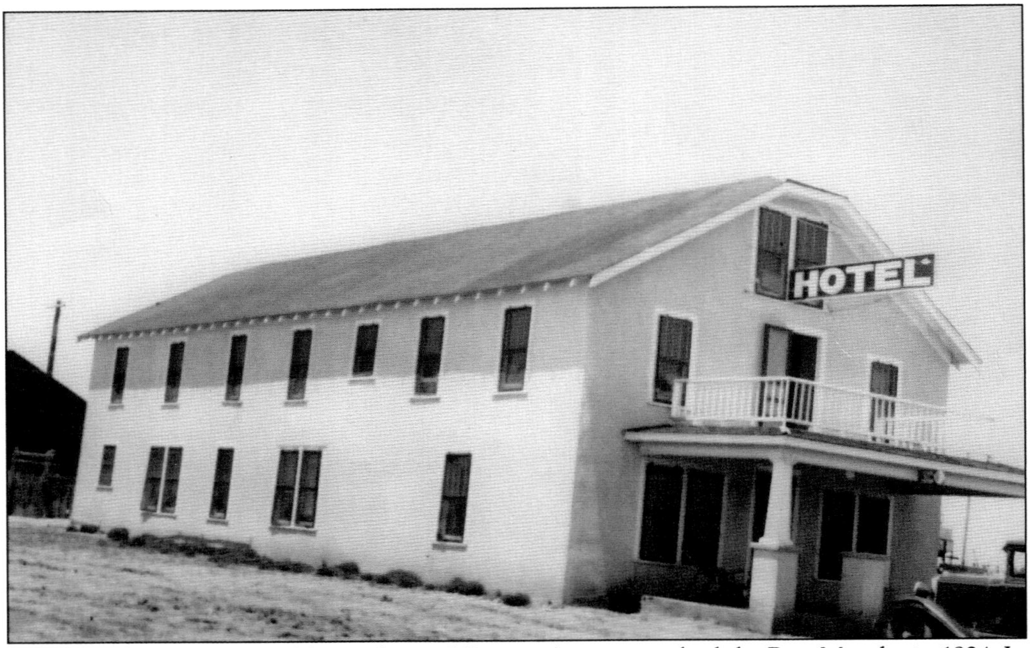

This two-story stucco hotel located at 805 Dumas Avenue was built by Bess Murphy in 1924. In about 1928, William D. Elliott bought the hotel and moved his wife and 13 children to Dumas. Two years later, Elliott died. His wife, Delia, ran the hotel until 1940. The Elliotts' son Floyd and his wife ran the hotel located on the northwest corner of Seventh Street and Dumas Avenue.

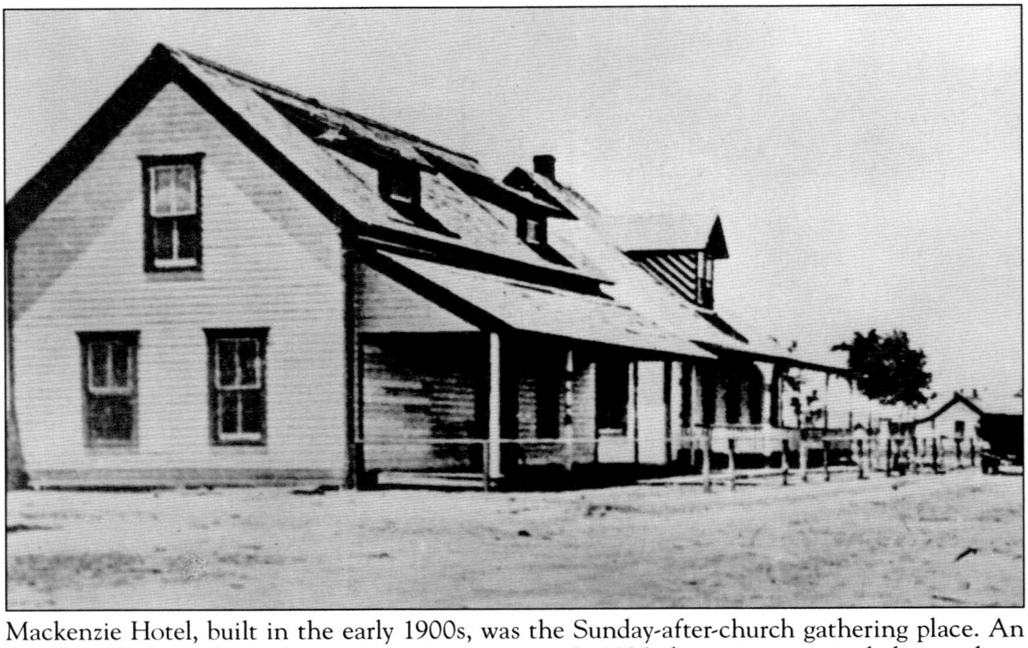

Mackenzie Hotel, built in the early 1900s, was the Sunday-after-church gathering place. An excellent chef and a Victrola were its main attractions. In 1926, the entire town, including students dismissed from classes, gathered to watch it burn. With no firefighting equipment and a high wind, nearby buildings were in jeopardy. Store owners hurriedly moved their merchandise into the street. Fortunately, the fire did not spread.

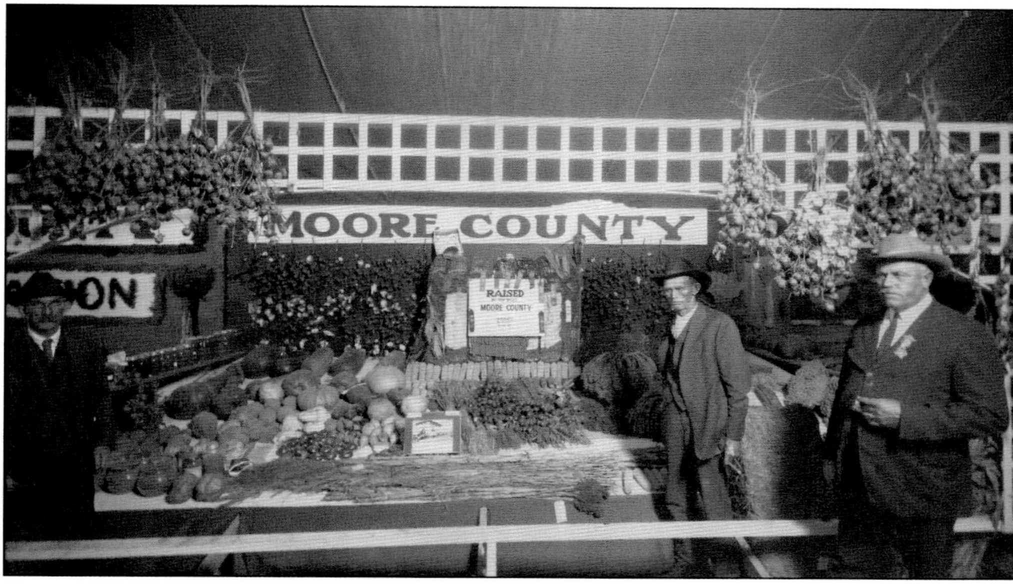

Cotton was not grown north of the Canadian River before O. B. "Ozy" Burnett grew six rows near Dumas. Needing another cash crop, in 1924, farmers planted 13,387 acres of cotton north of the river. Its success was advertised in Amarillo at the parade and this special booth at the fair. Note the cotton hanging in back. From left to right are Charles Dore, Burnett, and W. J. Morton. (Courtesy Harold Dean Morton.)

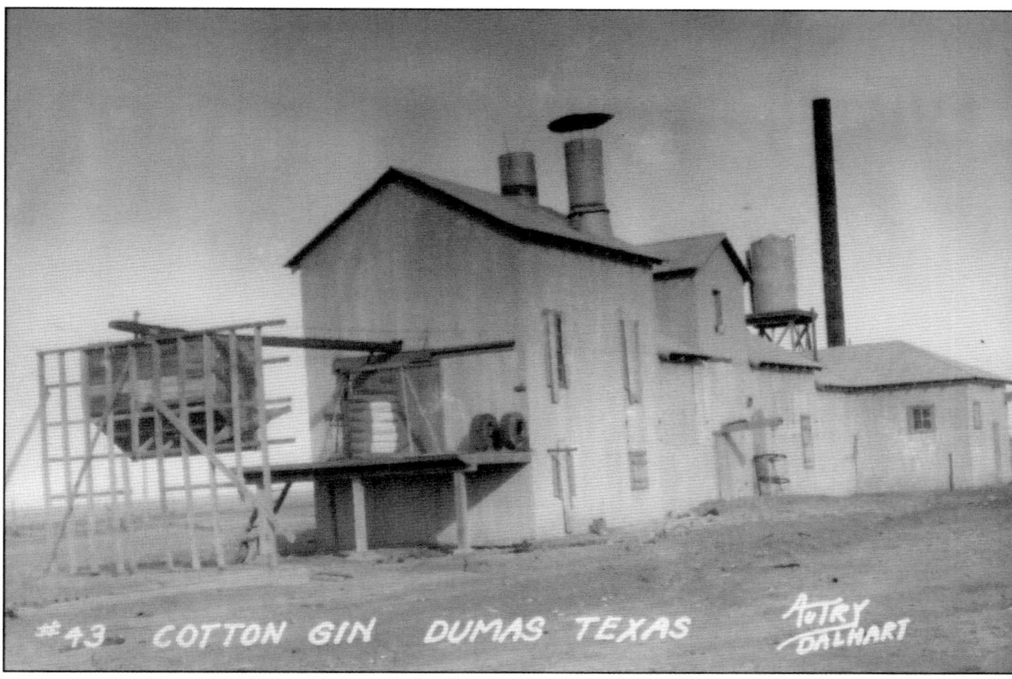

A gin was built in 1924 but was demolished in 1937 when there was not enough cotton to support it. A short growing season and shortage of workers were the two main causes for its demise. Most farmers went back to growing grain. A few had allotments, and some cotton was grown until about 1986. In Moore County, cotton was not grown again until after 2000.

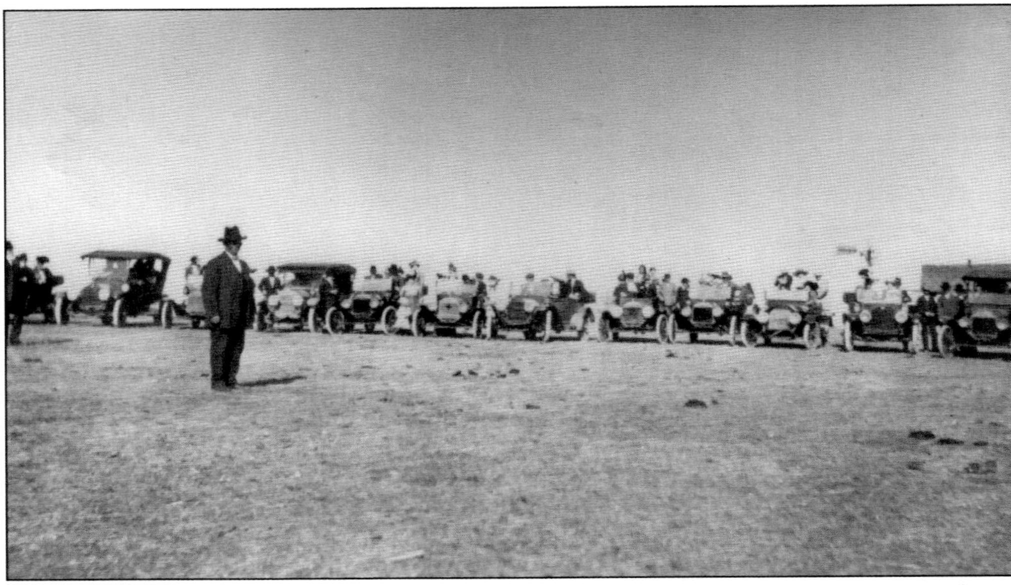

Most Dumas residents preferred their entertainment to be a little more peaceful than the dances held on the top floor of the courthouse. Parties in private homes or church-sponsored picnics and parties were their chief sources of entertainment. Occasionally, community leaders would organize a countywide event. Judging by the number of cars at an Easter egg hunt, this might have been one of those occasions.

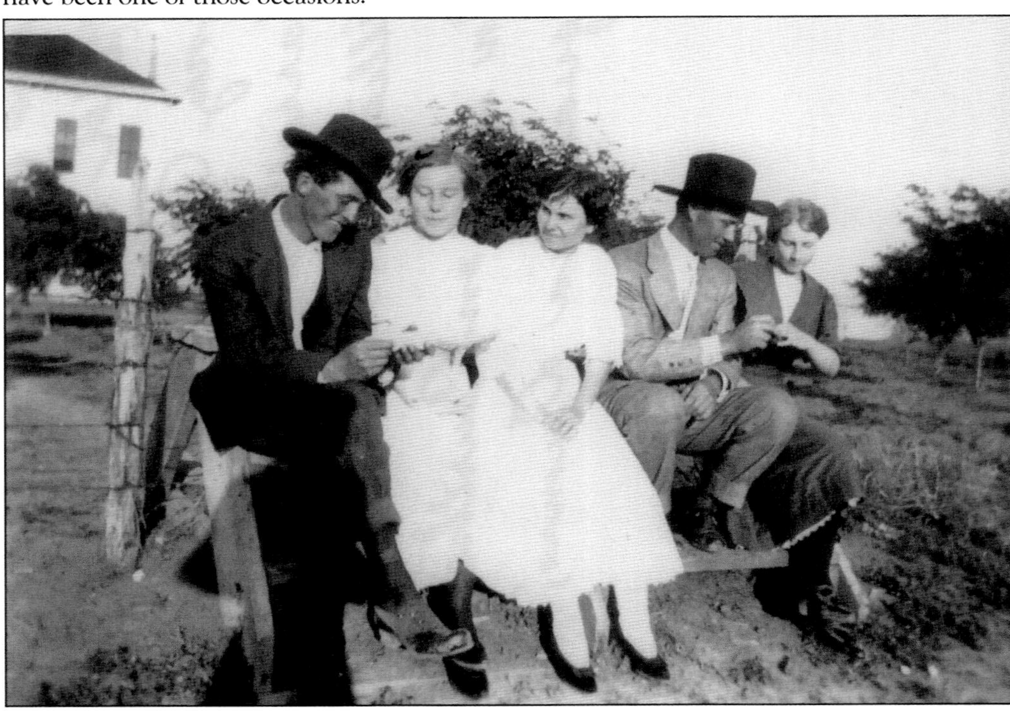

Two young ladies receive their engagement rings as a friend looks on. This happy occasion took place near the original courthouse, which can be seen in the upper left portion of the picture. The subjects were seated on a stile crossing the barbed-wire fence that surrounded the courthouse.

In 1917, Dumas students started school in a large two-story building on Seventh Street and Birge Street. Classrooms were on the lower floor, and the upper story was an auditorium. Later an auditorium was built next door, and senior high classes moved upstairs. A fire escape was built, and sometimes its purpose was ignored. Mil Boyd and a friend appear to be planning a slide down just for fun (below). J. T. Brown, who graduated in 1931, told of being upstairs in study hall when a plane flew over and landed just west of the school. He said, "We all hit that fire escape, all of us who were upstairs. Mr. Reid, the superintendent, was an aviator and he was right along with us." Classes were dismissed so everyone could go see the plane.

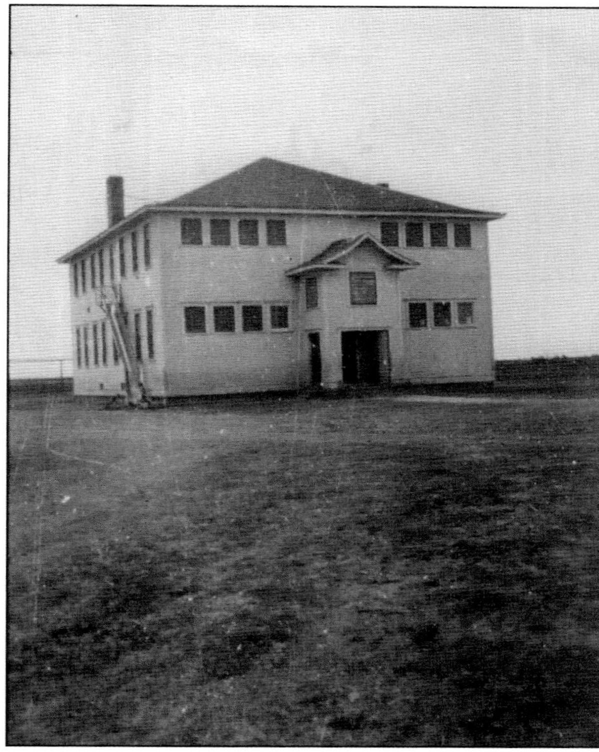

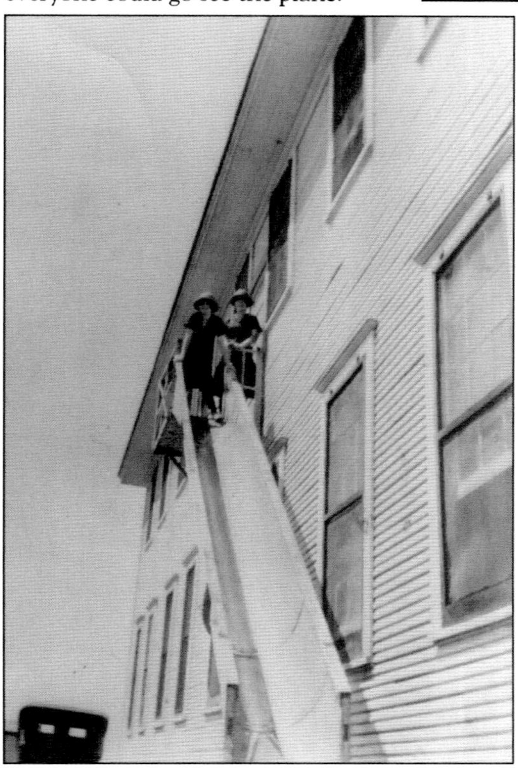

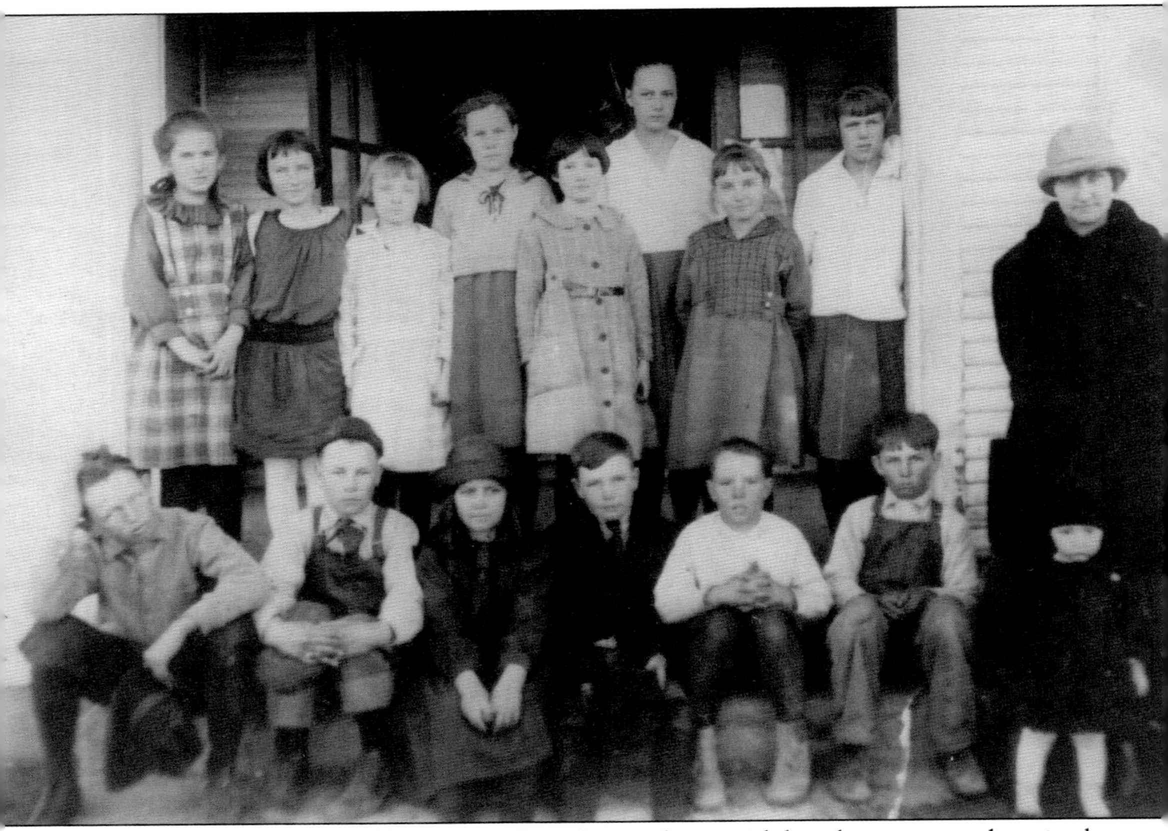

Mrs. Charles Manier and her son, on the right, are shown with her elementary students in about 1921. Gladys Makeig would replace Manier. In an interview with Gladys, when she was 95, she told of her experiences. She said, "I was 18 when I started teaching. . . . I taught fourth, fifth and sixth grade. There were eleven in the fifth grade, three in the sixth and four in the fourth. . . . I could tell you who all of them were, but that wouldn't be necessary. The students called me Gladys, but some of them called me Miss Gladys because their parents made them. They felt they would respect me more, but they did that anyway. When I told them something, I meant it and they knew it, and I didn't have to whip them either. I didn't have any trouble with them and I think they liked me about as well as I liked them. . . . Jessie Glenn and I taught together and we walked. We wore out a pair of those high topped overshoes; we walked so much through snow one year."

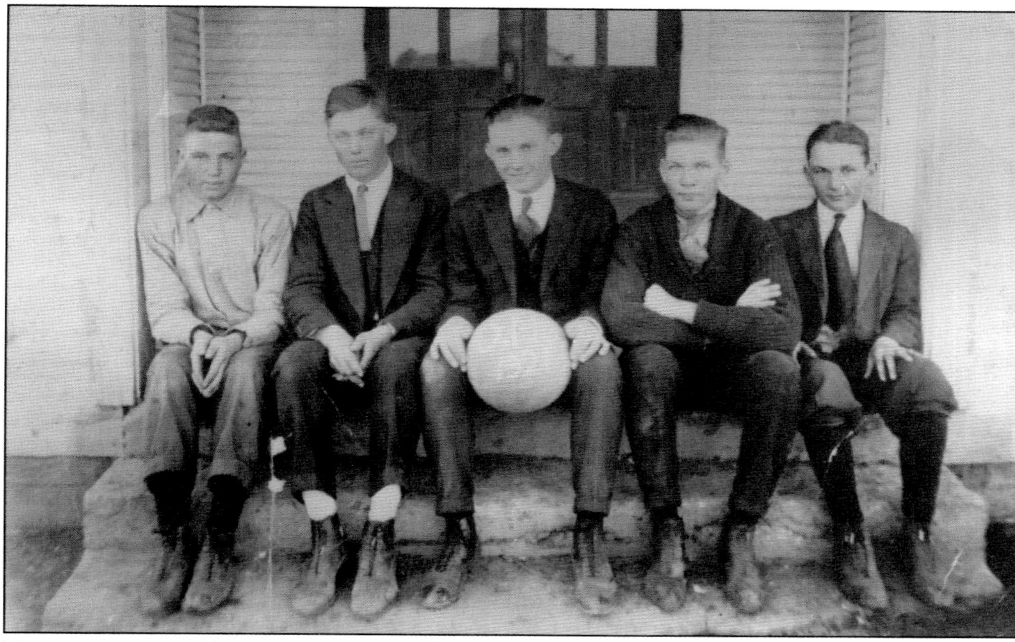

Dumas team sports began in 1910 with a baseball team that played Stratford and Channing. The job of coach fell to the high school principal or the school superintendent. At the time these photographs were made, games were played on outside basketball courts, both at home and in other small towns. School buses were not provided for transportation to out-of-town games at that time, but it appears one car could carry the whole team. The boys pictured here were the 1921 team. The photograph of the girls basketball team had no date, but it was taken about the same time. The uniforms reflect the modesty expected of girls at that time, but they appear to be having a good time anyway.

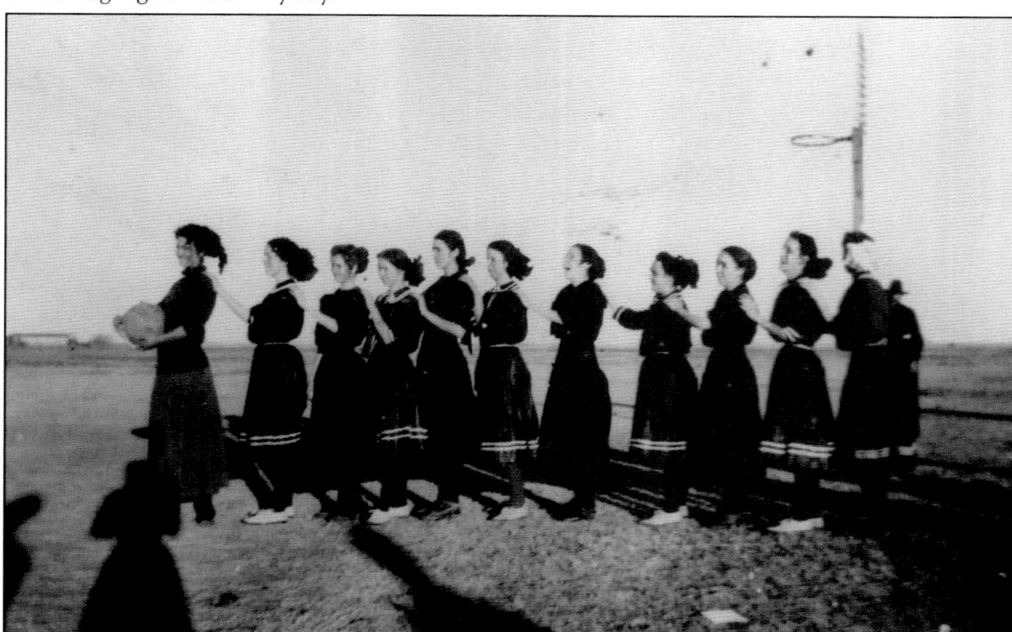

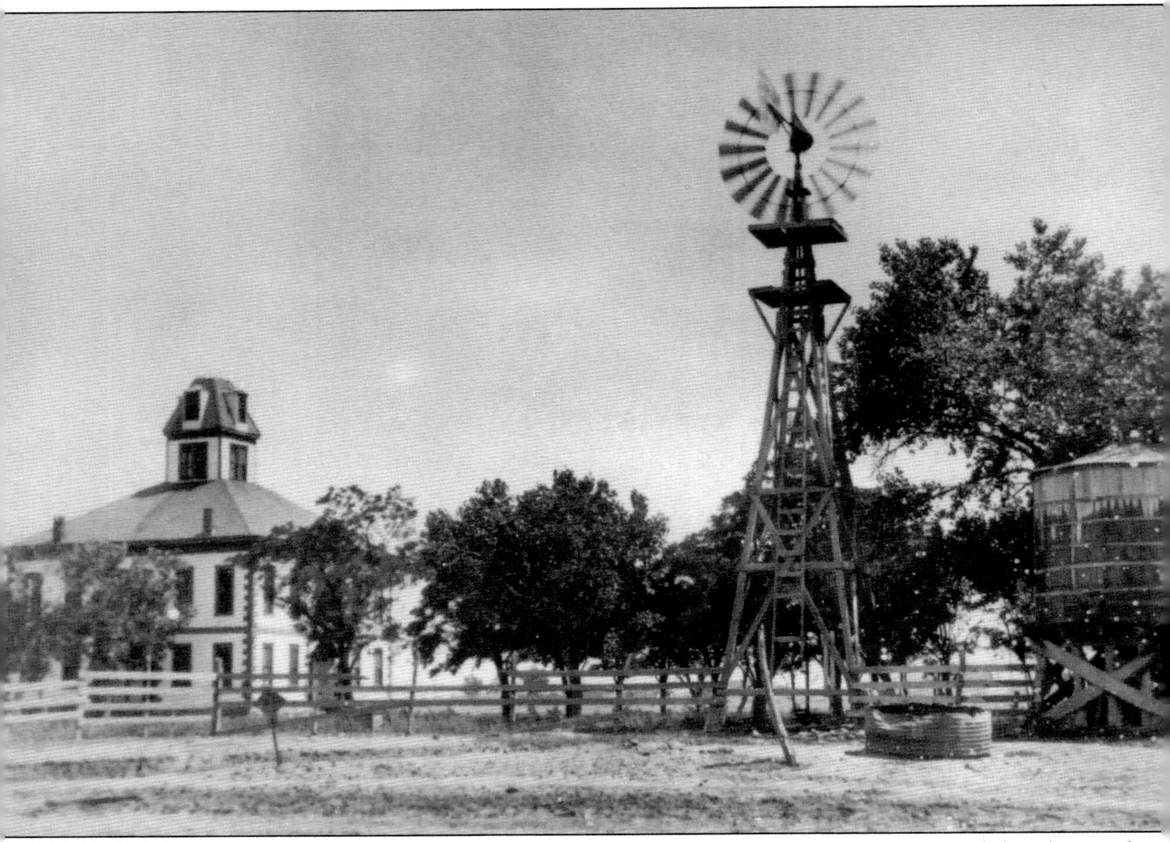

This photograph bears the name Dumas Water Works. It is also the subject of sketches and paintings by local artists. The well on the courthouse square was the town's only water supply for almost 30 years. From time to time in the early years of the well, homemakers complained that something had to be done. Kids were swimming in the tank and a dead bird was found now and again. When Myrtle Fox discovered that dogs were jumping in and out of the tank to cool off, she determined it was time for a solution to the problem. She took the complaint to the county commissioners. Soon thereafter, the tank was covered and elevated, to the relief of every homemaker in town. The well supplied water to the town's citizens until the late 1920s, when the discovery of gas and oil brought remarkable change to the small, quiet village.

Four

Boom and Bust

In 1918, a group drilled for oil about 20 miles south of Dumas in north Potter County, not far from the Moore County line. There was no oil, but a headline in the *Amarillo Daily News* read, "Remarkable Flow of Gas reported." It took years to realize the importance of that event, but it was the beginning of the transformation for the little town of Dumas.

Not until 1922, after wells were drilled in an ever-expanding area around that first one, was the Hugoton Gas Field delineated and determined to be the largest natural gas field in North America.

In 1927, a wildcat well drilled 7.5 miles northeast of Dumas became a 200-barrel-per-day oil producer. By 1930, fifty-seven wells had been drilled; 29 were gas producers and 20 were oil wells. The boom was on.

Population in Moore County more than doubled from 1920 to 1930 and stood at 1,555. The early 1930s were busy, exciting times for Dumas. Bonds were passed to build a courthouse and to pave roads. The city was incorporated and a fire truck was purchased; 28 houses were built in June and July 1930. The next year, a bond election approved the construction of a new school. Rock Island built a track across the northern portion of the county, and the Atchison, Topeka, and Santa Fe completed a line that came through Dumas going north.

Dumas had a number of new enterprises, including a newspaper, the *Moore County News*. Prospective advertisers included a theater, two cafés, two hotels, two drugstores, three general stores, a barbershop, and three filling stations with garages.

In the meantime, farmers and ranchers in the area were working quietly and diligently to grow the country's food. Crops were fairly good in 1928 and 1929.

Even after the Depression struck the rest of the country, Dumas and Moore County continued to enjoy prosperity. But by 1933, overproduction had stopped activity in the petroleum industry, and drought and dust storms had ravaged area farms. Dumas was facing tough times.

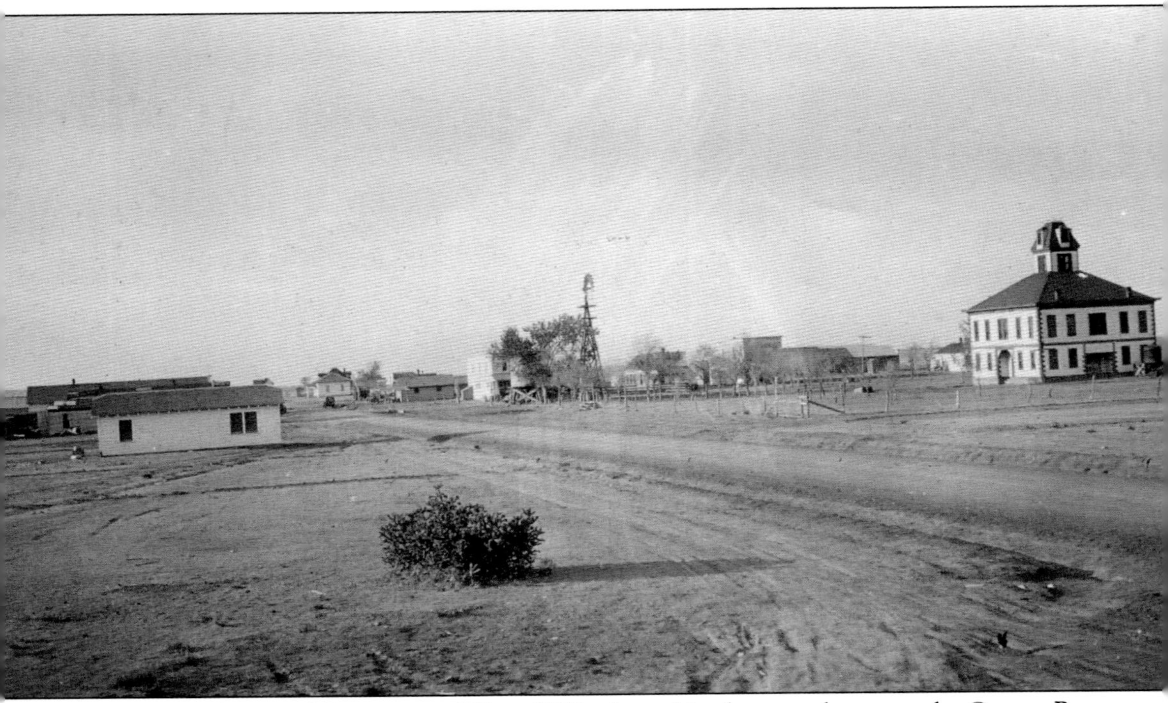

The population of Dumas was 250 in 1927, when this photograph was made. George Brown, longtime Moore County resident, remembered the town about that time. He said, "You could walk around the schoolhouse and count every house in Dumas. I can't remember now just how many; there was probably 18 or 20." Every house had a privy and a wash pot in the backyard, and most had a cow. The cow was free to wander within the fenced section of the town. A barbed-wire fence around the town square kept livestock from disrupting proceedings in the courthouse. The three churches in town, the Baptist, Methodist, and Church of Christ, struggled to keep their doors open. To stay in business, the few stores depended on cowboys and farmers. Dumas Avenue was difficult to travel after a good rain. Then the discovery of oil and gas changed the little town. Companies including Phillips, Shamrock, Sinclair, Magnolia, and Skelly came to participate in the exciting petroleum industry developments. Within three years, the population of Dumas would increase to 628 residents.

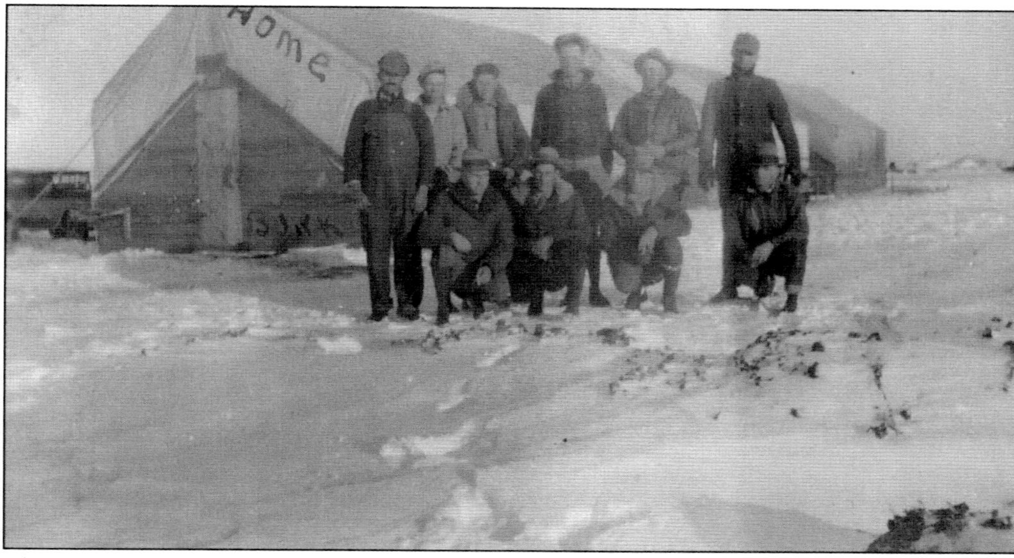

Three companies worked together in 1927 to build the first gasoline and compressor station in Moore County. Canadian River Gas was the first company to operate the plant located 16 miles south of Dumas. When construction began, approximately 160 workers lived in tents near the site. One of them labeled a tent "home" on his copy of this photograph.

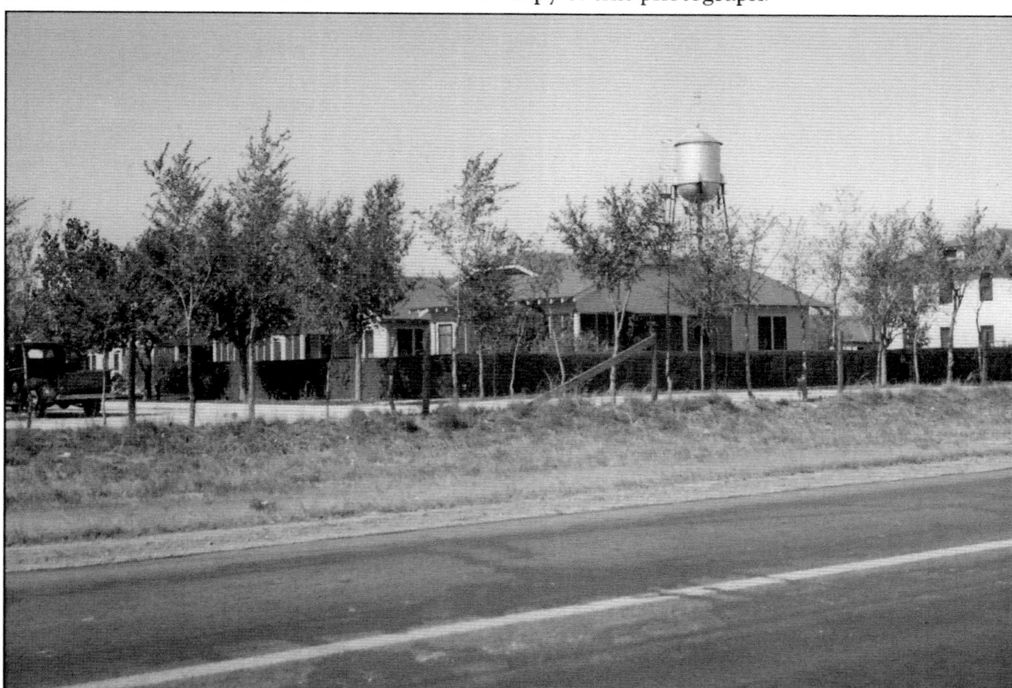

To be sure workers would be available when needed, 12 houses for families and a hotel for single workers were built nearby. Some called the housing area a "village," but "camp" became a more common term. In subsequent years, camps were scattered all across the county as plants for the production of petroleum and its by-products were built. Tremendous benefits to the economy of Dumas would result. (Courtesy Bureau of Mines.)

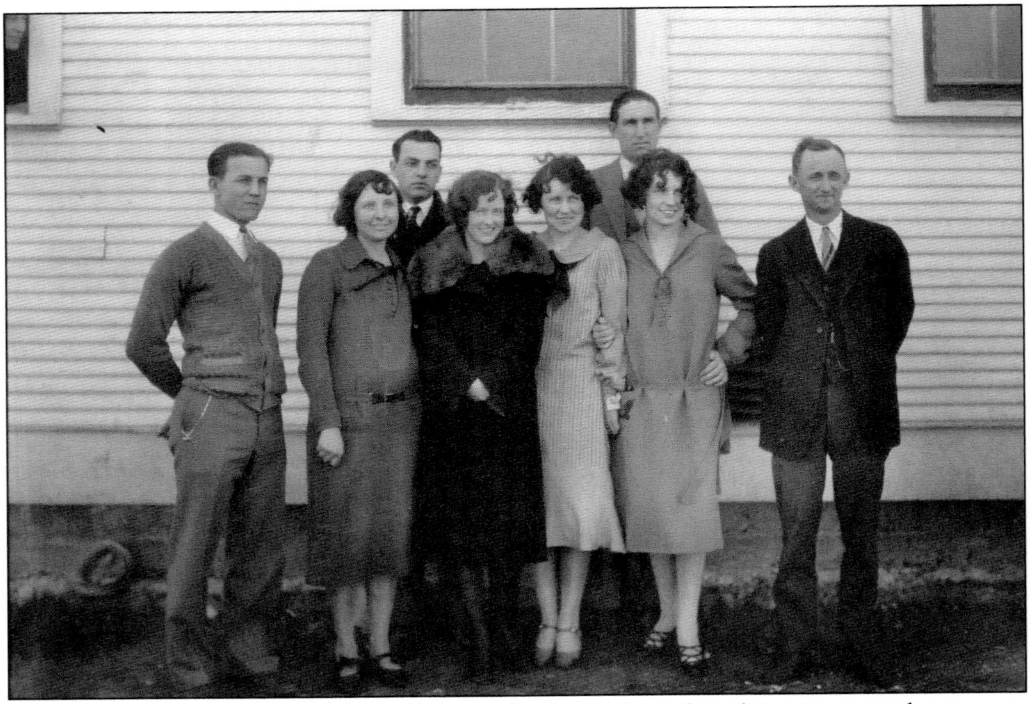

When R. C. Sampson (far right) was Dumas school superintendent, his primary goal was to get the school accredited. Seven teachers were assigned among the 11 grades, with some teaching as many as three grades in the elementary level. They all went to work to gain accreditation. From left to right, the teachers were John Henry Carver, Mrs. R. C. Sampson, Roy Carroll, Jessie Glynn Daugherty, Cecile Dowdy, Gene Byrd, and Gladys Makeig. Sampson is on the right.

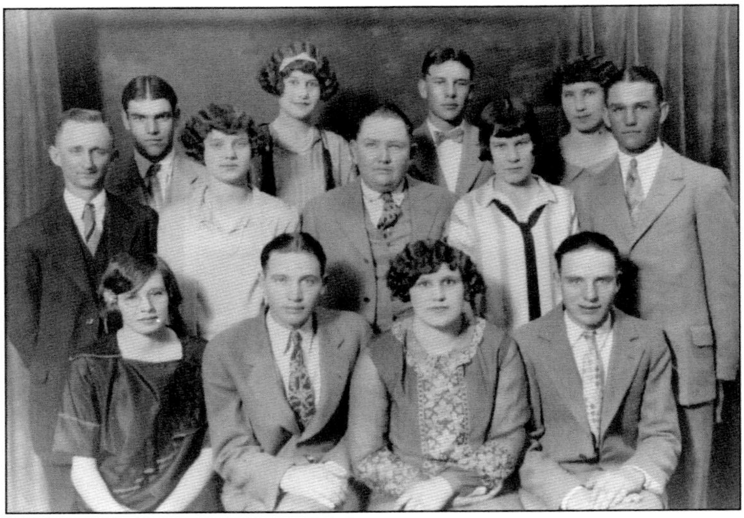

The class of 1926 was the first to graduate after completing 11 full grades. In an interview with the *Moore County News*, Hattie Byrd Huff said, "We were so proud of ourselves. Not everyone was privileged to graduate high school. . . . Students today have greater advantages. . . . I took a home economics class in sewing, but we didn't have any sewing machines."

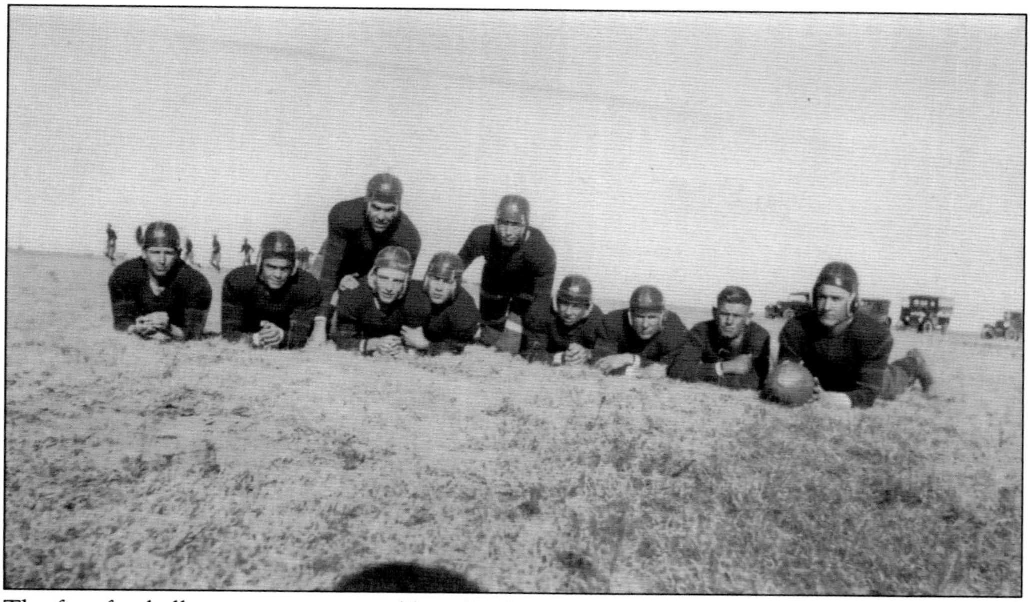

The first football team was organized by school principal John H. Carver in 1925. Games were played on a dirt field west of the school. The first few years saw more losses than victories. In 1928, Denny Denman followed Carver as principal and coach. Once when Denman was short one player, he suited up and played a position. He turned the team around, and there were more wins.

The school colors are orange and black. Denny Denman is credited for that choice. There are two versions as to how the teams were named Dumas Demons. One says it happened in 1926 in a team discussion, and the other claims it occurred in 1934 at a school assembly. Either way, the name inspires great pride in students, past and present. Girls' teams are Demonettes.

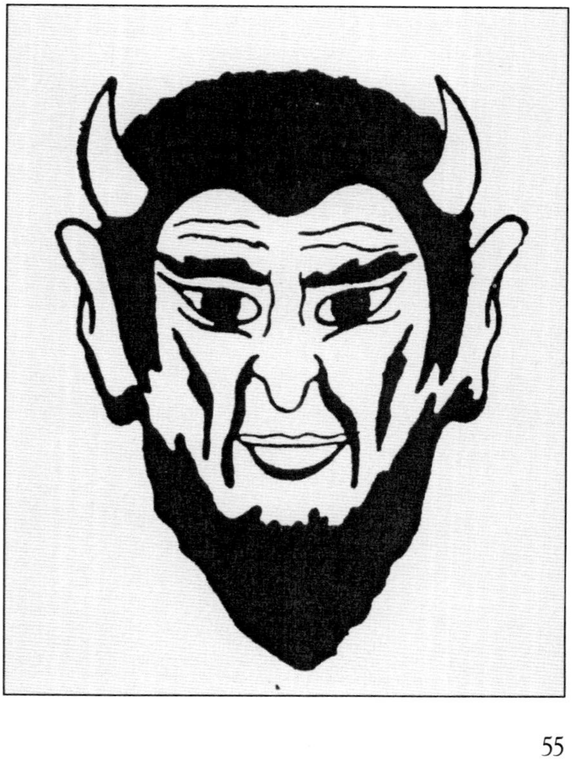

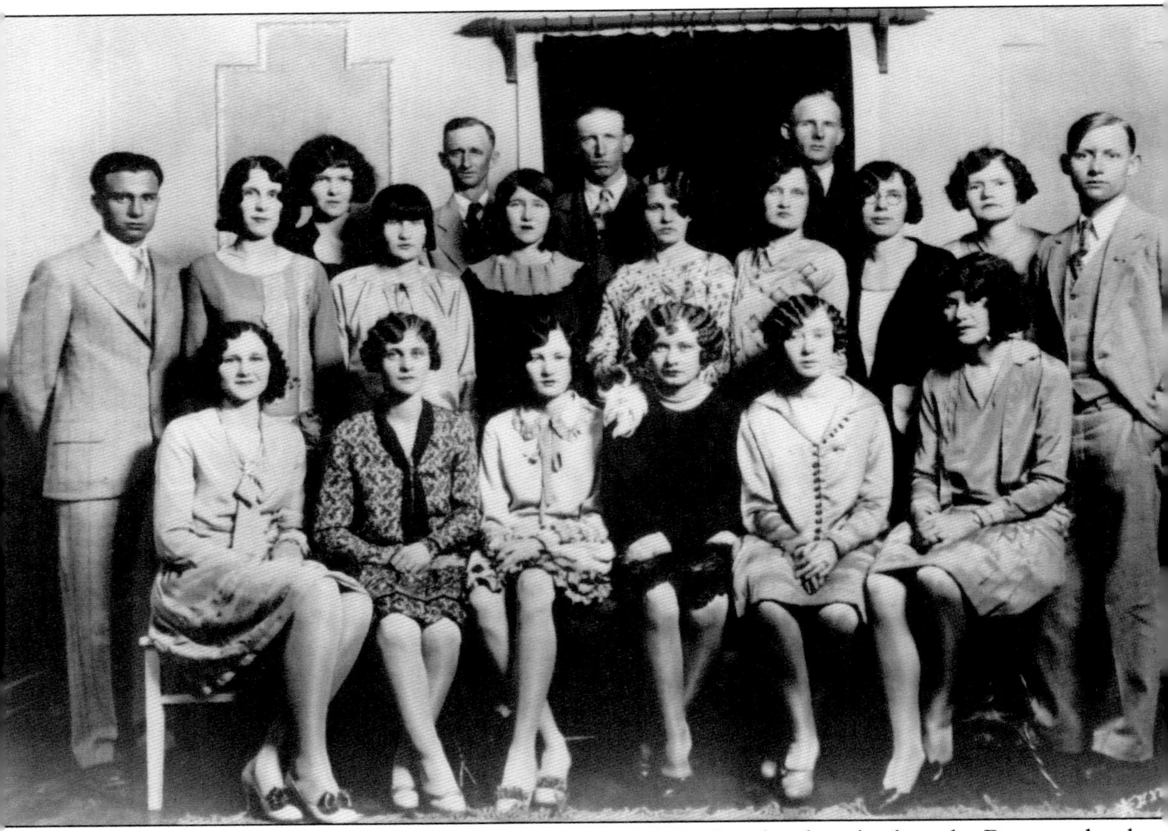

Sampson, the teachers, and students were rewarded for their hard work when the Dumas school became fully accredited. In a 1996 interview, Mil Burnett Boyd said, "Our class that graduated in 1928 was the first class in Dumas High School that was accredited, that could go to college without taking examinations. We had worked four years having a supervisor from Austin to come see the work we had done. Our work was put up on the blackboards for them to check. Believe me, our teachers had us do a lot of extra work to do that. But, we were proud of the fact that we could do it." Dumas High School had entered a new era.

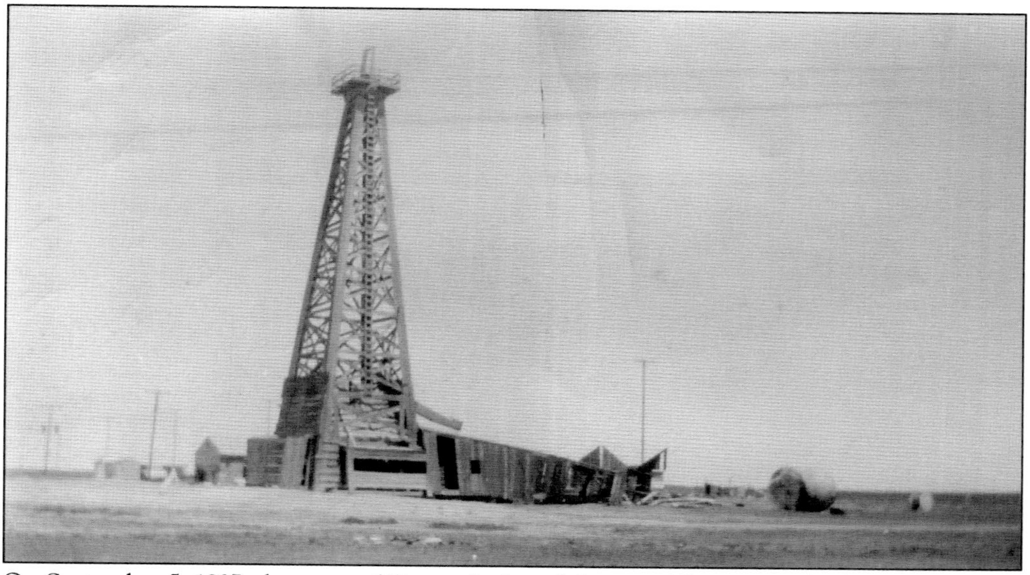

On September 5, 1927, the town of Dumas had a celebration. There was a barbecue, a baseball game, a rodeo, and a dance. The reason for the party was the gas well that had been drilled on the southeast corner of the original town. The well had a flow of 15 million cubic feet of natural gas. It still supplies natural gas to the city.

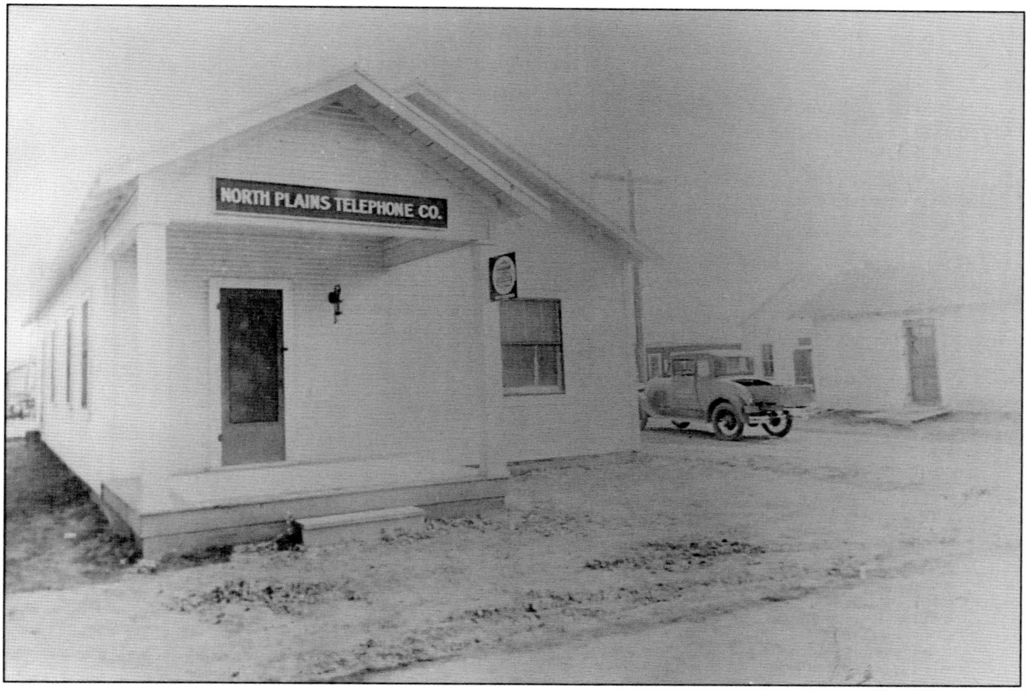

Telephone lines first came to Dumas in about 1905 when the Hartley-Dumas Telephone Company strung lines along barbed-wire fences. The exchange was sold in 1927 to two businessmen who soon found other interests. The following year, R. L. Spencer bought the company and announced a new building and a new name. North Plains Telephone Company served Moore County residents for 34 years.

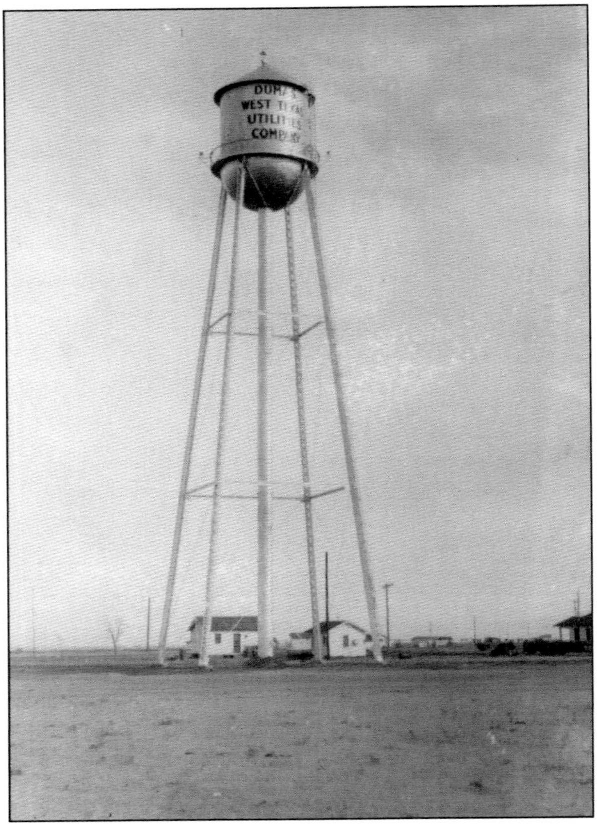

After the Dumas city gas well was drilled, a franchise was granted to W. L. Felts to provide lights, gas, and water to residents in the city. In 1930, West Texas Utilities of Abilene bought out Felts's business and quickly updated equipment and improved service. This water tower was located on the northeast corner of Second Street and Porter Avenue.

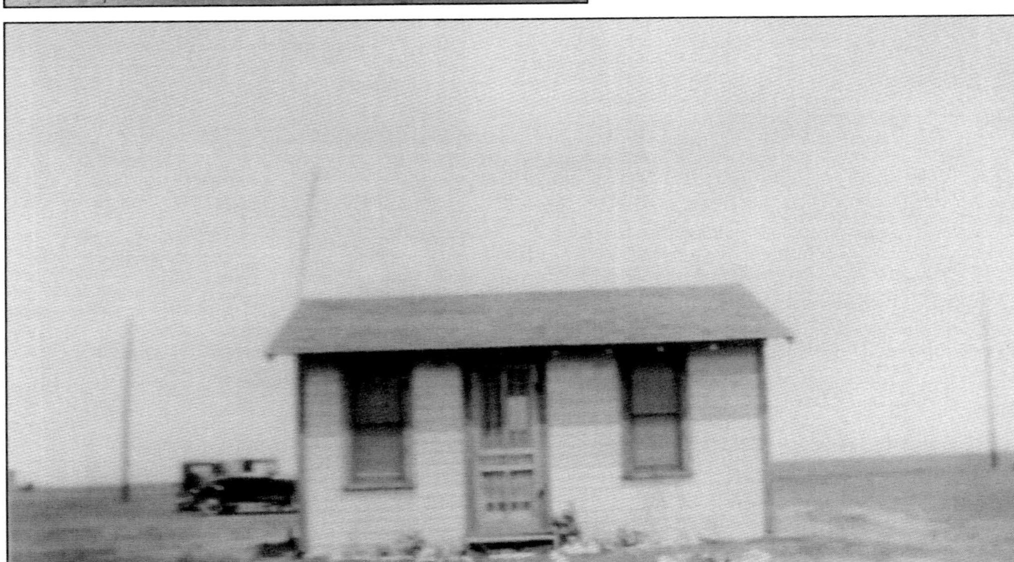

Earl and Alpha Rauh married in the early 1930s. They bought this house on South Bliss Avenue and paid $100 down and $6.25 a week. When the Depression caught up with Moore County, jobs were scare. For a time, Rauh worked for the Works Progress Administration (WPA). As part of the job he helped build the sidewalk in front of his little house. (Courtesy Earl Rauh.)

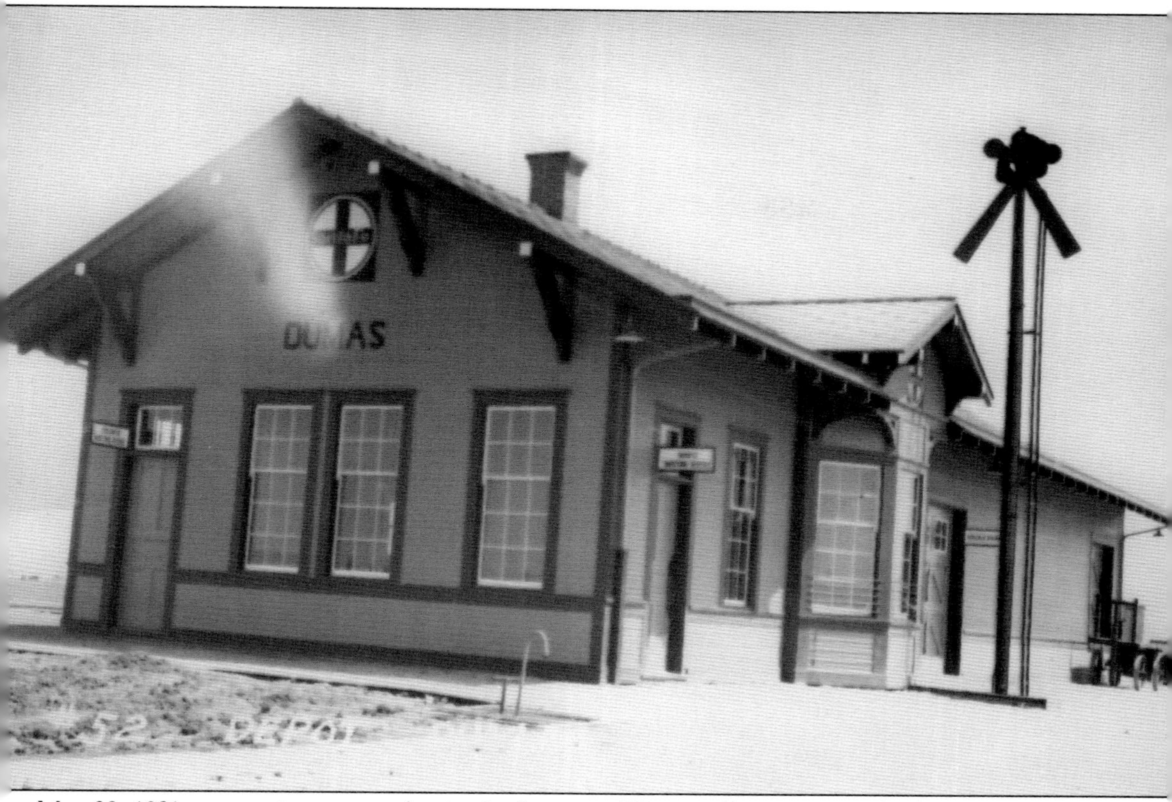

May 29, 1931, was an important day in the history of Dumas. Businesses and schools closed. Delegations from all over the panhandle, including 200 people from Dalhart and 160 from Amarillo, came to help celebrate. The cause for this celebration was the long-awaited arrival of the first train to come puffing into town. Farmers and ranchers enthusiastically welcomed the railroad to Dumas. For ranchers, it meant a quicker and easier way to get their cattle to market. For farmers, it ended long trips to elevators in Hartley or Channing to sell their grain. Three elevators were built alongside the tracks and were in operation by July 1931. (Courtesy Library of Congress.)

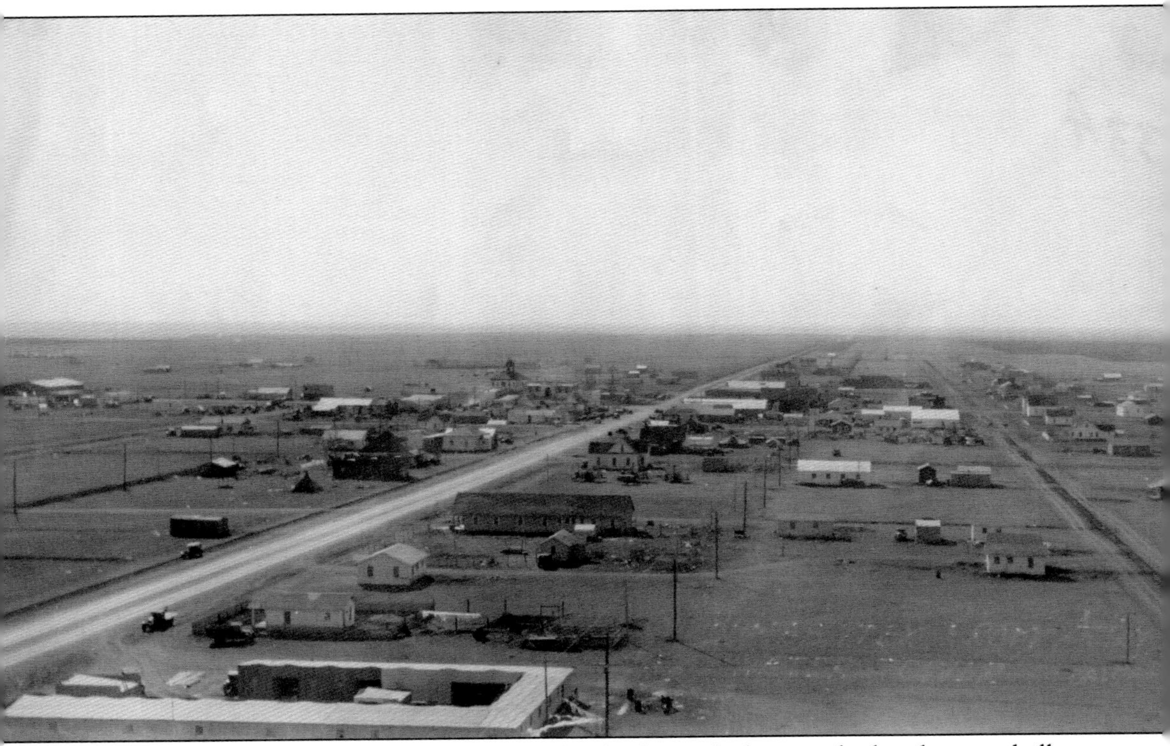

Taken from the new water tower on the north side of town, looking south, this photograph illustrates how quickly changes came to Dumas. The 28 new houses and 8 new downtown buildings had transformed the village into a town. But before this photograph was made, the Depression caught up with Dumas. There weren't enough jobs, and Central Charity was organized. On January 22, 1932, an excerpt from the *Moore County News* read, "For years the streets of Dumas have been a quagmire of mud following any heavy moisture." When Central Charity ran out of funds, businessmen found solutions for both problems. They raised funds to buy caliche and pay workers $1 per day to pave the roads. Newly topped Dumas Avenue begins in the lower left corner of the picture. The original courthouse is to the left of Dumas Avenue. In front of it, construction on the new one is proceeding. Later that year, work began on paving north to Sherman County and south to Potter County. Dumas Avenue would finally be paved.

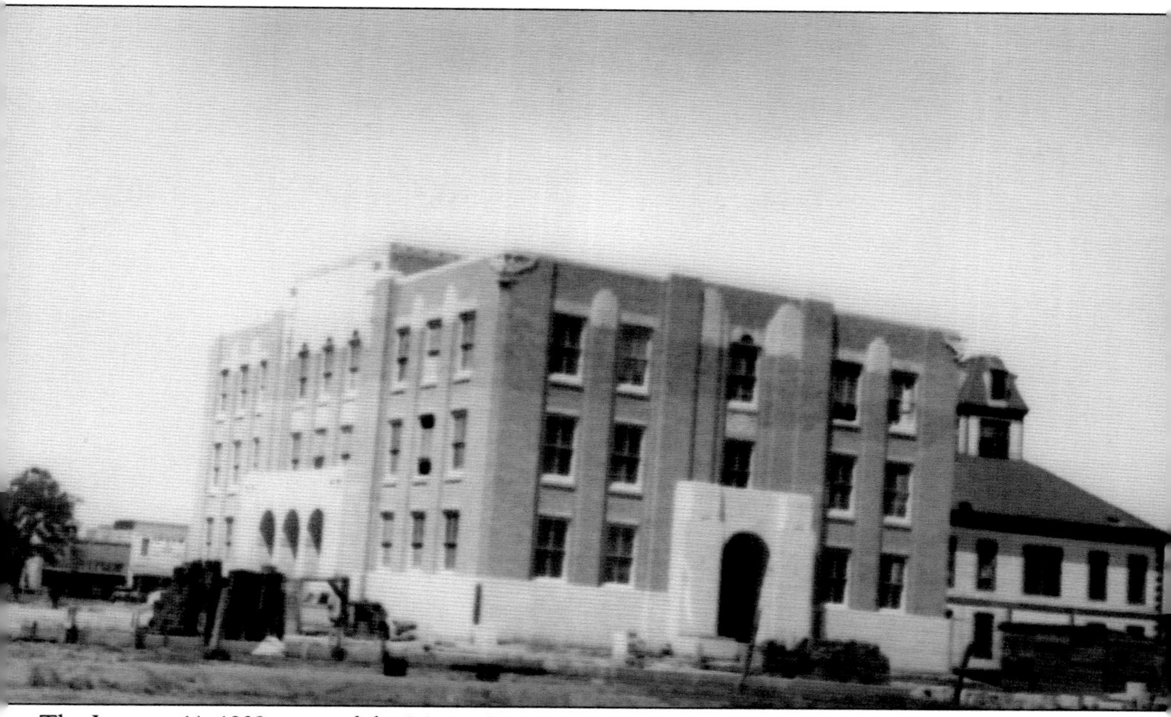

The January 11, 1929, issue of the *Moore County News* reported that the chamber of commerce had started a petition to build a new courthouse. It took more than a year, but their efforts were rewarded when a vote in May 1930 approved bonds of $1.5 million for the project. The fence around the courthouse had to come down. An ordinance was passed in January 1931 to prohibit livestock from roaming freely as they had always done. Surface privies were also outlawed that year. When the building was finished, county offices were on the first floor, and the county judge and justice of the peace were on the second. The third floor held the jail and the sheriff's apartment. On August 7, 1931, the paper reported that during the preceding week, county officials moved into their offices. That weekend, the annual reunion was held along with the usual picnic and rodeo. An article in the next paper read, "Only three 'guests' were 'invited' to the new jail."

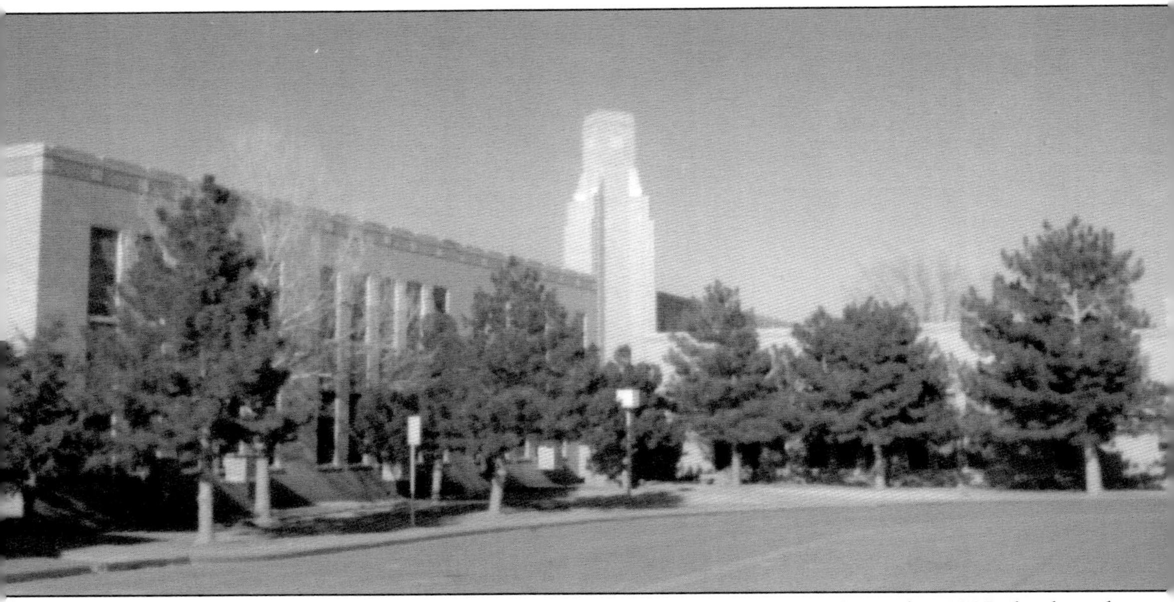

The high school newspaper, the *Prairie Cloud*, published an essay in November 1927 pleading the case for a new school. There was no quick response, but in 1929, enrollment jumped from 200 to 310. The announcement of a railroad promised another increase. In a 1931 election, bonds in the amount of $150,000 were passed for a new school building for all grades. The school was the first to have electricity. It also had a laboratory and an auditorium. The PTA raised $700 for a grand piano as an extra for the auditorium. The football stadium built two years earlier had only one small section of bleachers, but since the school sat on two blocks of land, there was plenty of room for fans to park their cars around it to watch games. The spacious new school building was occupied in April 1932.

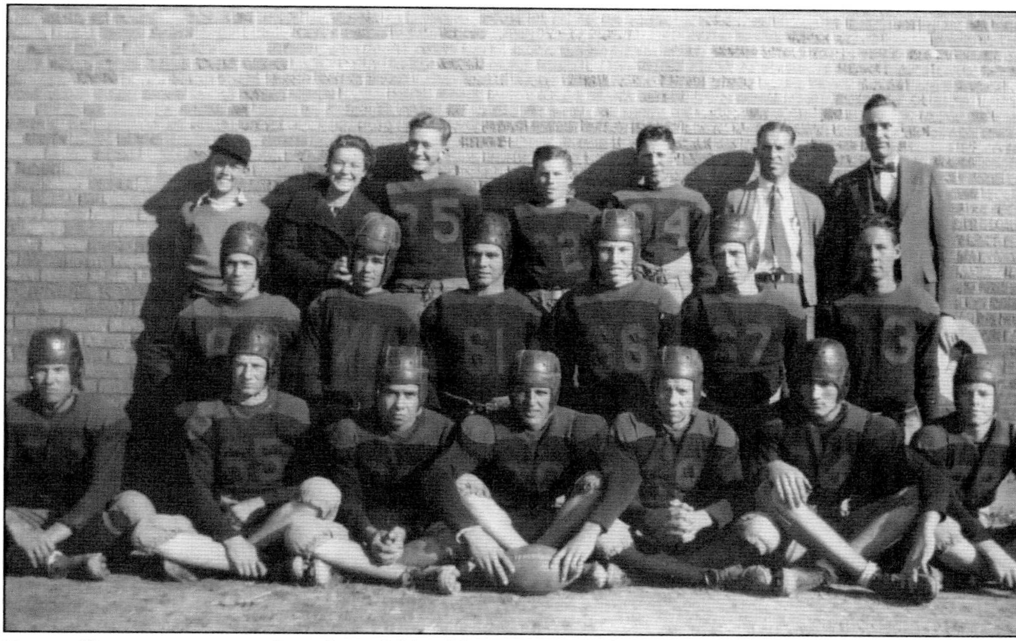

Denny Denman was coach and would lead his team to a district championship in 1935 that year. Standing on the far right is Ted Reid, school superintendent and assistant coach, with Denman to his left. The football queen poses with the Dumas Demons. Denman left his coaching job in 1938 to become postmaster with the post office. He continued working with Dumas youth through the Scouting program.

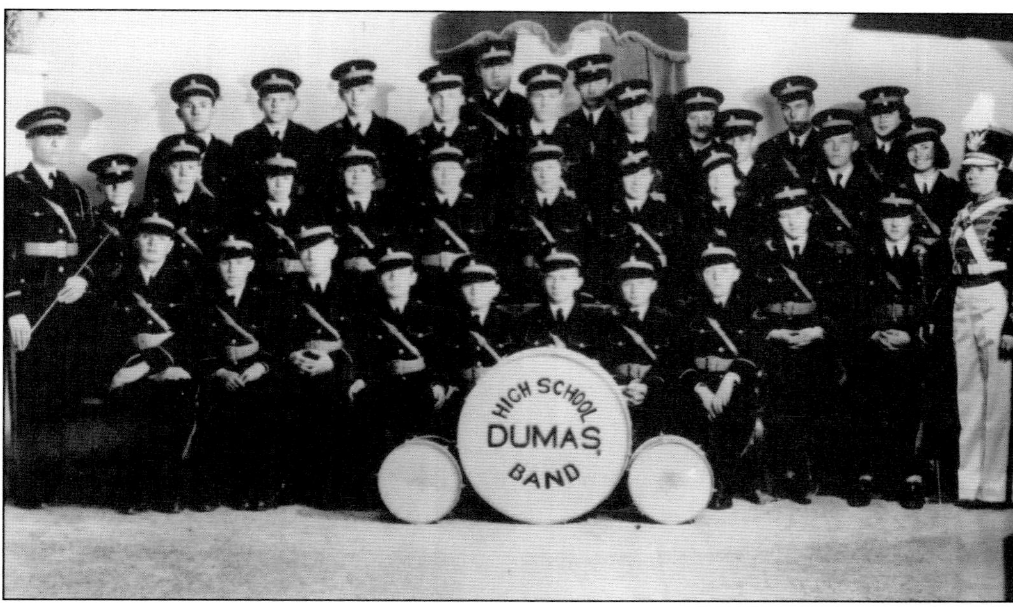

The Dumas Civic Club was organized in 1935 and focused on industrial development in the area, but it did not neglect the cultural development of the community. The members sponsored the fair and pushed for the organization of a high school band. The band was organized in 1937. Here members proudly display their brand-new uniforms.

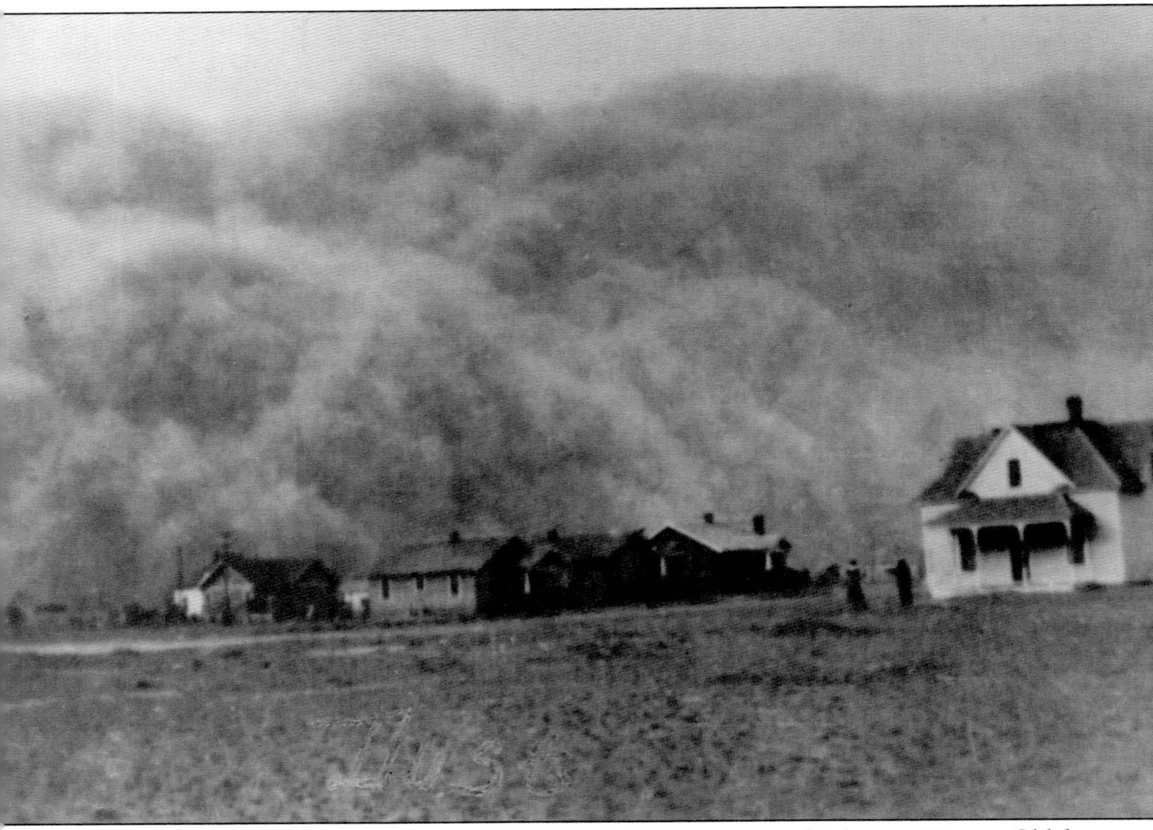

By the thousands, settlers poured into the Southern Plains states of Arkansas, Kansas, Oklahoma, and Texas during the late 1800s and early 1900s. For most, the land they plowed provided a good living until 1931, when the rains stopped and the wind started. The eight-year drought that followed devastated the land and its owners. As the drought took its toll, families were forced to leave and seek another way to make a living. The soil from those plowed fields was picked up and carried by tremendous wind until its energy was spent. It is hard to imagine the scope of the storms. This photograph and the one on the following page were both made as the April 14, 1935, storm approached Dumas. Photographs made on that day in Dodge City, Kansas; Cimarron County, Oklahoma; and Dallam and Gray Counties in Texas all look the same.

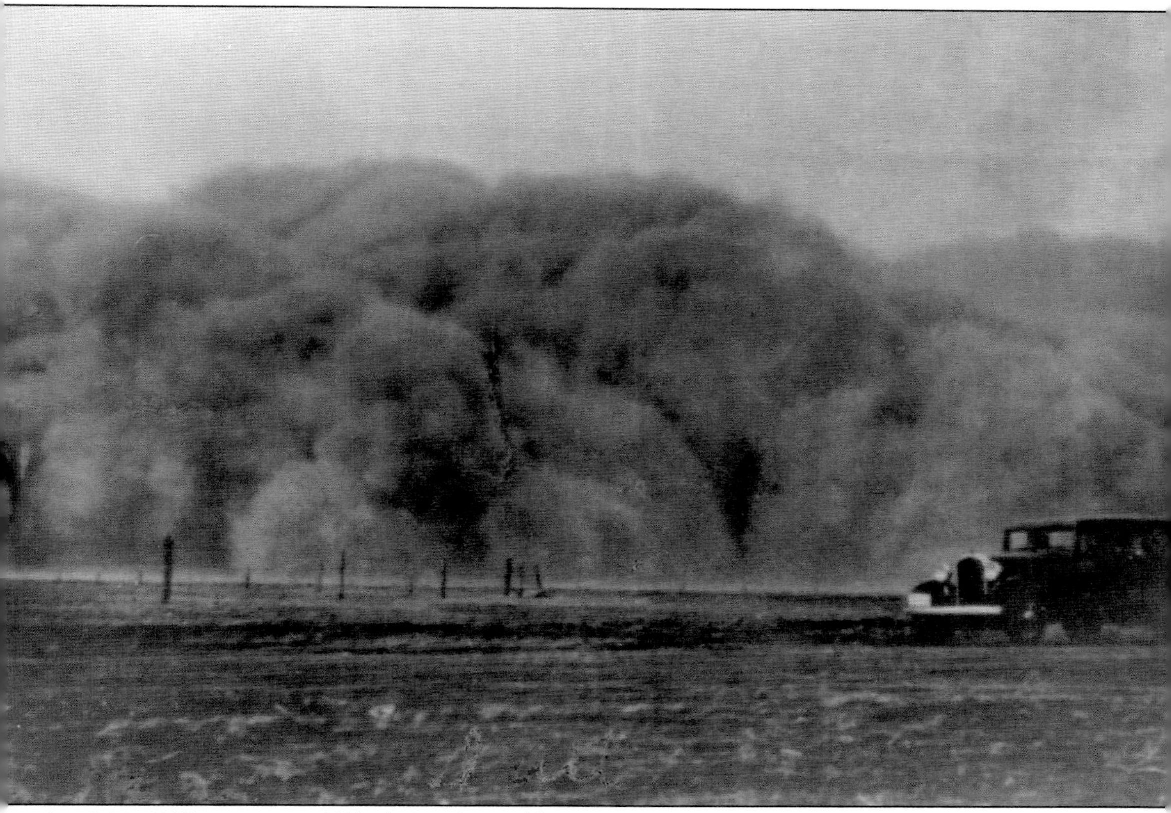

April 14, 1935, was named Black Sunday. Old-timers refer to that storm as the "Granddaddy of them all." It extended from eastern New Mexico to western Oklahoma, from southwestern Kansas to the south plains of Texas, and lasted for hours. Ola Covey, a longtime Texas Panhandle resident, described it: "That thing rolled in and it wasn't like a dust cloud, coming from out of the sky. It was like something creeping along on the ground, just turning over and over and over. We watched it until it hit the school building there and it just simply rolled over it. . . . One minute you could see the school building and the next minute, you couldn't. . . . It just simply covered the thing over. It was just an amazing thing to watch. . . . There were a whole lot of stories told about that storm, about how people got scared and got religion and everything else. People really got scared. It was a scary thing."

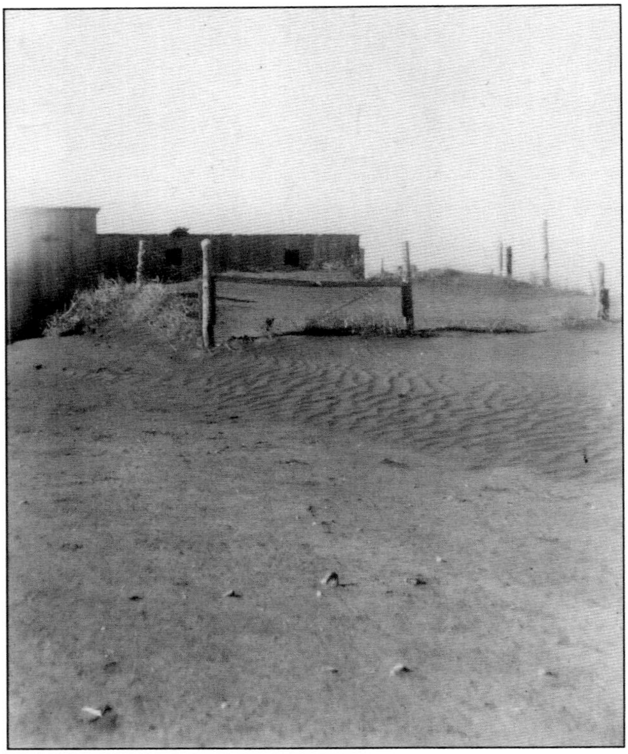

Fierce wind piled sand along fence lines so that cattle and horses walked over them. In other places, soil was stripped down to the hardpan. In *100 Moore Years*, Fred Squyres wrote, "The depression was bad enough, but to have the years of drought that helped create the Dust Bowl was more than many Moore County farmers and ranchers could endure." If farmers stayed, a few had money coming from oil companies; some received enough from federal relief programs to survive; and some received help from local merchants who "carried" them when they couldn't pay their debts. Squyres quoted an oft-told story about the owners of the general store, a filling station, and the blacksmith shop: "The ones who didn't owe Jake Phillips, owed Jim Crabb, and they all owed Frank Anderson." (Both courtesy Freda Keeney.)

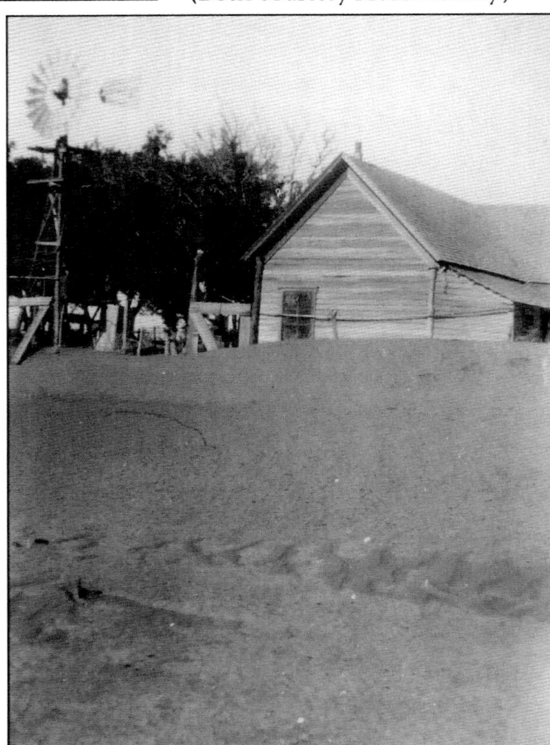

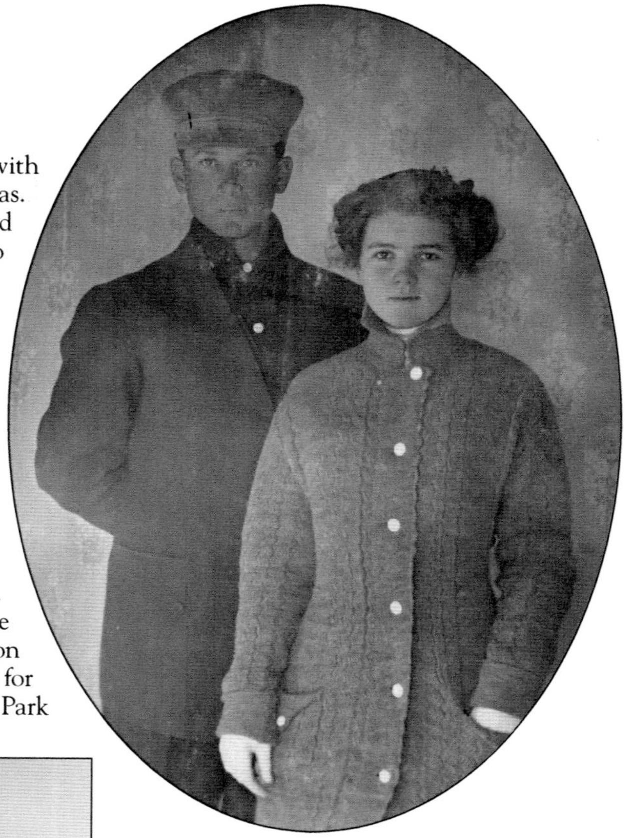

As a teenager, Noel McDade moved with his family to a farm southeast of Dumas. Shown with his bride in 1909, he farmed until 1919 when the couple moved into Dumas. He ran a grocery store for a time then went to work in a bank. In 1928, he bought the bank. He spearheaded efforts to incorporate Dumas in 1930, became the first mayor, and led the city through the Depression. He and area leaders met with senators and bank officials in Washington to successfully plead for relief for area farmers facing foreclosure. With farmers' input, he wrote a plan to prevent wind erosion. It was, in large part, adopted by the state as the Soil Conservation Wind Erosion Act. McDade served as county judge for 10 years beginning in 1935. McDade Park honors his leadership.

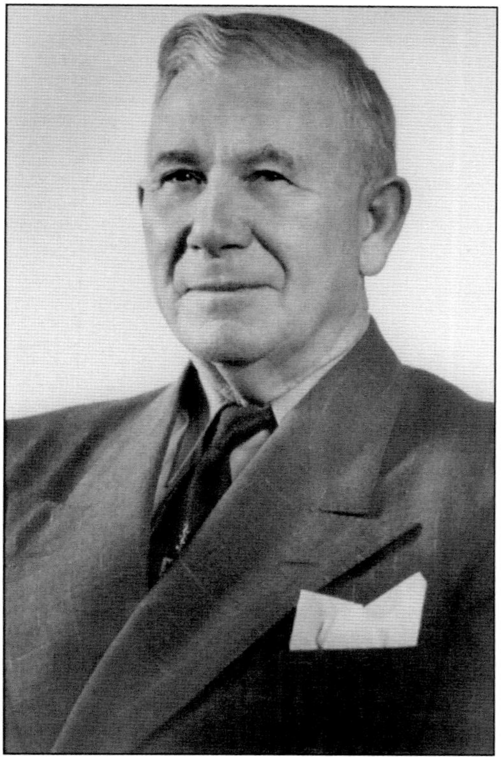

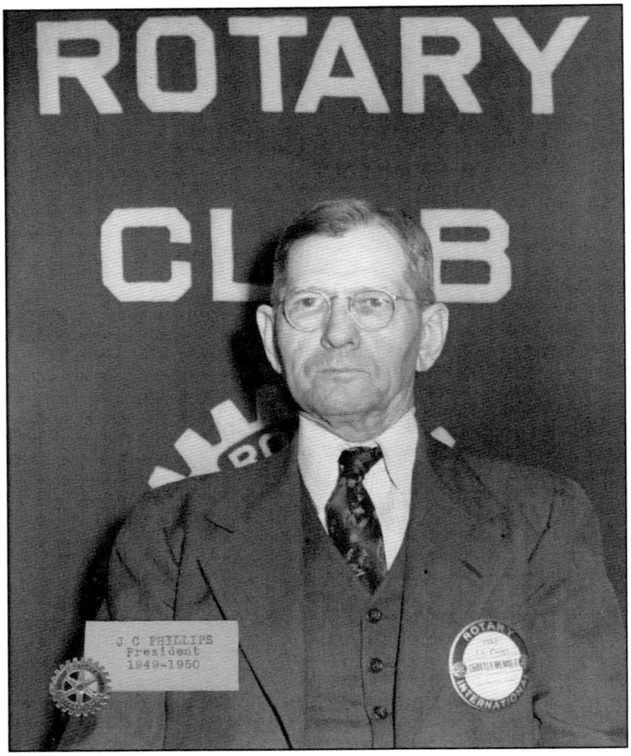

In 1913, Jacob Collier "Jake" Phillips took over his family's general store. During the Depression, he sold goods on credit to customers and "carried" their indebtedness. In *100 Moore Years*, Fred Squyres wrote, "One common story is that Jake Phillips could have owned half the farms in Moore County if he had wanted to." Phillips ran the store until his death in 1956.

Chester Logue faced unusual challenges when he was elected sheriff in 1928. Prohibition was in effect and so was bootlegging. He said most of his troubles were over when Prohibition was over. Belle Plain, where rough boomtown characters exiled from Borger had settled, occasionally required his attention. In one raid, three women and one man were charged with vagrancy. In 1936, Logue left the job for a quiet farm.

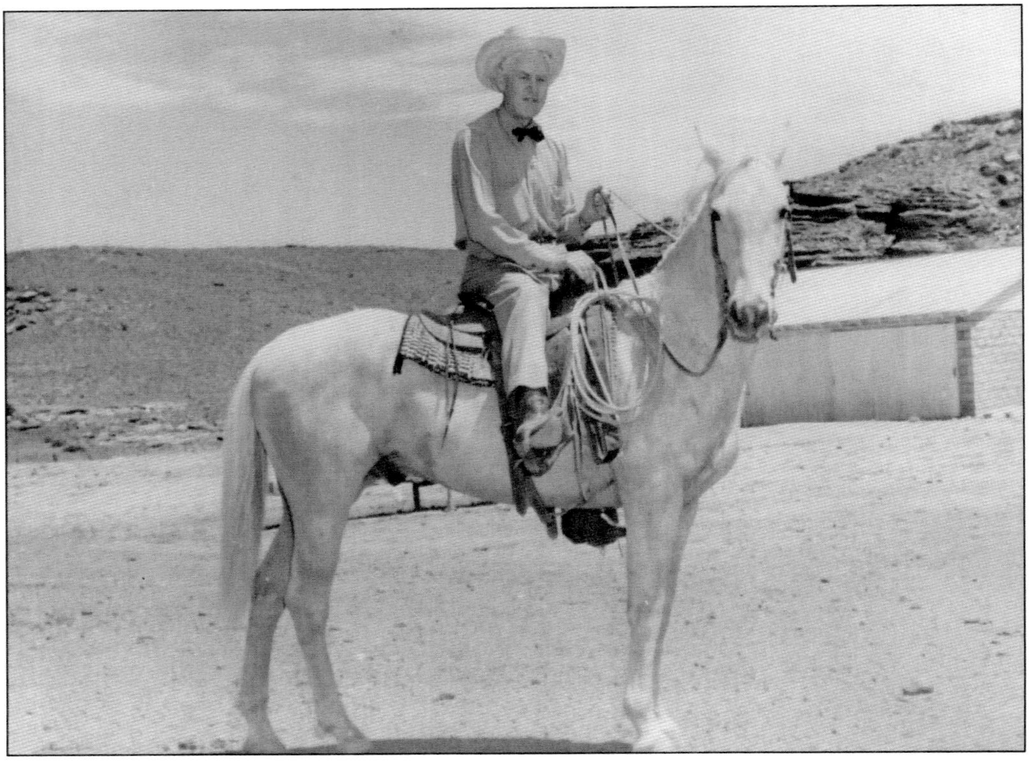

Five

Busy Years

By 1935, better times were on the horizon. Several petroleum companies announced their intentions to drill for oil. The following year, two large carbon plants and a zinc smelter were built and began operations. Shamrock Oil and Gas announced an expansion and construction of a large carbon plant. Paving was completed between Dumas and Hartley and Dumas and Sunray. All those activities created a new prosperity for Dumas. In 1936, it cost about $3,000 to build a six-room house. A total of $50,030 in building permits was issued in the first half of the year.

Area farmers had to wait a while longer before they realized better times. Not until August 1939 did they relish a 4.5-inch rain. A foot of snow in December was further relief. Normal rainfall returned then, and the drought was finally over.

Pres. Franklin D. Roosevelt proposed a peacetime draft in the summer of 1940. In November, the first two Dumas men left for the army. Within weeks, five other inductees and two volunteers left.

The attack on Pearl Harbor on December 7, 1941, stunned Dumas residents as it did the nation. The first casualty from Dumas was killed that day at Hickham Field. Before World War II was finished, around 700 Moore County residents volunteered for or were drafted into service. Like other Americans, Dumas residents endured rationing, bought victory bonds, and supported war efforts in every way they could.

In 1942, Cactus Ordnance Works construction began, and the town of Cactus came into being. While the plant was being built, its purpose was kept secret. Construction on another plant south of Dumas started that year—its purpose also secret. Expansions and constructions continued, and before the end of World War II, at least 14 plants, with camps nearby, were scattered across the county.

Activities slowed for a short time after the war was over, but another surge soon followed. During the decade beginning in 1940, population in Dumas increased from 2,117 to 6,127. Those were truly busy years.

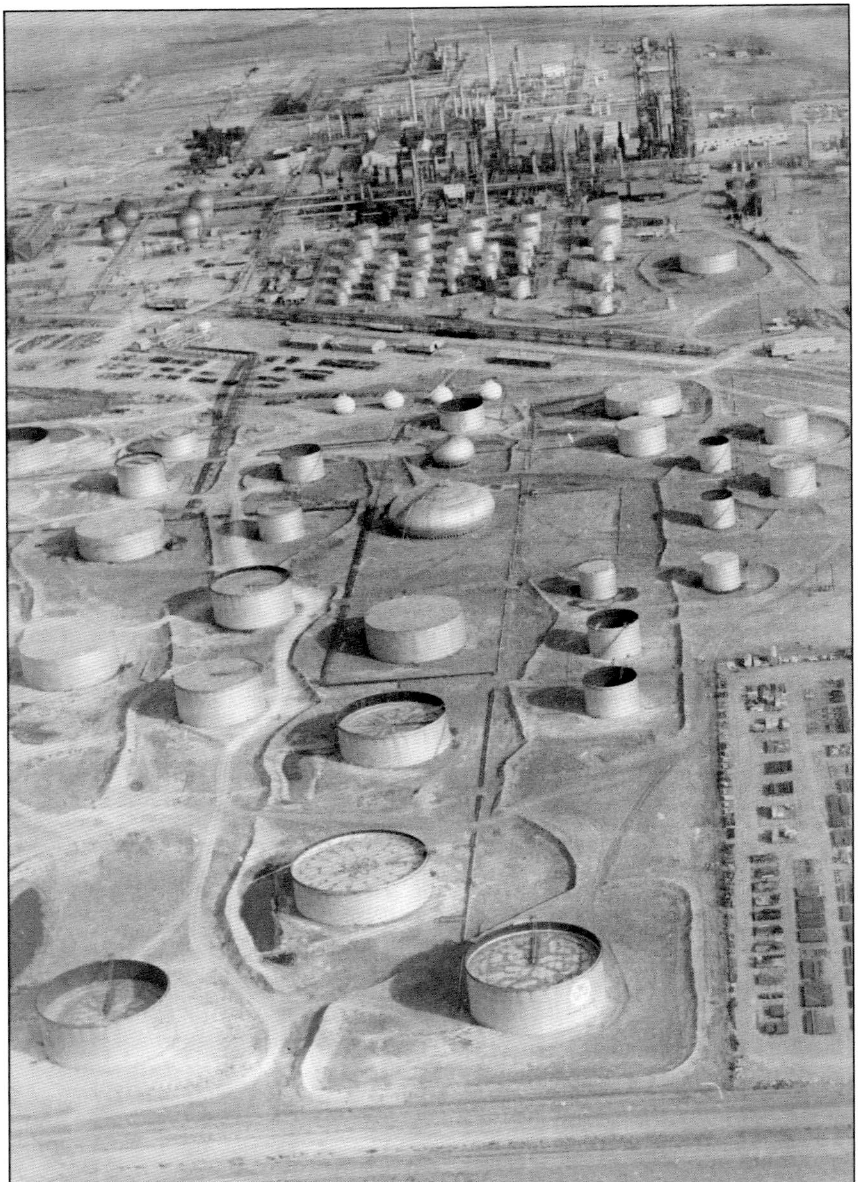

John J. Sherrin named his central and north Texas oil promotion company Shamrock. The company was incorporated as Shamrock Oil and Gas, Inc., when he came to the panhandle in 1927 to lease land for exploration. Early efforts in Gray County resulted in finding significant amounts of gas for which there was no market. Sherrin built a refinery southwest of Pampa and continued the search for oil. In August 1930, they had oil when the No. 1 Brumley, northeast of Dumas, came in. Soon more oil was discovered. In 1932, the company bought a small refinery near Sunray, renovated it, and provided 25 much-needed jobs. Next they announced plans to build a plant on the McKee lease northeast of Dumas. In 1934, with Reliance Carbon Company, Shamrock built a carbon black plant near the McKee refinery. Additional expansions increased production from the plant's original 60 million cubic feet of gas to 250 million cubic feet. This photograph taken in 1970 illustrates further growth.

In 1936, Shamrock, Continental Oil Company, and R. I. Wishnick formed Continental Carbon. A plant was constructed north of the McKee Refinery. Carbon black, manufactured from natural gas, is used in ink, tires, and paint. Workers powdered their faces in an effort to keep the black off. As seen in the photograph of W. M. Chambless, it didn't work perfectly. (Courtesy Judy Garmany.)

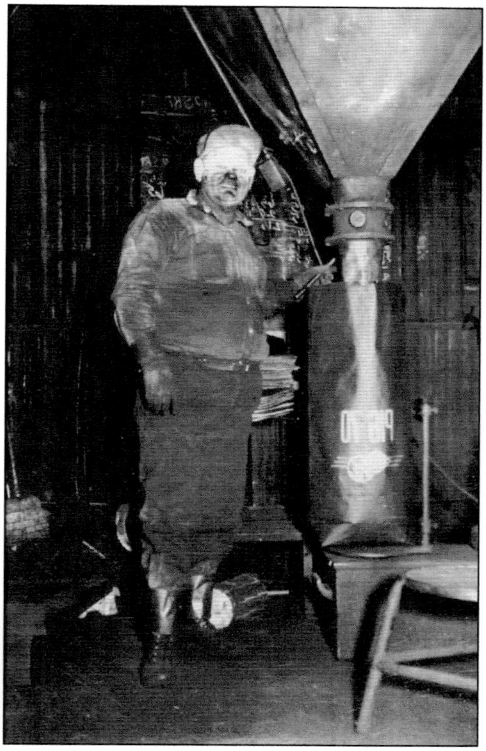

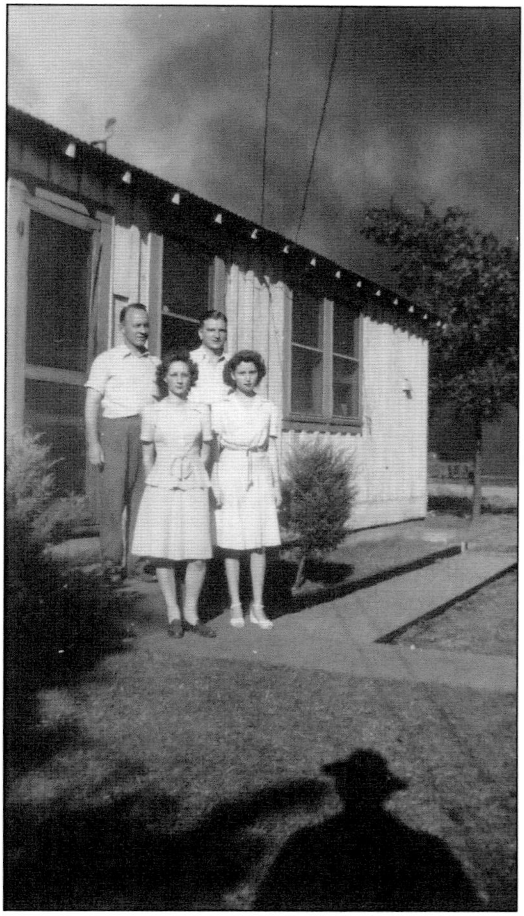

The office staff of Continental Carbon stands in front of the office. From left to right, they are Ross Reding, Shelby ?, Jereline Musick, and Totsie Williams. The "clouds" behind them are actually smoke emanating from the plant. There were 40 homes in the camp near the plant. Homemakers had to check the direction of the wind before hanging their laundry. (Courtesy Jereline Musick.)

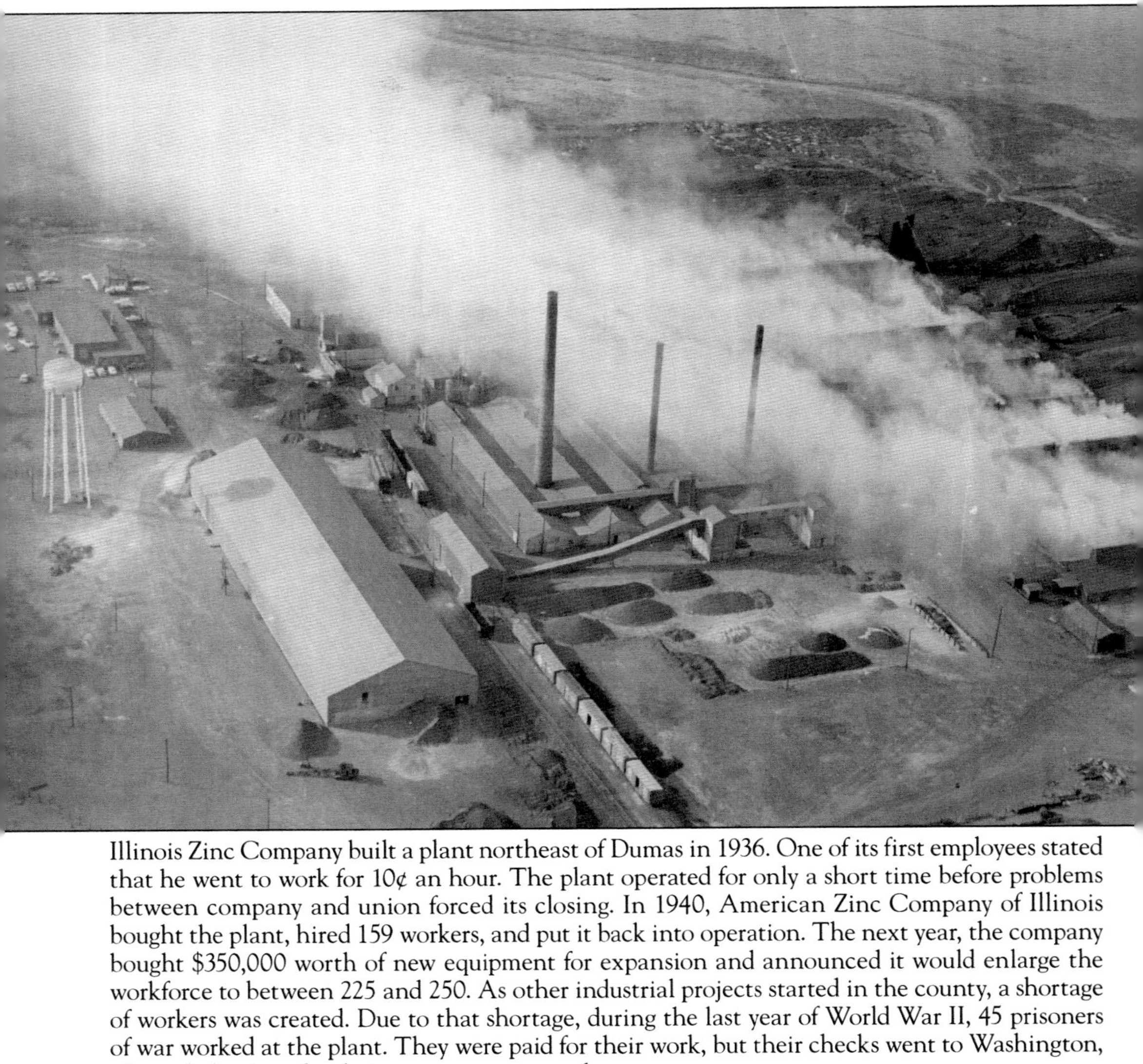

Illinois Zinc Company built a plant northeast of Dumas in 1936. One of its first employees stated that he went to work for 10¢ an hour. The plant operated for only a short time before problems between company and union forced its closing. In 1940, American Zinc Company of Illinois bought the plant, hired 159 workers, and put it back into operation. The next year, the company bought $350,000 worth of new equipment for expansion and announced it would enlarge the workforce to between 225 and 250. As other industrial projects started in the county, a shortage of workers was created. Due to that shortage, during the last year of World War II, 45 prisoners of war worked at the plant. They were paid for their work, but their checks went to Washington, where deductions for their expenses were made.

Zinc is used for galvanizing, die casting, and brass production. The zinc concentrate was obtained primarily from Mexico and the southwestern United States. This worker has been to the furnace to fill the bucket with molten zinc, which he is pouring into the molds to form 60-pound blocks.

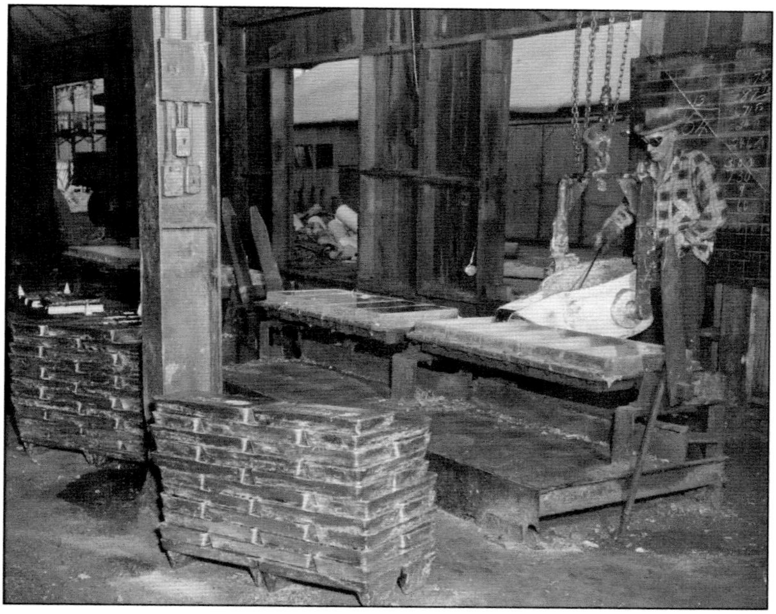

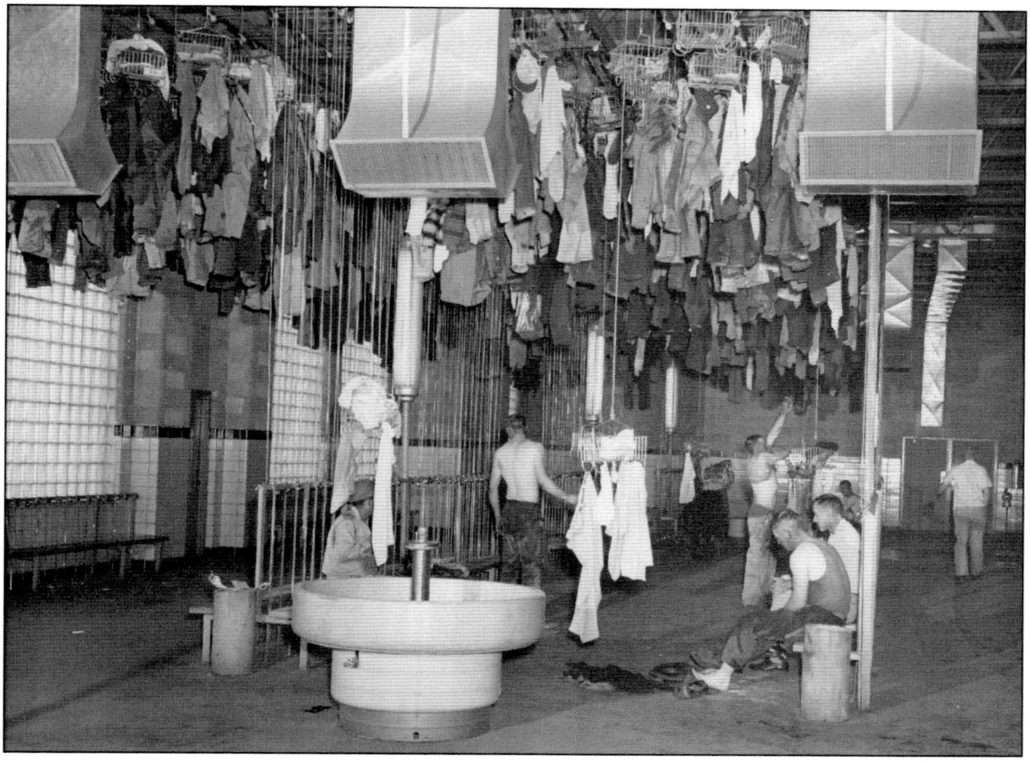

Over the years, an average of 350 employees kept the zinc plant running seven days a week, 24 hours a day. The men worked in extremely hot conditions. After a shift, a shower and a change of clothing were necessary. There was not enough floor space to store all the baskets, so they were stored overhead. A hook on the side of the basket allowed the men to hang their wet clothes to dry for the next shift.

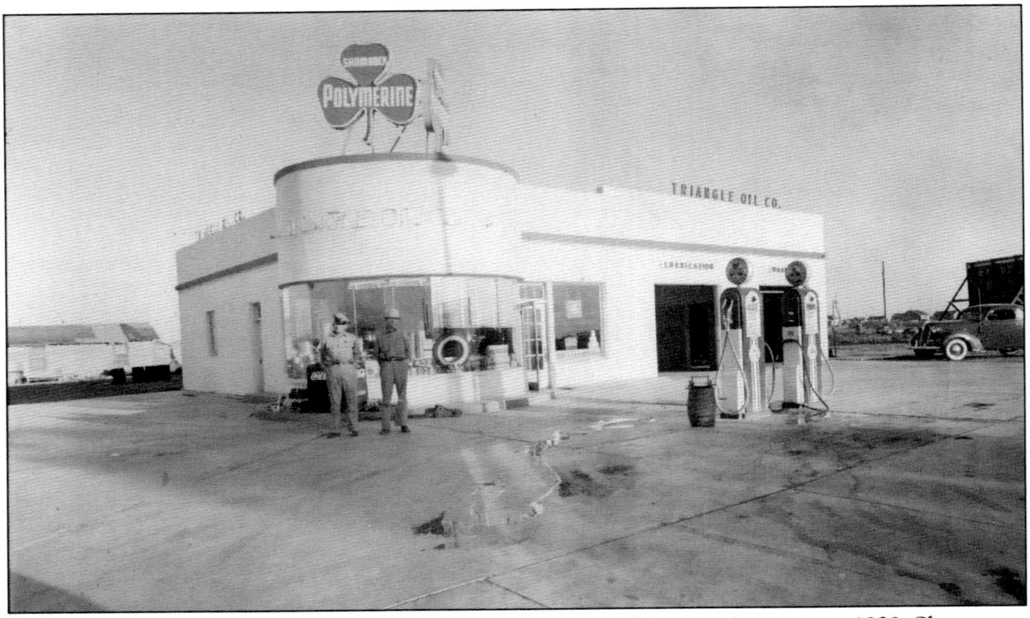

James Morton "Jim" Crabb built a new building at First and Dumas Avenues in 1939. Shown are Dan Trayler (left) and Crabb. When he started the business in 1930, he bought gasoline for less than 2¢ a gallon from Borger's McMillen Refinery. Later he bought and hauled gasoline from the Apache Refinery at Sunray. He received invoice No. 1 on gasoline purchased from Shamrock's McKee plant. He and his son, Jimmy, ran the business for almost 60 years.

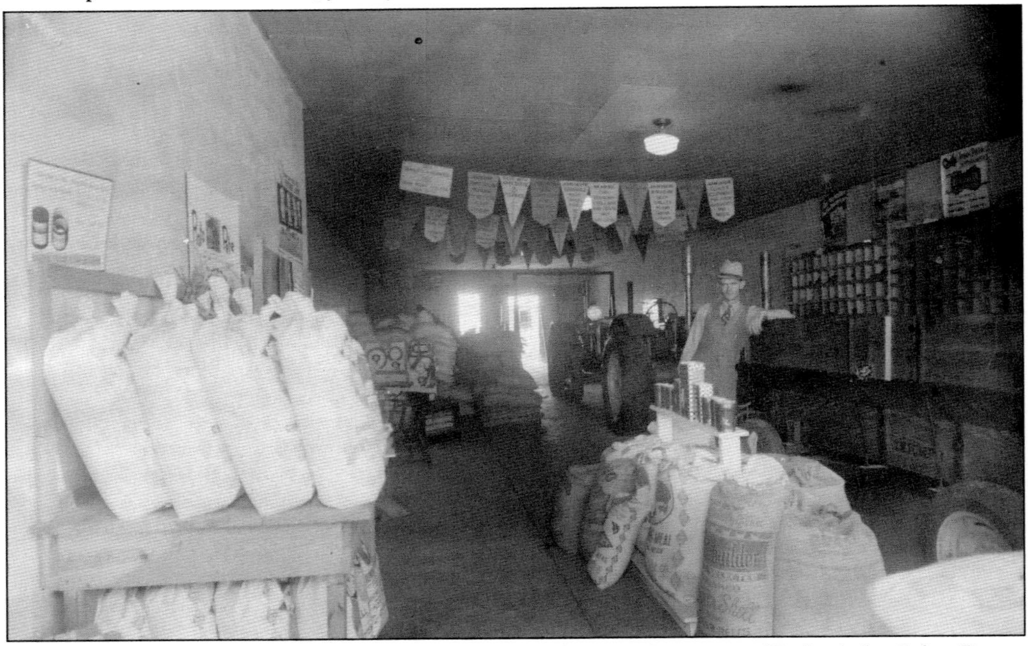

A. B. "Chink" Burnett operated the Burnett Machinery Company. He had the John Deere dealership and worked as a mechanic. He ground feed for local farmers and ranchers and labeled it "Burnett's Best." This photograph dated June 1939 shows Burnett inside his store in the Smith Building in the 700 block of Dumas Avenue.

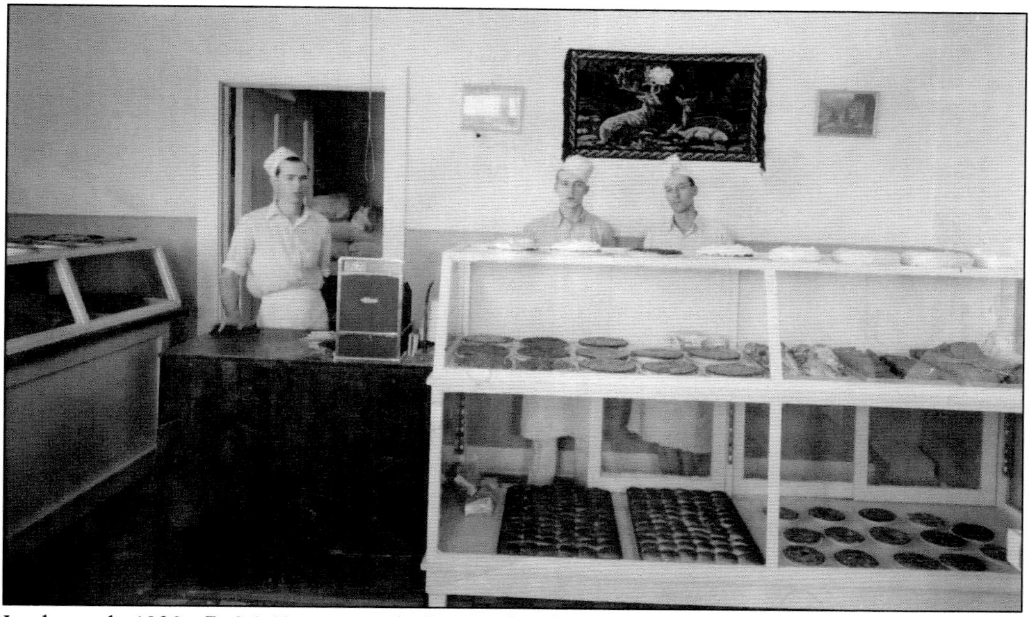

In the early 1930s, R. M. Keeney worked in his brother's bakery in Amarillo. In 1934, an elderly couple wanted to sell their bakery in Dumas and retire. R. M. bought it and survived some of the worst years of the Depression. He kept gaining customers, and by the mid-1940s, he had eight employees and four delivery trucks. He sold wholesale and retail to cafés, schools, and grocery stores. (Courtesy Mert Keeney.)

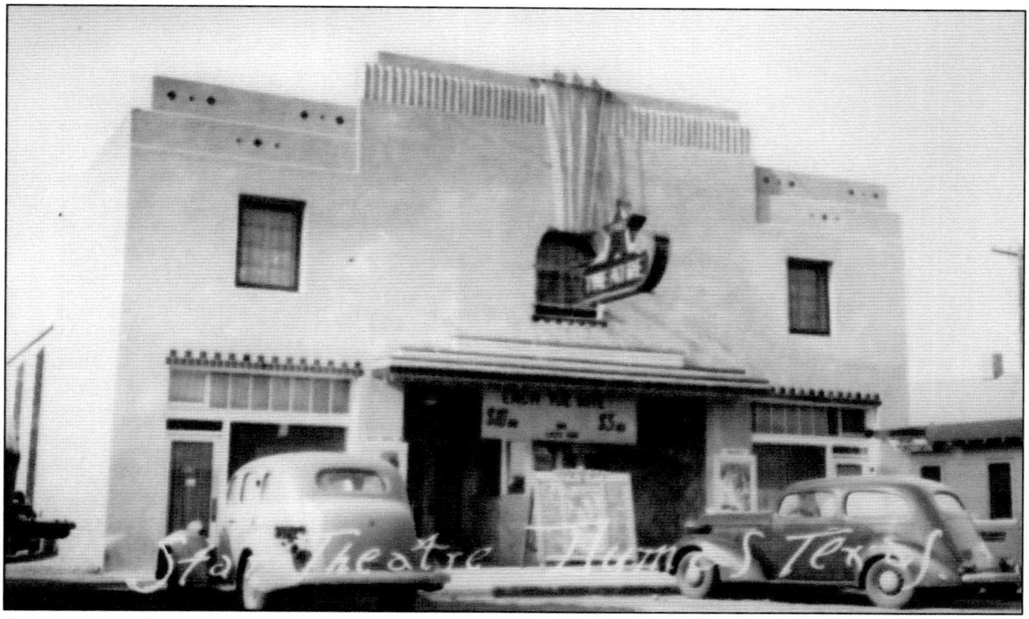

Another small business that survived the Depression was the theater. Bob Powell bought the Gem Theater at Seventh Street and Dumas Avenue in 1930. Later it was moved to 117 West Seventh Street. In 1937, Powell opened the brand-new air-conditioned Star Theater across the street. During World War II, crowds swarmed the theater in search of a pleasant diversion. Adult tickets were about 50¢, drinks and popcorn 10¢.

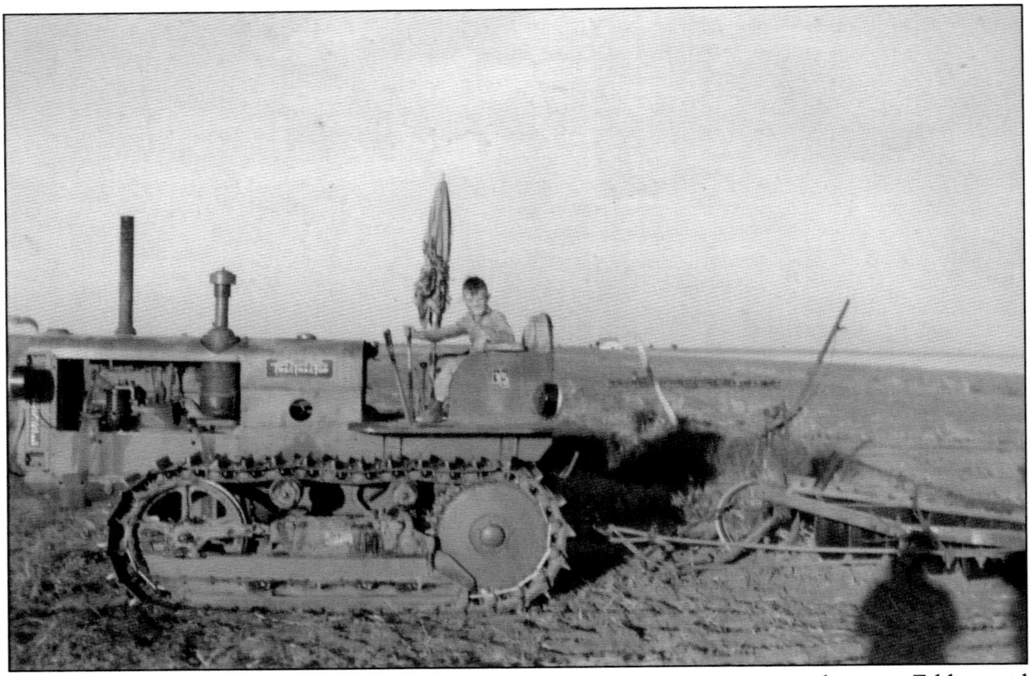

Ed Stallwitz farmed a section of land southwest of Dumas. In an interview, his son, Eddie, said that all through the 1930s, his father could not grow enough wheat to have seed for the next year's crop. He worked other jobs that included highway construction and measuring land, and he kept on farming. In 1939, he bought an International Harvester TD35 crawler from Jake Phillips General Store. Eddie, age 7, tried it out. (Courtesy Eddie Stallwitz.)

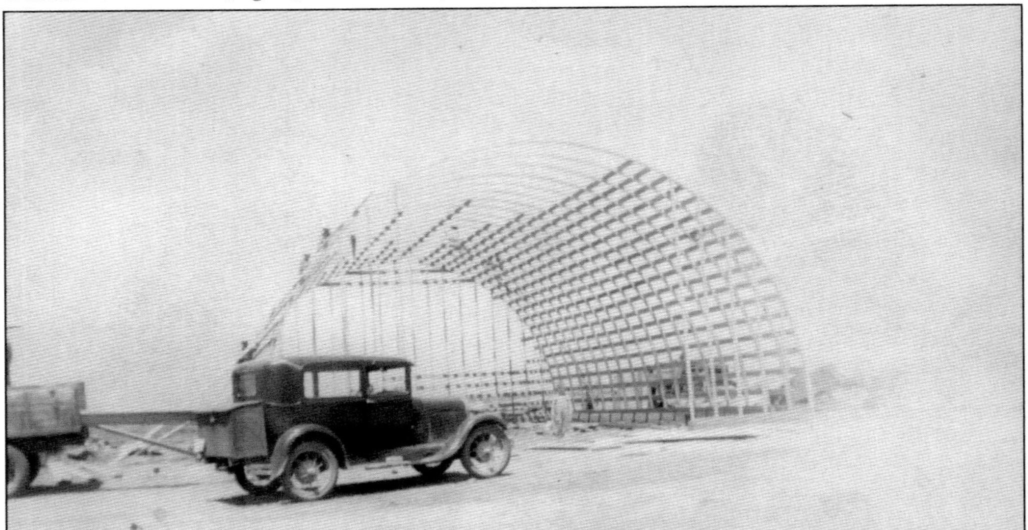

Quonset hut barns became popular after World War II. Stallwitz was ahead of the trend. He built his in 1939. Unlike those built later with metal frames, his barn had a wooden frame. It was enclosed with tin. His son said there was one problem with that barn—it leaked like a sieve. (Courtesy Eddie Stallwitz.)

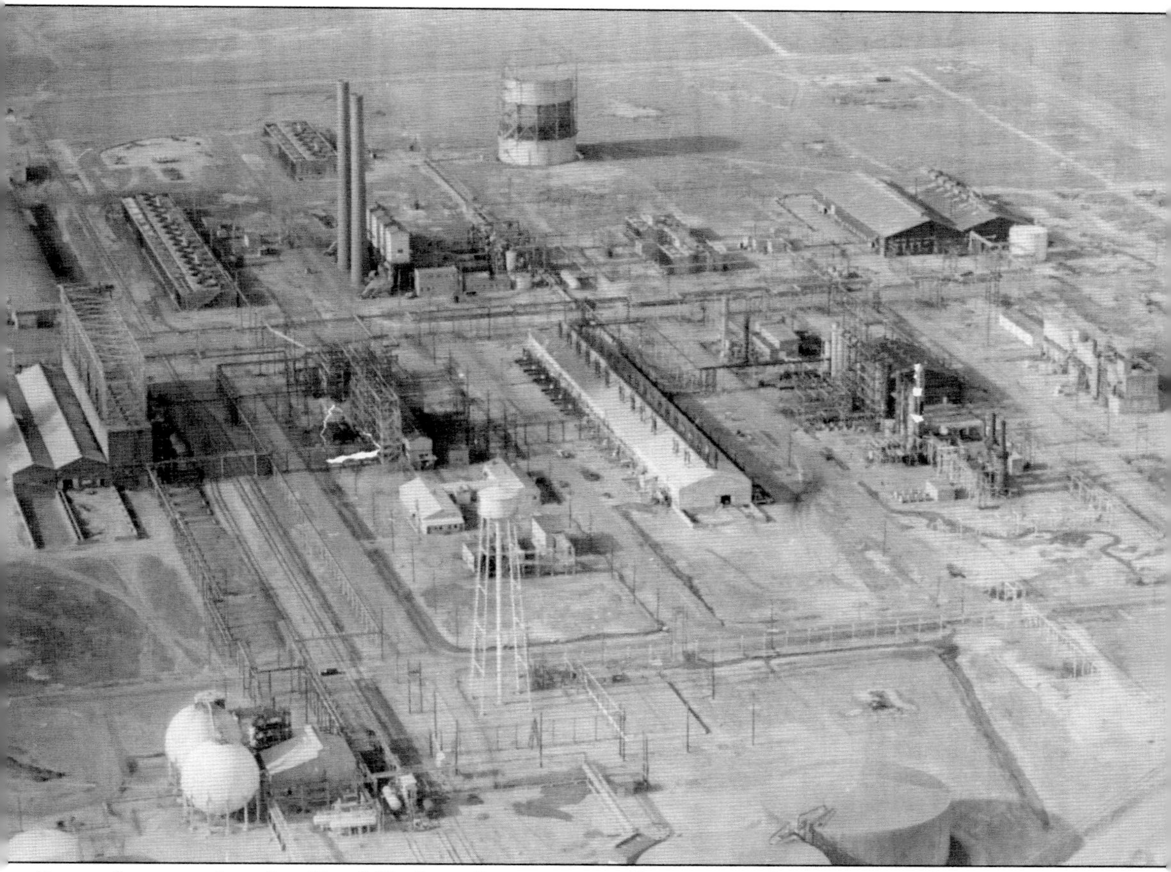

Just a few months after Pearl Harbor, Congressman Eugene Worley announced a contract with Chemical Construction Company to build a plant in Moore County. The product to be manufactured was not named, nor was the plant's exact location. Activities 12 miles north of Dumas, such as surveying and drilling of water wells, gave away its location. The U.S. Army Corps of Engineers arrived to supervise the project, which came to be known at Cactus Ordnance Works. Plans called for 35 staff houses, five 63-man dormitories, 2 women's dormitories, and 75 two-family duplexes along with a cafeteria, canteen, and fire station. Subcontractor Brown and Root Construction built much of the plant, intended to produce ammonia from natural gas for use in making munitions. Employment was over 2,000 and the plant 85 percent complete in May 1943, when Washington decided the product was no longer needed and ordered the plant liquidated. Other companies tried to keep the plant running but were unsuccessful until 1949, when Phillips Petroleum bought the plant to continue producing ammonia and to make a commercial fertilizer.

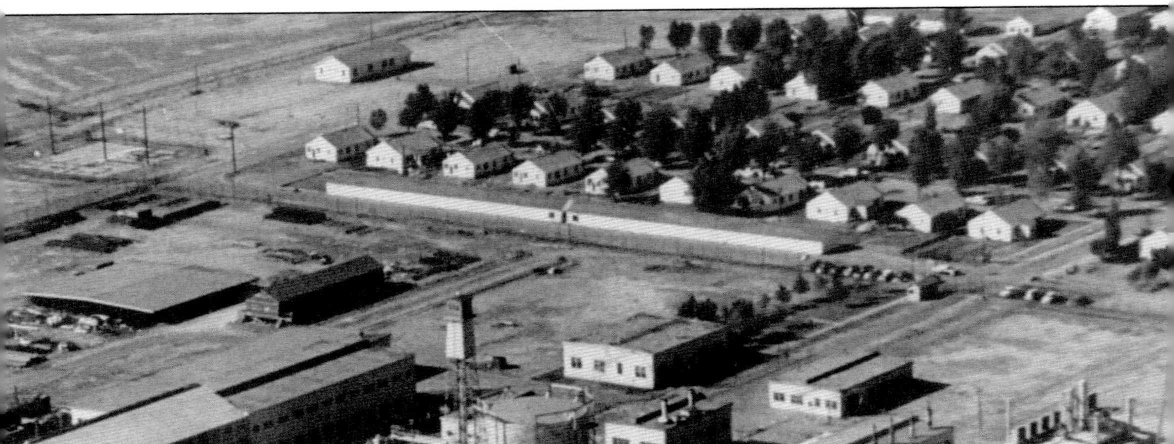

In March 1942, the Department of the Interior purchased land from J. W. Crawford on which to build a helium plant 17 miles south of Dumas. The next month, construction contracts were delivered to Stearns-Rogers Manufacturing Company of Denver. The secret project got one announcement in the *Moore County News*. It stated only that a plant was being built in the panhandle. Even after the plant was completed, its location was classified. Construction proceeded at the fastest possible rate to meet the navy's dire need for helium. The Bureau of Mines was responsible for the plant's operation, and by March 1942, it was producing helium. Security was tight during the early years of the plant. Note the old oil field derrick in the center of this photograph. It was used as a watchtower and had a guard on duty around the clock. The plant was named Exell Helium Plant. (Courtesy Bureau of Mines.)

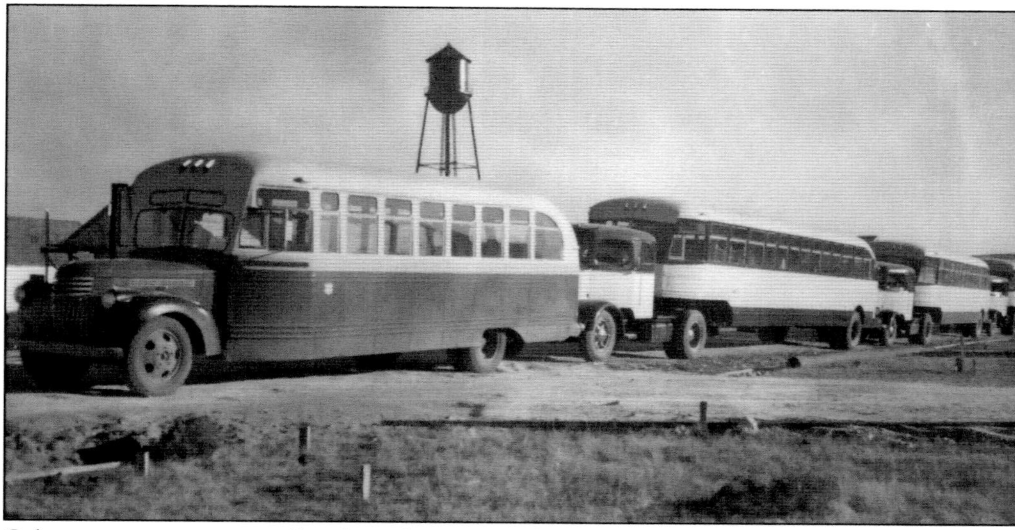

Other wartime projects offered employment to both skilled and unskilled laborers, and the workforce was a fraction of what it had been a few years earlier. Even so, this line of 72-passenger buses indicates a sizable number of workers. In addition to the helium plant, 75 houses, a recreation hall, and long garages to be shared by residents were built within a matter of months. (Courtesy Bureau of Mines.)

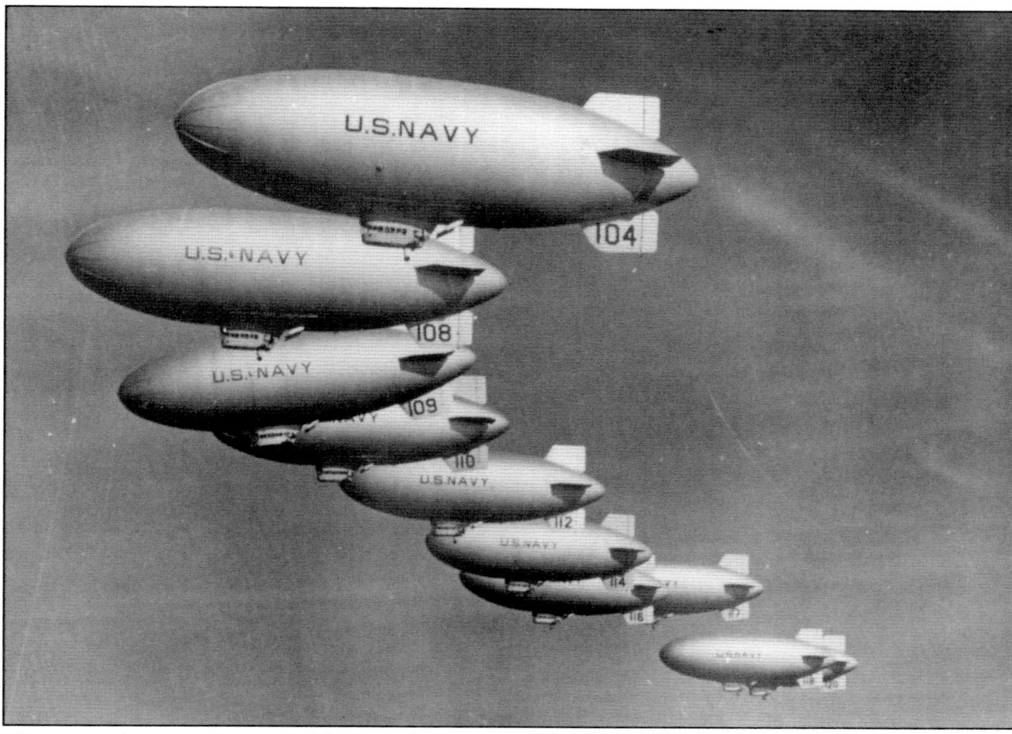

The navy desperately needed helium for its blimp antisubmarine patrol service. Between 1942 and 1945, these dirigibles escorted 89,000 ships loaded with troops, military equipment, and supplies without the loss of a single ship to the enemy. This picture was captioned "March of the Mammoths." (Courtesy Bureau of Mines.)

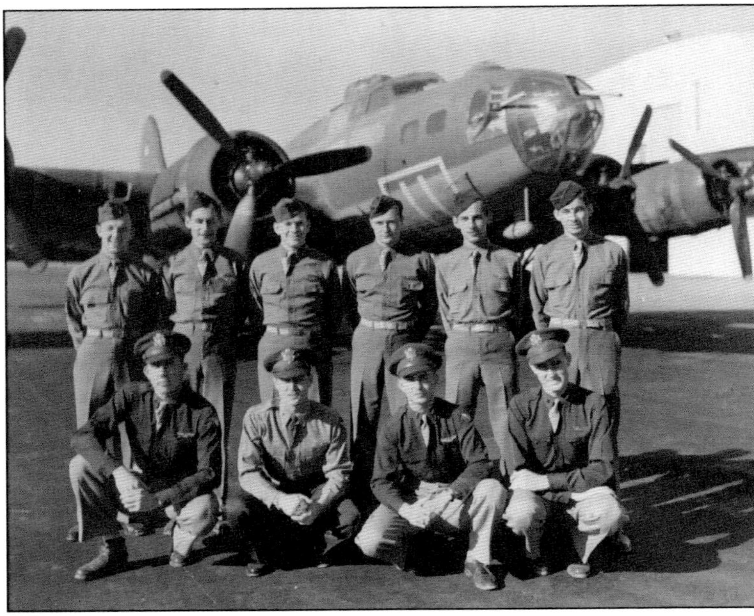

Forrest Clayton Piatt worked for Shamrock Oil and Gas when he registered for the draft on July 1, 1941. He went into the U.S. Air Force in 1942 and became a navigator. He completed 50 missions on the Flying Fortress *Joanne* and won a number of decorations, including the Distinguished Flying Cross and an Air Medal with three Oak Clusters. Piatt is the first man kneeling on the left.

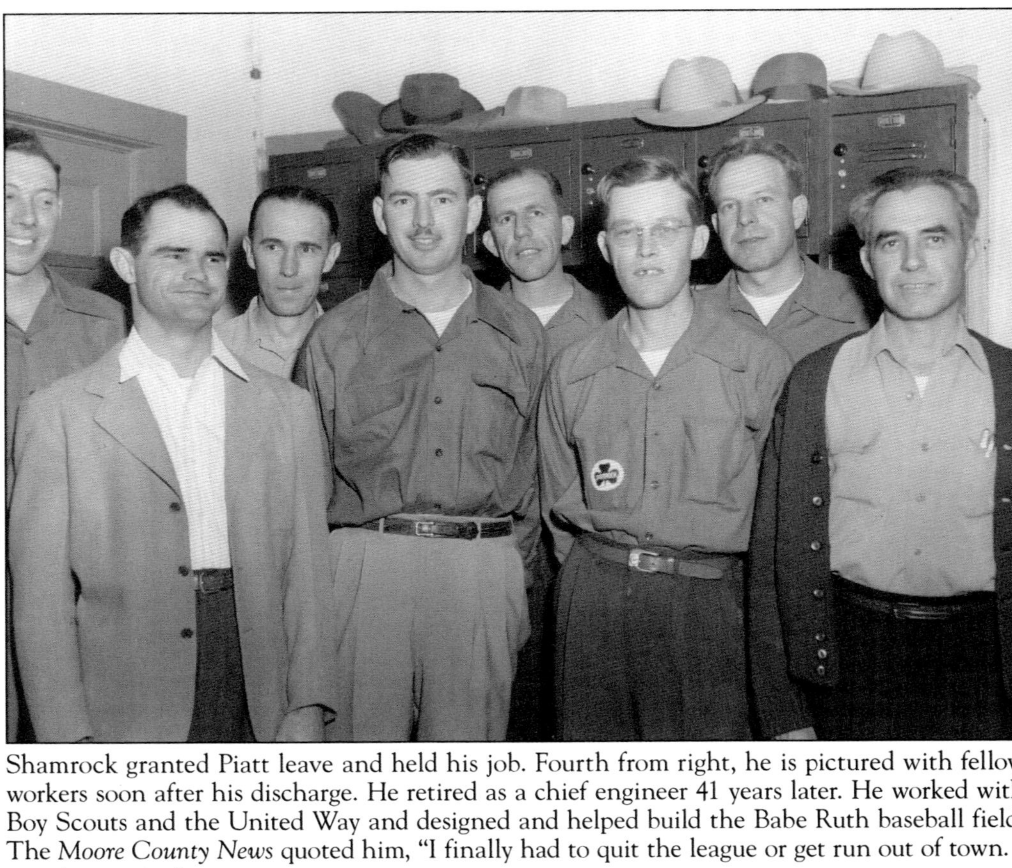

Shamrock granted Piatt leave and held his job. Fourth from right, he is pictured with fellow workers soon after his discharge. He retired as a chief engineer 41 years later. He worked with Boy Scouts and the United Way and designed and helped build the Babe Ruth baseball field. The *Moore County News* quoted him, "I finally had to quit the league or get run out of town. I was the umpire."

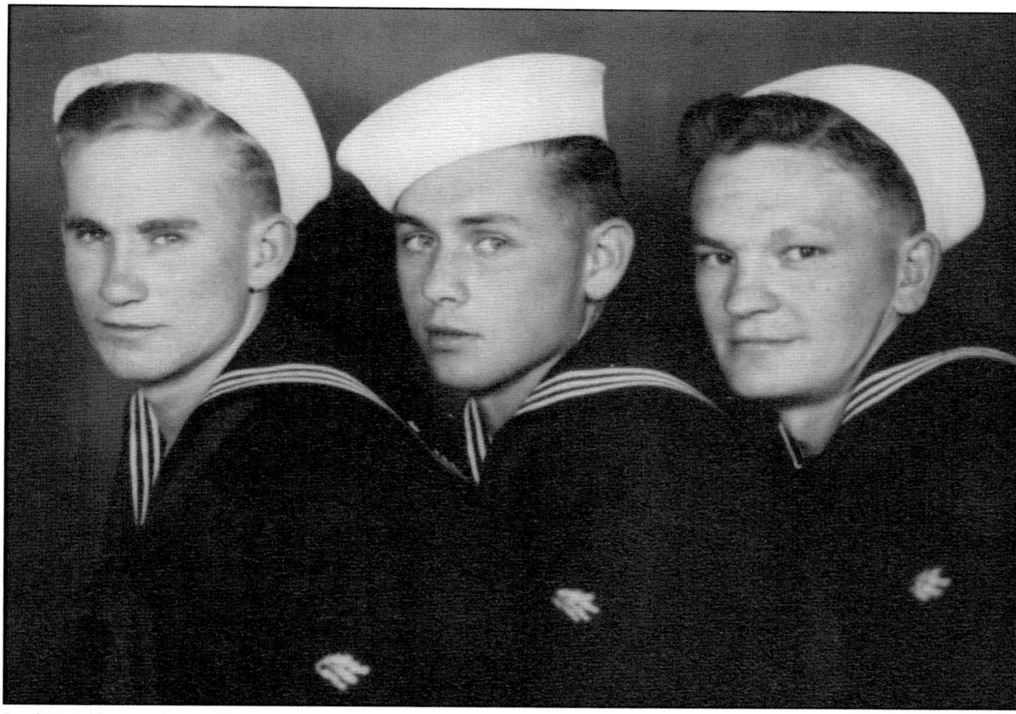

Jack Mills graduated Dumas High School in 1943, attended one semester at A&M, and then enlisted in the navy. A radioman, he was stationed in San Diego. While away from base on an assignment from his commanding officer, his unit shipped out for duty somewhere in the Pacific. Mills, on the left in this photograph, wrote on the back, "These are a couple of my bosom buddies and yours truly." In 1946, he returned and married Naomi Ruth "Boots" Hilton, the girl to whom he sent the picture. (Courtesy Boots Mills.)

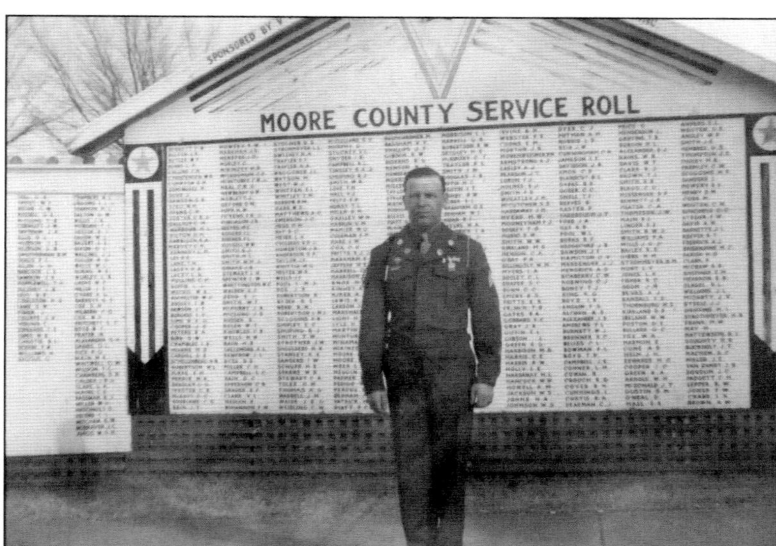

To honor all Moore County men and women serving during World War II, their names were posted on the Moore County Service Roll. The Veterans of Foreign Wars erected the board on the courthouse square in 1945. Elmer Fox, a returning veteran, stands in front of the board. (Courtesy Mert Keeney.)

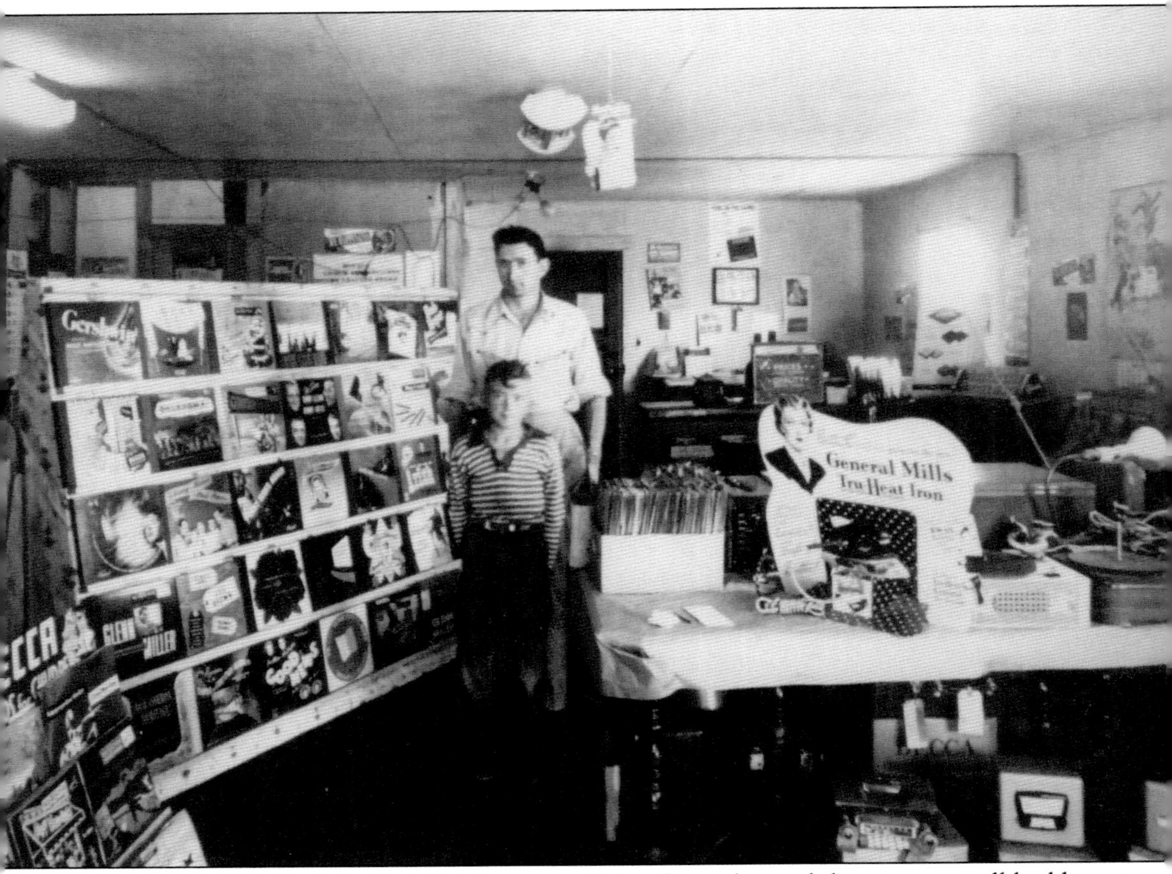

In the early 1940s, John D. McVicker moved his radio and record shop into a small building at Fourth Street and Dumas Avenues. It had a house for his family of six. After a time, the landlord decided to move the house and rent it out. McVicker wasted no time in building a concrete block addition for his family. Army blankets served as some partitions. Building materials were in short supply. McVicker's daughter Bonnie Corbin states she and her siblings, bucket by bucket, poured cement into a mold to make the blocks used to build a bathhouse About 6 by 6 feet, it had only a sink, shower, and commode. When newcomers filled the town to overflowing, some needed a place to park a trailer house. Before long, three small and two large ones were parked on the small lot with McVicker's shop. Six families, including his own, used the bathhouse. In 2002, McVicker visited Dumas and was pleased to see the building and bathhouse still standing—right across the street from the Sonic on Dumas Avenue. (Courtesy Bonnie Corbin.)

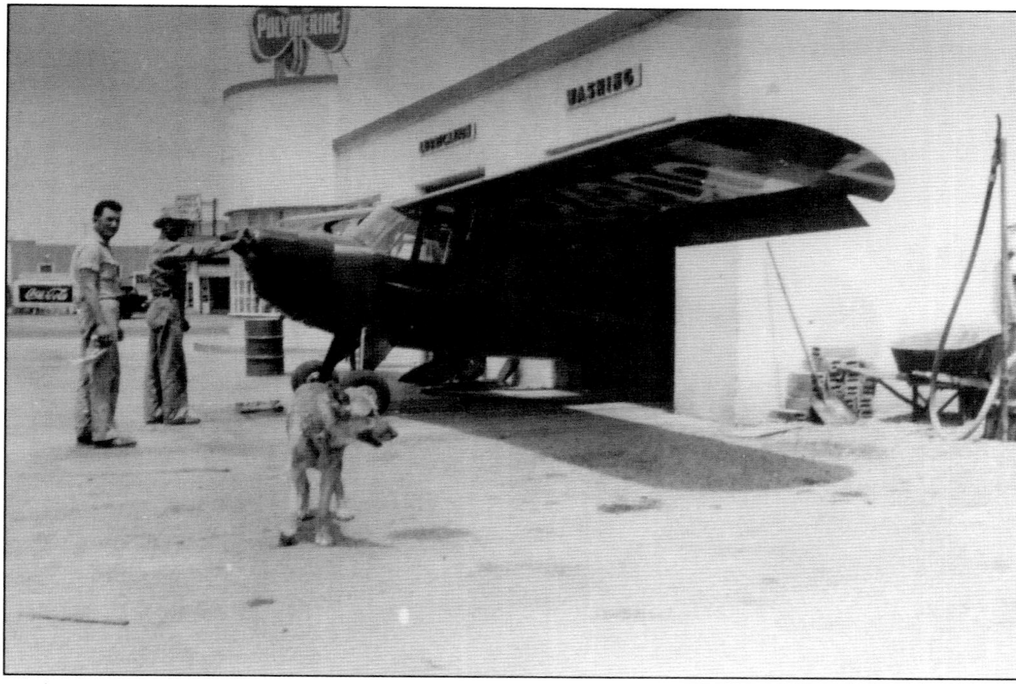

In the 1940s, a small airstrip ran parallel to the south edge of town. Dr. T. G. "Doc" Brown, who had the town's only medical clinic, owned a small plane to fly to outlying areas to care for patients. When his plane needed servicing, he simply drove it from the strip through city streets to the north end of town, where Jim Crabb and his assistant waited to do the work.

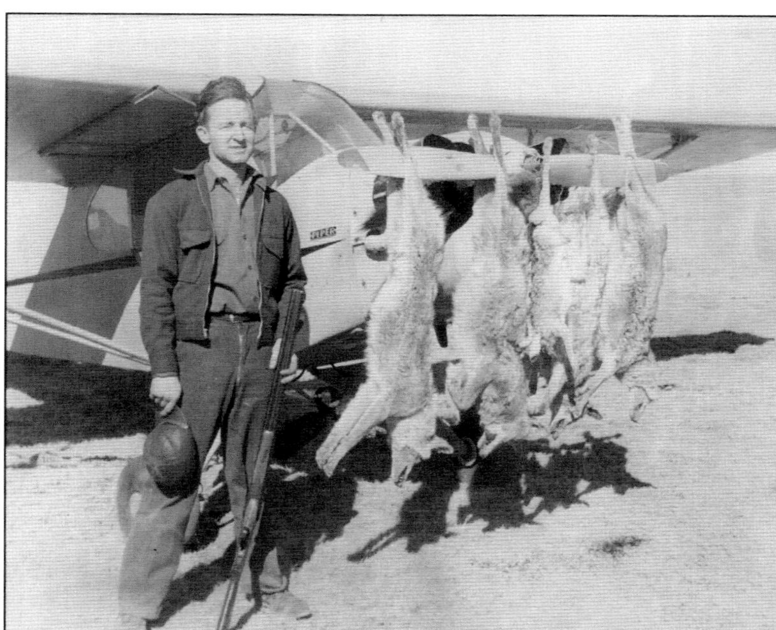

Coyotes have always been a problem for area ranchers. From time to time over the years, the county has paid a bounty for coyote ears. It is not known whether Johnny Lowry ever collected a bounty after this hunt in his Piper Cub.

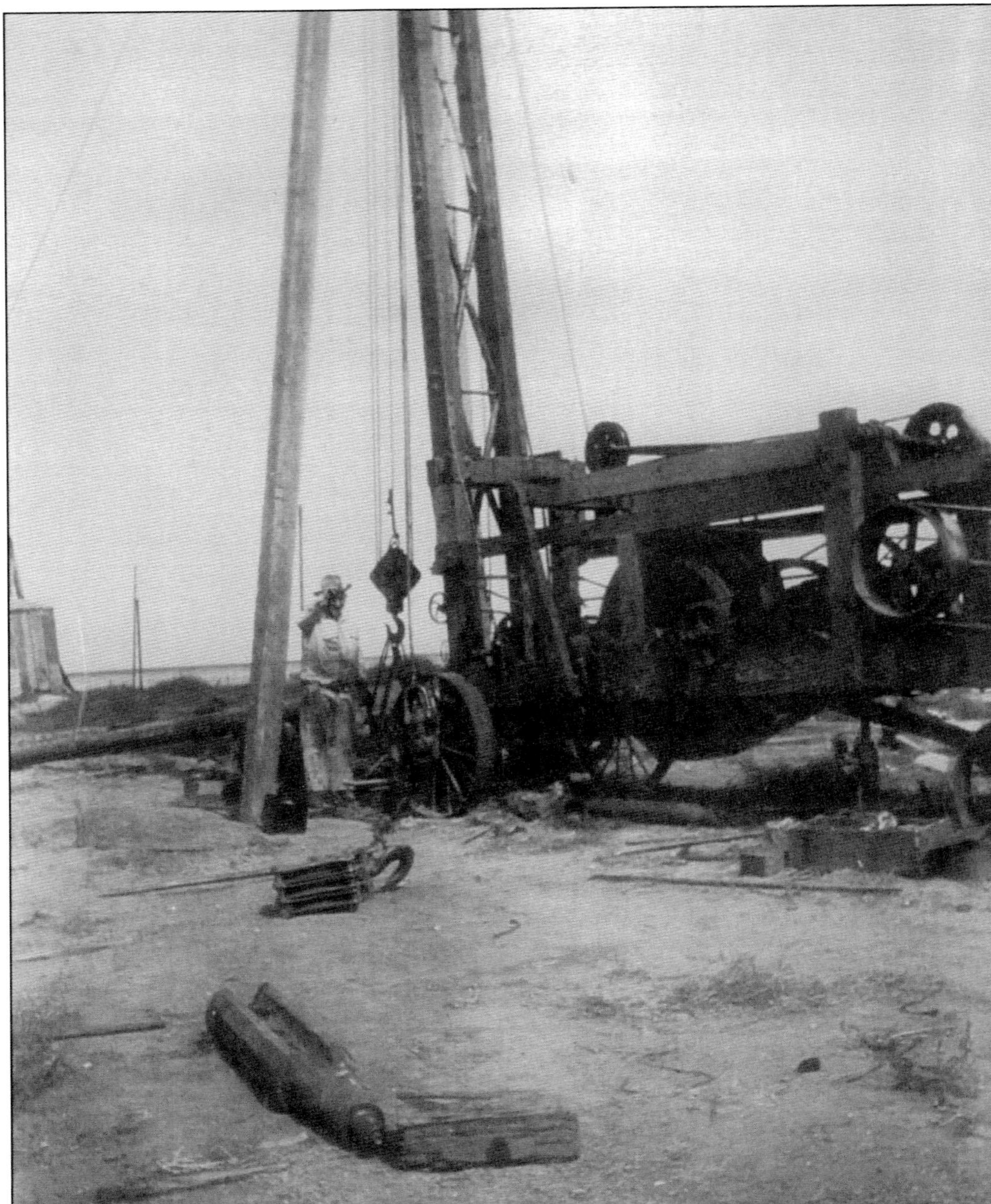

Charlie Jameson was a young boy in 1901 when his family moved onto a farm 5 miles southwest of Dumas. When he was old enough, he learned water well drilling by working with an older brother. He bought his own rig in 1916. In 1976, Jameson wrote a family sketch for the book *The Windswept Land* in which he described his early experience in that occupation: "The wells were pretty far apart—maybe 50 miles away. The rigs were moved with horses and wagons. When we dug 30 or 40 feet a day, we thought we had done a big job. There was a difference in the equipment too. It's all push button now, but then we hooked mules up—that was the horsepower, and we would go round and round. I have walked as far as from here to New York and back walking that team." Jameson drilled wells into the 1970s.

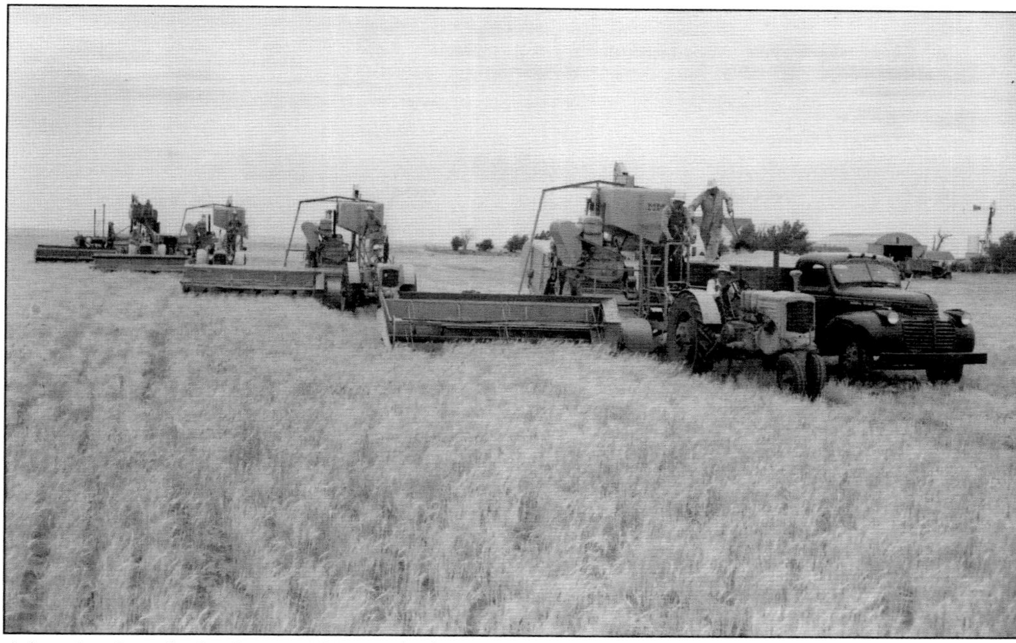

After the drought broke in 1939, good wheat crops were harvested all through the 1940s. In this photograph, a harvest crew is cutting wheat on the Stallwitz place in about 1946. Some grain sorghum and sugar cane were grown, and occasionally oats and barley, but wheat was by far the biggest crop grown in the area at that time.

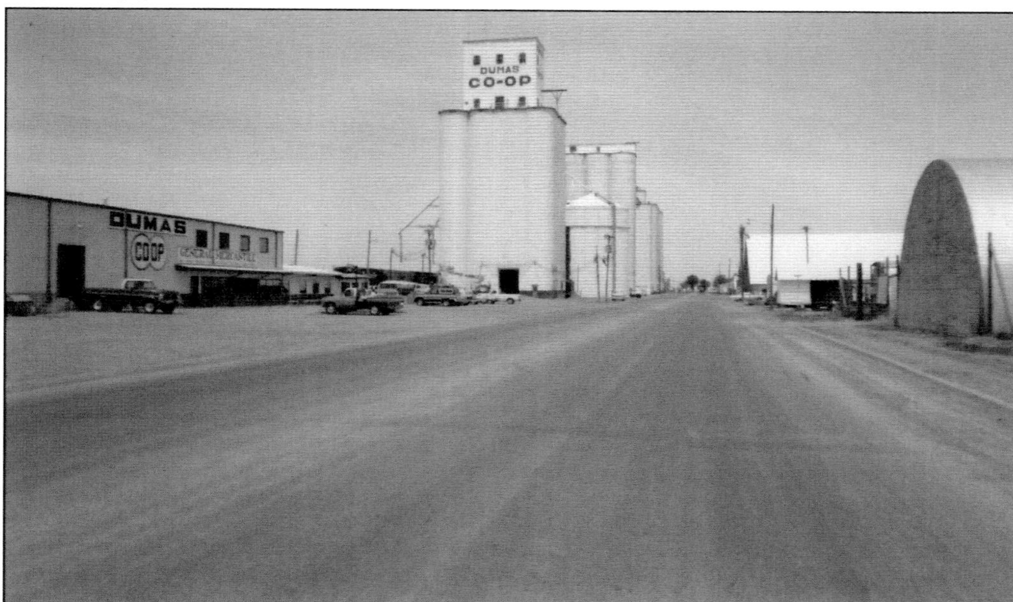

On May 30, 1947, Farmers Elevator Company sold its 24,000-bushel grain elevator after a group agreed to form a co-op to process, store, and market agricultural products and to furnish supplies and services to its members. Dumas Co-op began that day with election of a board of directors and a manager being hired. The construction of a 300,000-bushel elevator the following year was only the beginning for Dumas Co-op.

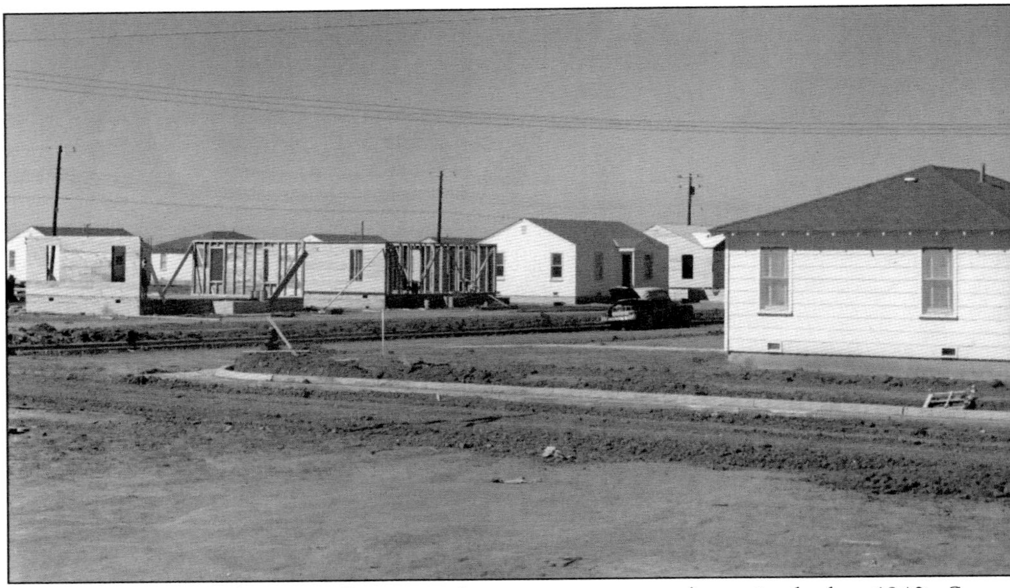

Construction of new homes in Dumas took an immense upward turn in the late 1940s. Several factors brought about the trend. Some plants expanded and hired workers, while others ceased operations and closed employee housing. Others continued production but closed their camps. Some residents bought company houses and moved them to town or had homes built. Phillips Petroleum was renovating the plant in Cactus and had large amounts of scrap lumber. A few individuals built their homes out of that lumber, sold for $1 a pickup load.

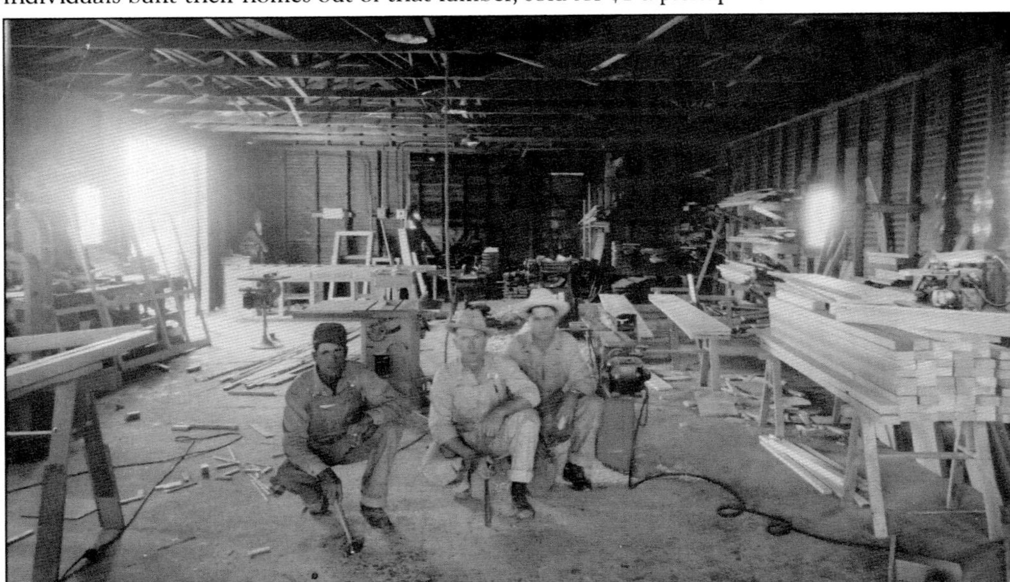

Banner Construction was in on the building boom. Taking a break are, from left to right, Bill Beck, Bob Moore, and Vic Lewis in about 1949. With the influx of residents came new businesses. Vic Lewis states that both residential and commercial building kept them busy for several years.

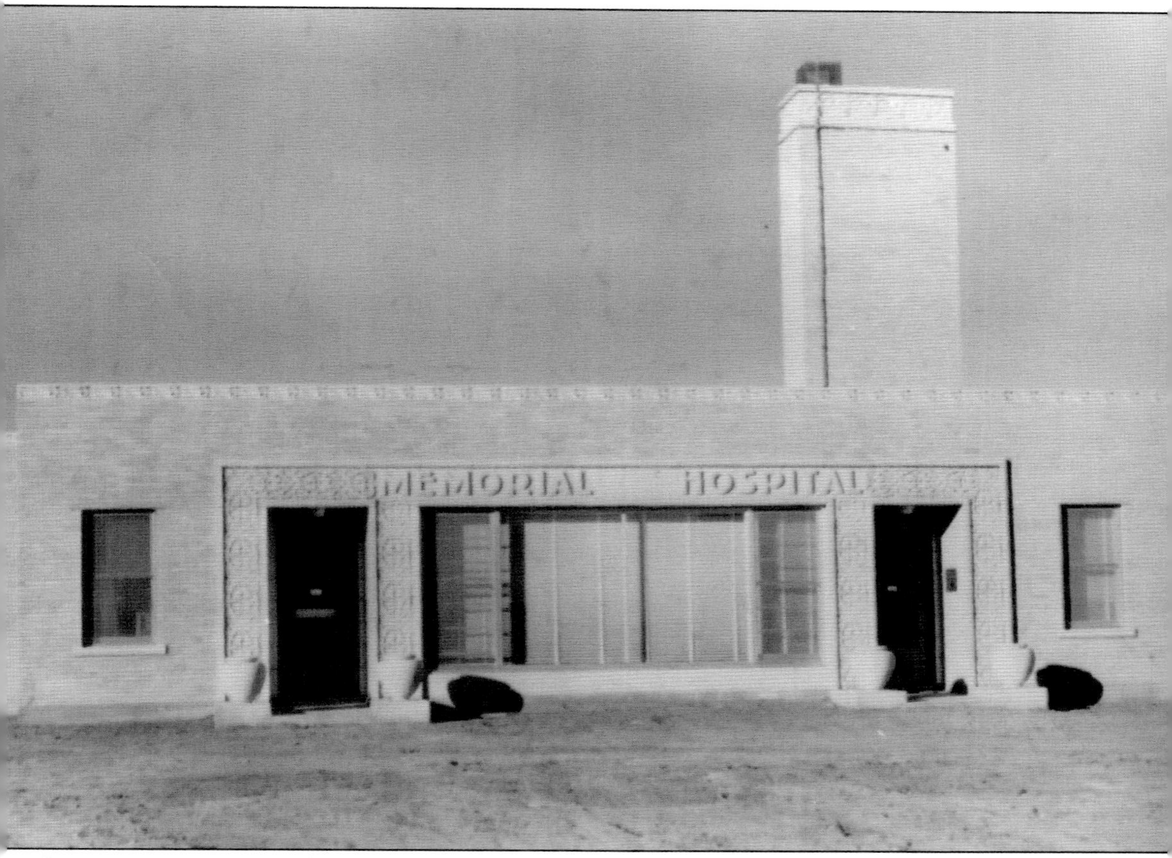

Dr. T. G. "Doc" Brown's clinic was the nearest thing to a hospital Dumas had in 1947. Josie Walker decided it was time for that to change. She talked with her brother W. J. Morton Jr. He took up the cause, organized a committee, and circulated petitions for an election to build a county-owned hospital. The election passed, and the 22-bed Memorial Hospital opened on September 9, 1948. Frank Cheevers was administrator and held the position for more than 30 years. Morton was elected as chairman of the board and served for 19 years. Over the years, the two men worked together to make improvements, such as adding an obstetrical wing in 1949 and air-conditioning in 1953. Their legacy, one of determined effort to provide a first-class medical facility for the community, is still being acted out at Memorial Hospital.

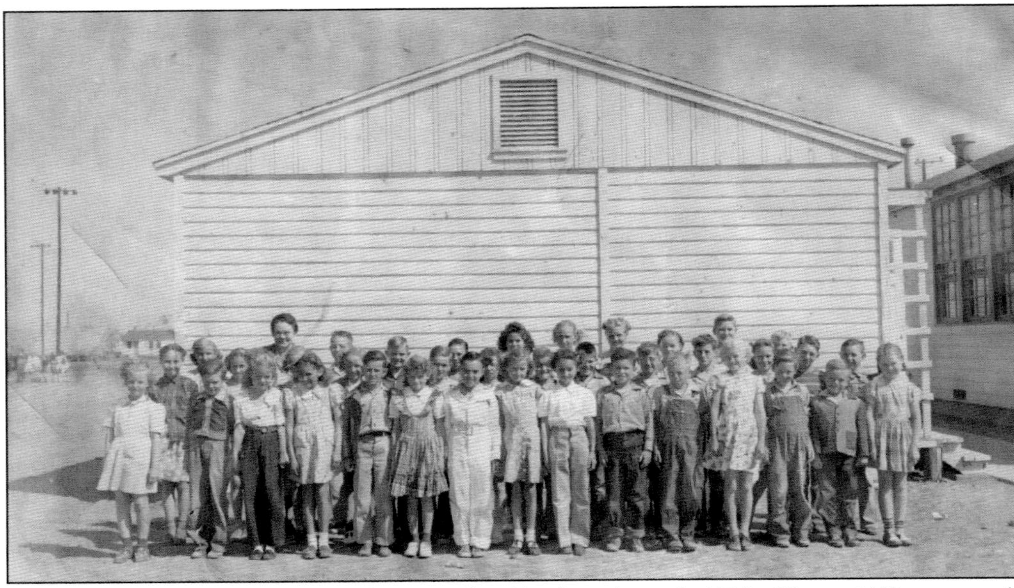

Some folks were against building the new school back in the early 1930s. They said Dumas would never need that much space. In 1940, the population of Dumas was 2,117. By 1950, it was 6,127. In the early 1940s, a barrack was moved in for classes. This faded photograph of Velma Steiner's 1949 class of nearly 40 students was taken in front of that building.

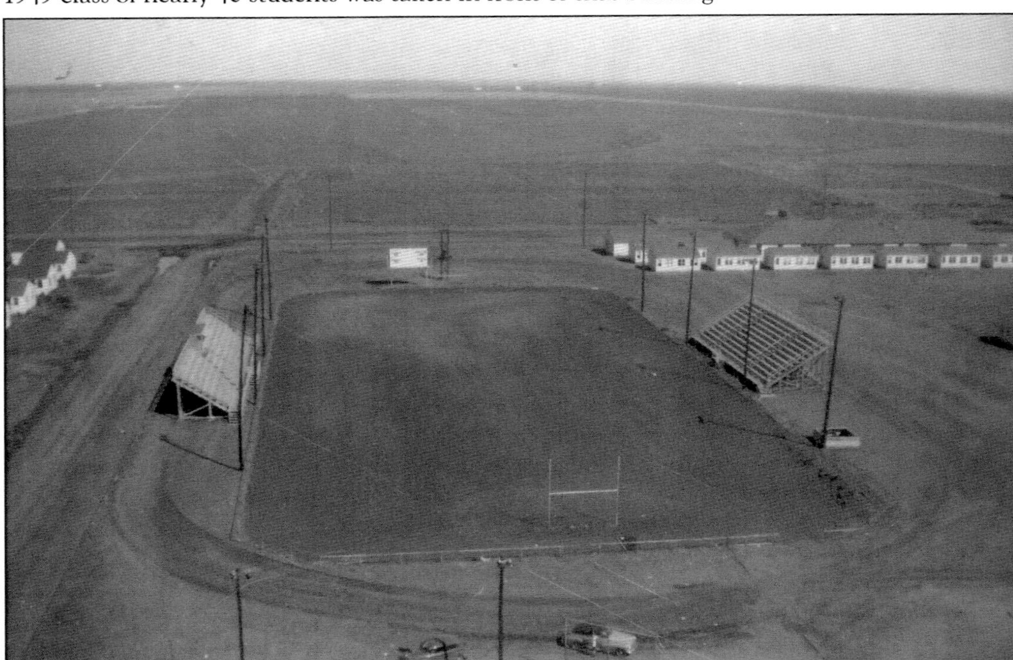

The football stadium had been improved with the addition of a second row of bleachers when this photograph was made in about 1949. Classrooms were so crowded in 1946 that seven prefabricated 20-by-28-foot buildings were bought. Some of those buildings appear in the upper right-hand corner of this photograph. On the left are some of the 100 Coronado homes hurriedly constructed during the early 1940s.

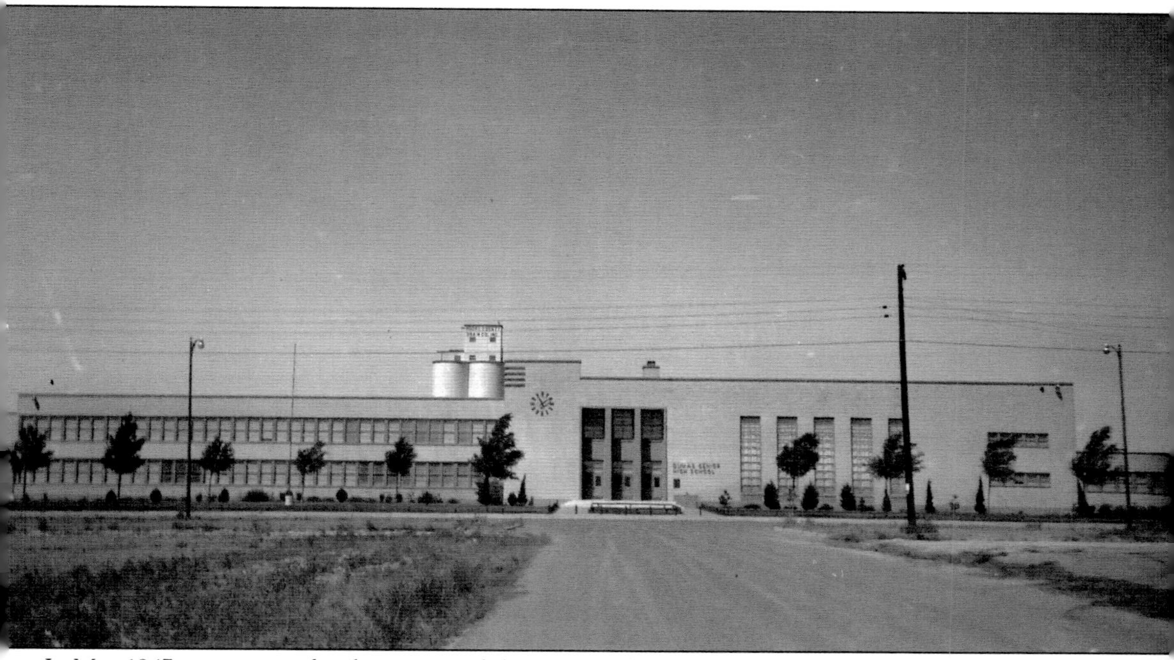

In May 1947, voters were firmly convinced that a new school building was needed. They approved bonds in the amount of $700,000 to build a new high school. Construction began early the next year, but the building was not finished in time for the fall term in 1949, when school enrollment jumped from 1,475 the previous year to 1,866. While construction continued, classes were moved to the new school. It was six weeks before the cafeteria was finished and even longer before the gym was completed. The first three basketball games were played in the old gym. In the meantime, at the old building, the anticipated extra room was hardly noticed because of the large increase in the number of students. The number of teachers in Dumas schools also grew from 51 to 70. By the time construction of the new high school was finished, the total cost had risen to nearly $1 million. Ten years later, voters approved another $1 million for expansion of the building.

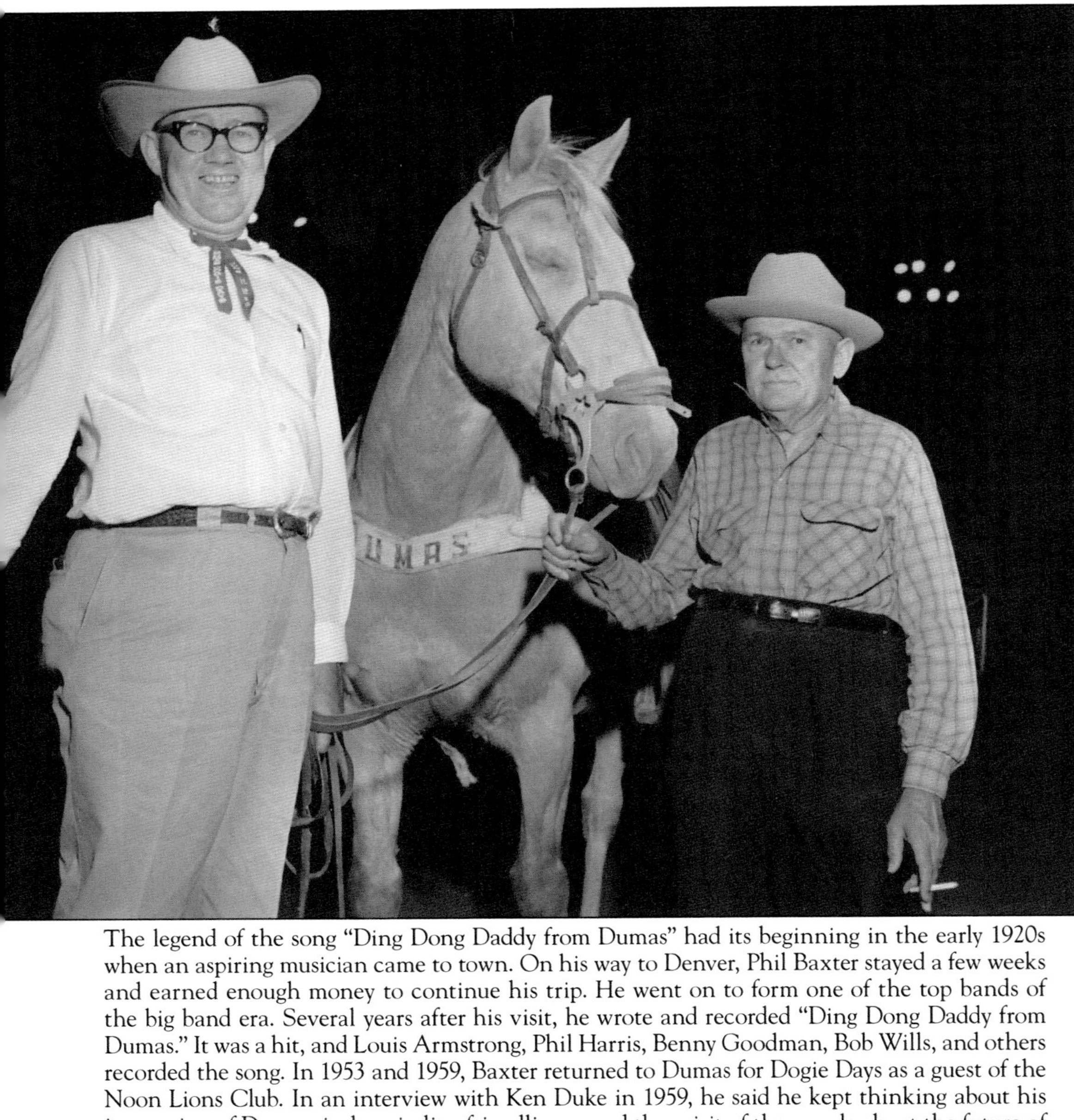

The legend of the song "Ding Dong Daddy from Dumas" had its beginning in the early 1920s when an aspiring musician came to town. On his way to Denver, Phil Baxter stayed a few weeks and earned enough money to continue his trip. He went on to form one of the top bands of the big band era. Several years after his visit, he wrote and recorded "Ding Dong Daddy from Dumas." It was a hit, and Louis Armstrong, Phil Harris, Benny Goodman, Bob Wills, and others recorded the song. In 1953 and 1959, Baxter returned to Dumas for Dogie Days as a guest of the Noon Lions Club. In an interview with Ken Duke in 1959, he said he kept thinking about his impression of Dumas, its hospitality, friendliness, and the spirit of the people about the future of the city and was inspired to write the song. Here he and soon-to-be mayor Mutt McMurry pose for a photograph after the Dogie Days parade in 1953.

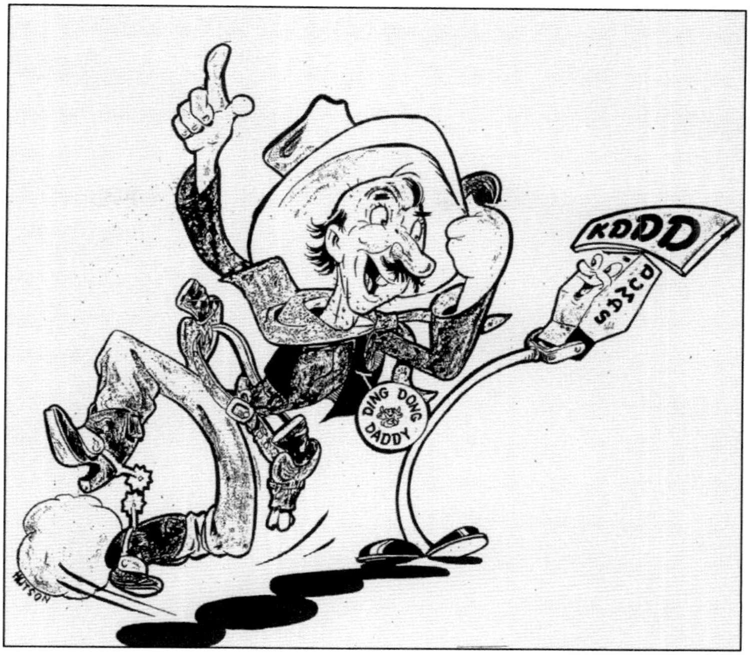

Lucian Spencer and 29 other stockholders in North Plains Broadcasting were issued a permit for a radio station in 1948. Its call letters became KDDD. Ken Duke became manager in February 1949. Duke, a strong supporter of his town, commissioned Amarillo artist Hut Hutson to create the image of Dumas's Ding Dong Daddy. The original drawing is displayed at Window on the Plains Museum.

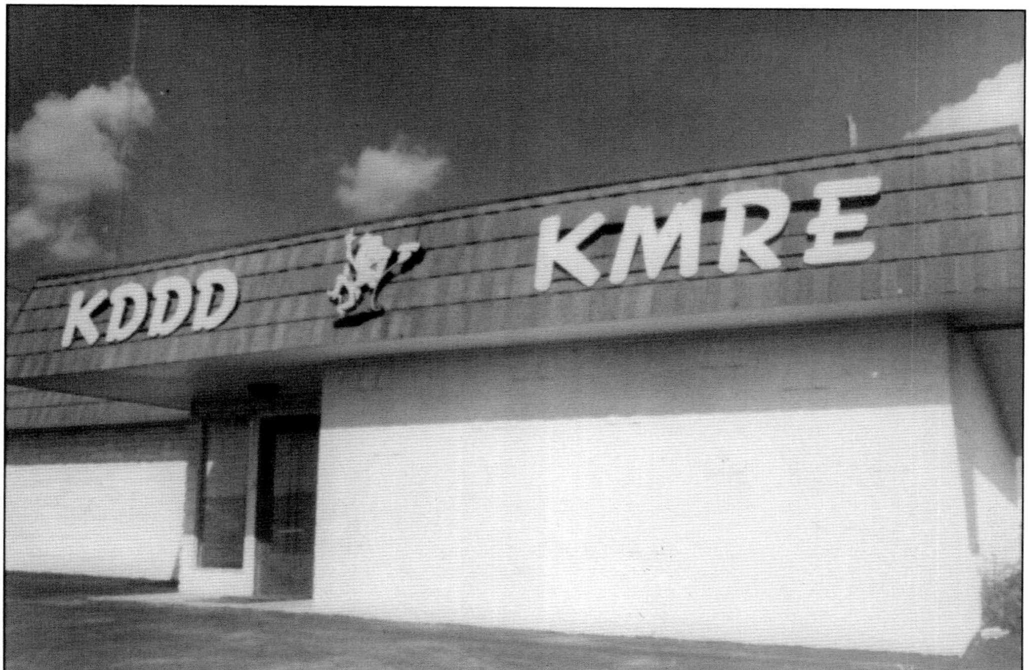

Ken Duke hired Al Trimble as newsman/salesman in 1950. In the mid-1950s, they both left the station but later returned and under the name Dumas Broadcasters, Inc., they bought it. An FM station was added in 1960 with call letters KDDD-FM. In 1975, the station's operations expanded and it was changed to KMRE-FM.

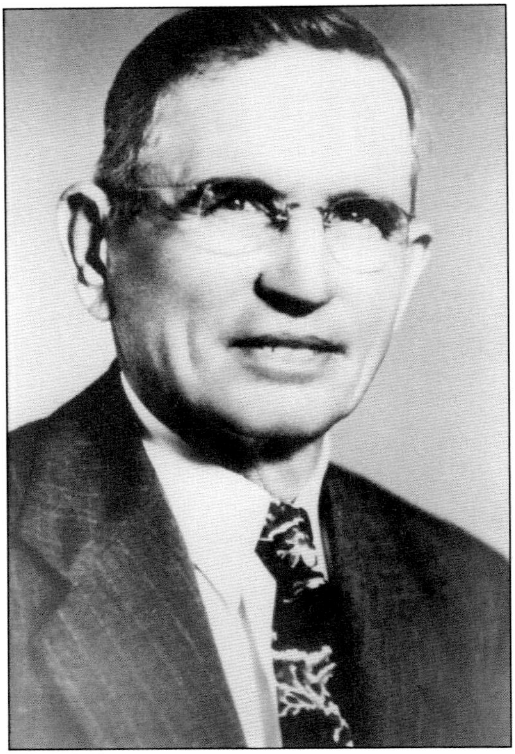

When Fred Makeig was elected mayor in 1939, city employees were being paid in scrip warrants because of the city's poor financial condition. When he left the office in 1949, the warrants had been paid off and gas service and a water system bought. The city hall and equipment for police and fire departments were purchased. As evidence of his dedication to his community, Mayor Makeig worked three years without salary.

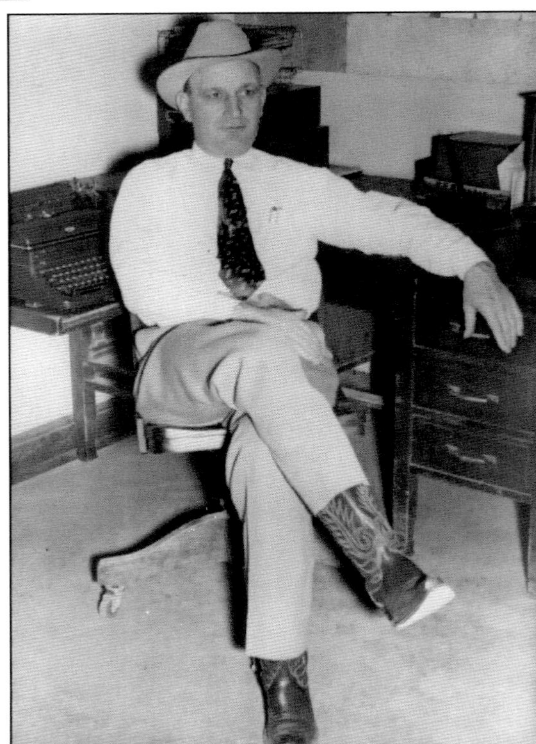

P. F. Younger was elected sheriff in 1936. Since Prohibition was over and a degree of economic stability restored, he may have thought his job would be a little tamer than that of his predecessor. Challenges came when the population more than doubled within a few months in the early 1940s. But the people of Moore County approved the way he met those challenges. They elected him six times to two-year terms.

Maud Spencer never intended to manage a business. Her husband, Robert, became owner and manager of North Plains Telephone in Dumas in 1930. Four years later, he died suddenly. Maud took over management and led the company to further growth. Gradually her son Robert Jr. took over responsibility. In 1947, he died in an automobile accident. Once again, Maud took over until her son Lucian learned the business.

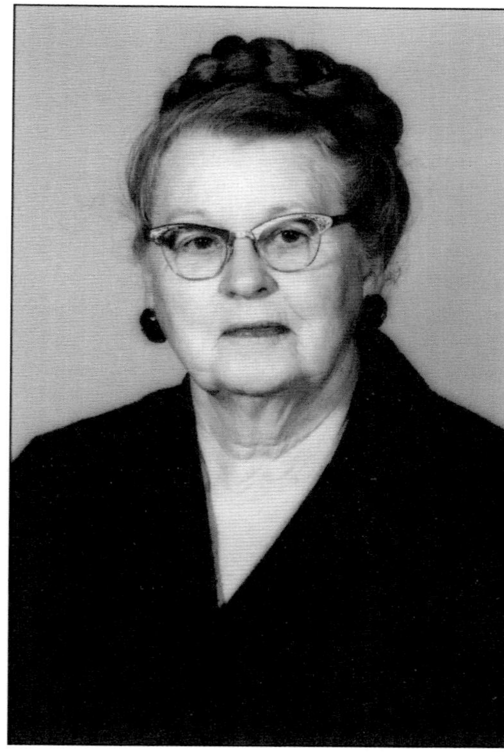

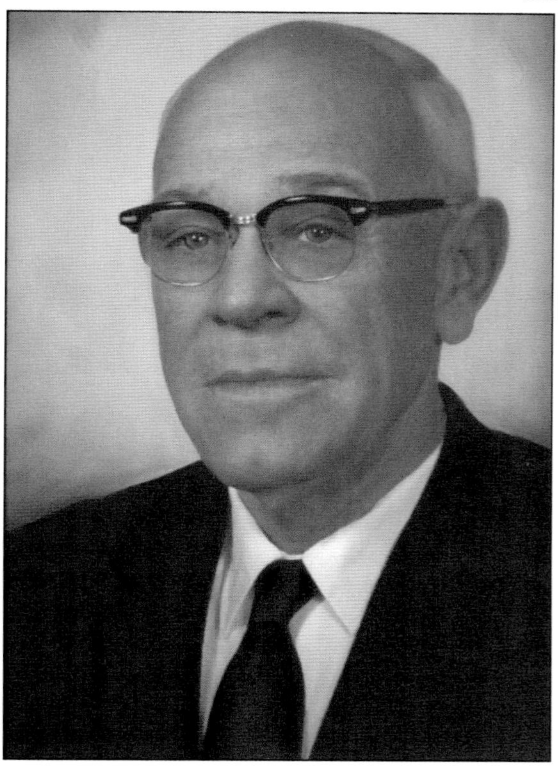

W. J. Morton Jr. worked for the betterment of his community for many years. In the 1930s, he served on the wind erosion committee. In the 1940s, he led the drive for the hospital. In the 1960s, he was instrumental in securing the community building. He worked for legislation to allow use of natural gas for irrigation engine fuel. Dumas Chamber of Commerce honored him as Man of the Year in 1966.

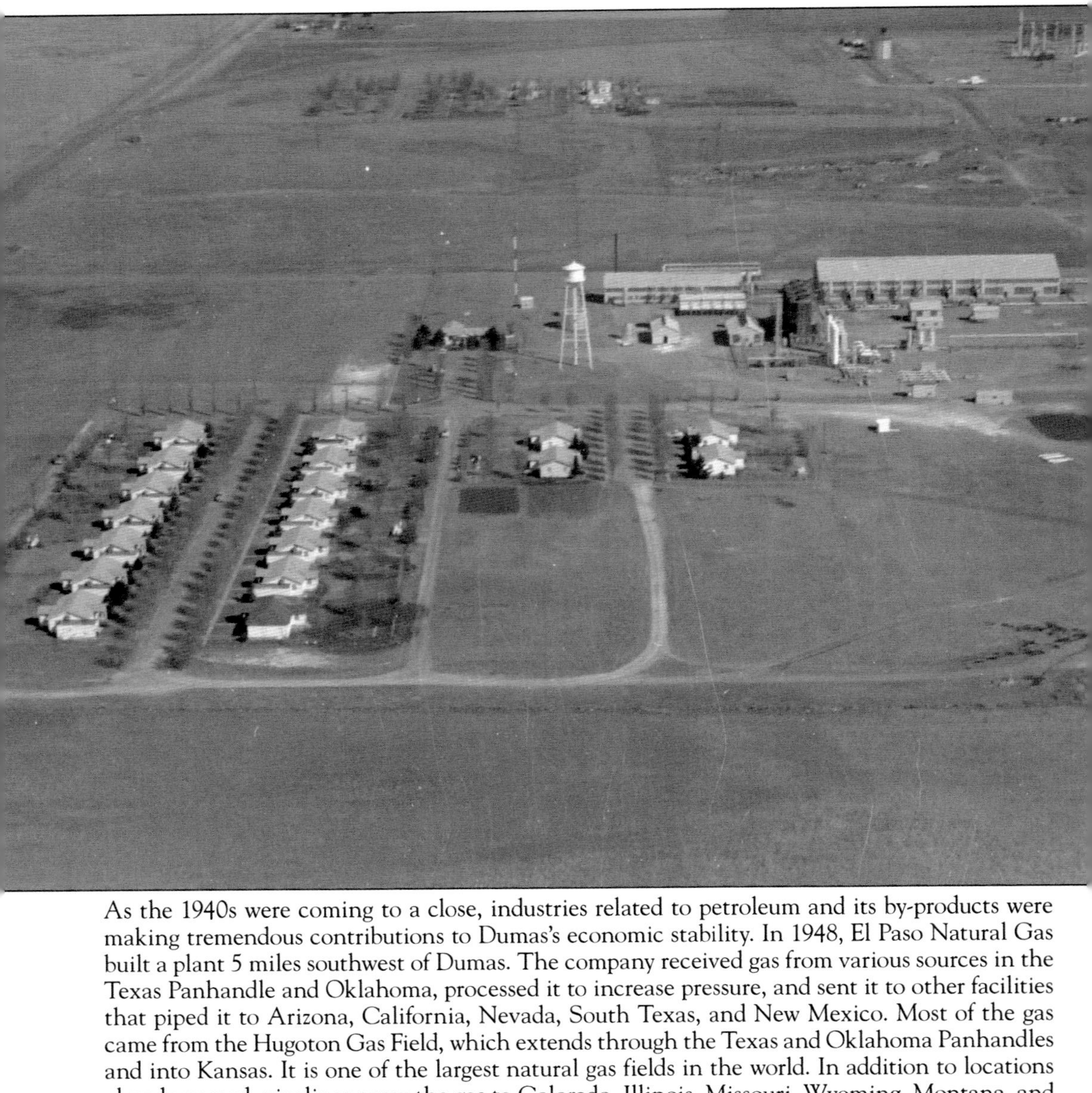

As the 1940s were coming to a close, industries related to petroleum and its by-products were making tremendous contributions to Dumas's economic stability. In 1948, El Paso Natural Gas built a plant 5 miles southwest of Dumas. The company received gas from various sources in the Texas Panhandle and Oklahoma, processed it to increase pressure, and sent it to other facilities that piped it to Arizona, California, Nevada, South Texas, and New Mexico. Most of the gas came from the Hugoton Gas Field, which extends through the Texas and Oklahoma Panhandles and into Kansas. It is one of the largest natural gas fields in the world. In addition to locations already named, pipelines carry the gas to Colorado, Illinois, Missouri, Wyoming, Montana, and the list goes on. Not conforming to the trend other companies were following of closing employee housing, El Paso Natural Gas built 17 homes near the plant. Housing shortages in Dumas may have been the basis for that decision. Camp residents were part of the community in Dumas and brought benefits beyond the economic impact to the city.

Six

The Last 60 Years

The first half of Dumas's history was full of extremes, from almost ceasing to exist to overwhelming influx. The last half has had its ups and downs, but it has not been as volatile. Some small industries have come and gone; farmers have had good years and bad; the petroleum industry has declined, then slowly revived. Local retailers suffered painful losses as chain stores came to entice the growing population.

A drought that lasted for five years began in 1951, but irrigation advancements in the early 1950s lessened some of the effects. As irrigation became common, the number of acres farmed steadily increased. In the mid-1960s, corn and hybrid seed became major crops in the area. Other crops were tried, including vegetables, soybeans, sunflowers, castor beans, sugar beets, and pinto beans. The Texas Tech Research Field Unit, with the purpose of testing new crops, was dedicated in 1964. The first cattle feedlot started in 1960. Cotton returned to Moore County in 2000 with 137.5 acres being planted. Acres have increased to about 11,000.

Shamrock Oil and Gas merged with Diamond Alkali and became Diamond Shamrock, was bought out by Ultramar, and now belongs to Valero. Other plants' histories are similar. American Zinc, Exell Helium, Phillips at Cactus, and four carbon black plants were all shut down. A large beef-packing plant, industries related to it, and other businesses have provided jobs and kept the economy strong.

New industries brought changes of all sorts. The nearly 100-percent Caucasian population of previous years began to change with the coming of hybrid seed. Summer months brought hundreds of migrant workers to rogue maize (remove unwanted plants). Some stayed and became a part of the community. Other industries brought workers from as close as Mexico and as far away as Sudan.

Today, along with the diverse economy, there is a diverse citizenry of about 17,000 that keeps Dumas growing and prospering.

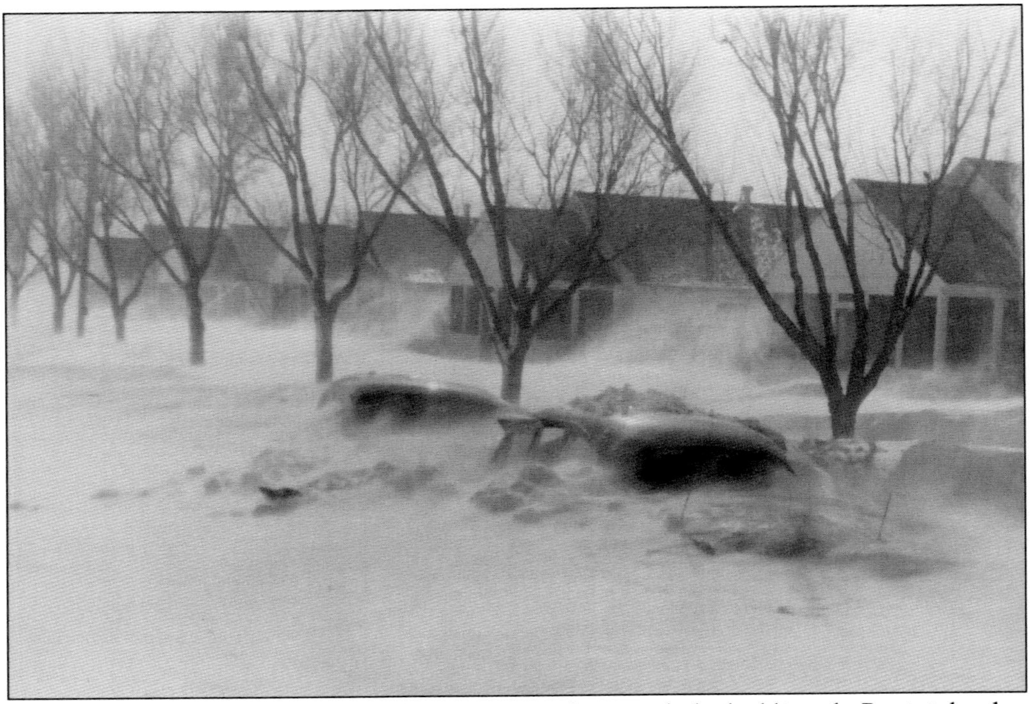

Weather in the Texas Panhandle is often exaggerated, particularly the blizzards. But it is hard to exaggerate the blizzard in March 1957. Stranded travelers experienced hospitality from perfect strangers, who opened their homes when motels, churches, schools, and the YMCA were filled to capacity. Plant workers were stranded on the job when their relief could not get to work. Cattle strayed miles from their owners' property, and about 2,000 died. Roofs of commercial buildings collapsed, as did ceilings in homes where snow blew into attics. (Courtesy Claude Pickett.)

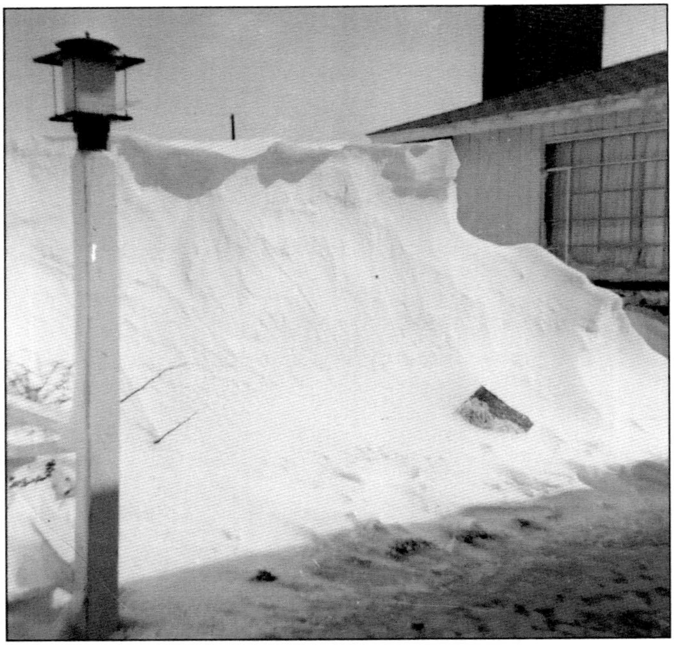

The storm lasted three days. Howling winds of up to 75 miles per hour formed remarkable drifts. Children enjoyed walking up a drift to the roof of their home to look the world over. They also enjoyed a few days of vacation from school. (Courtesy Mert Keeney.)

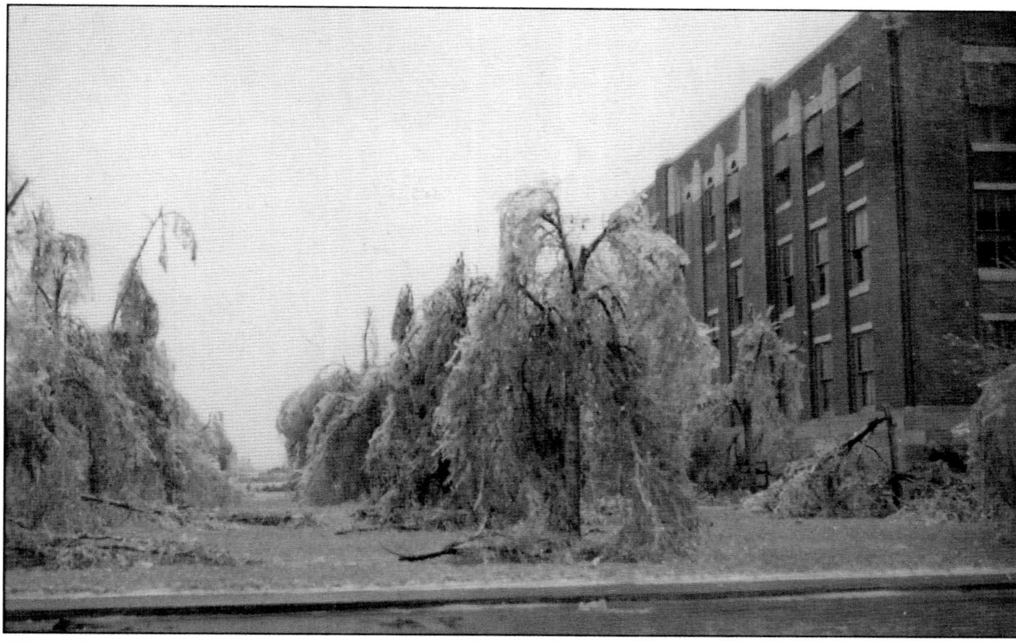

Blizzards with drifting snow are common in the wintertime, but occasionally there is an ice storm that provides tree trimmers with work not usually available in the winter months. The one captured in this photograph occurred on Thanksgiving Day. (Courtesy Eddie Stallwitz.)

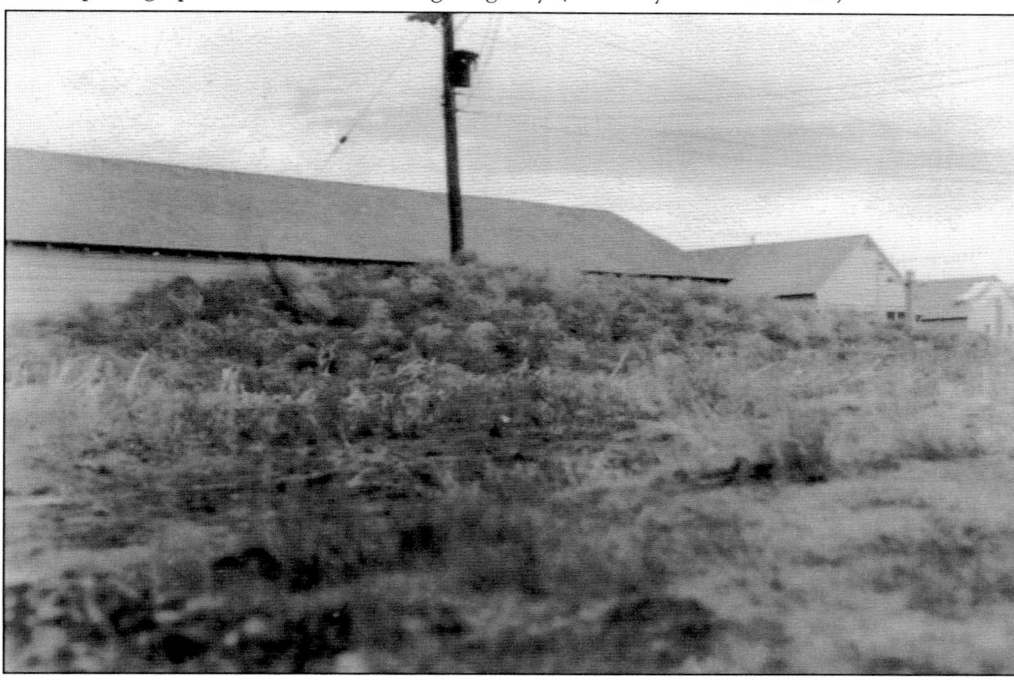

Tumbleweeds will grow when and where nothing else will. In the fall, a tumbleweed plant breaks off from its root at the ground and goes wherever the wind carries it, all the while scattering its millions of seeds. The wind sometimes piles the weeds up along fences and buildings, as it did in this photograph labeled "tumbleweed blizzard." (Courtesy Bureau of Mines.)

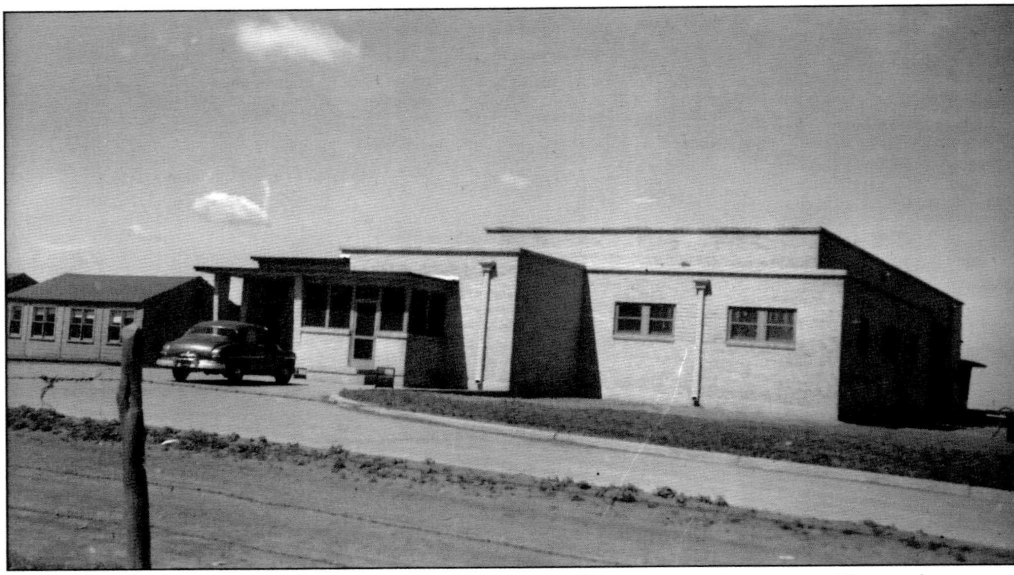

By the early 1950s, the two schools were once again bursting at the seams. Three elementary schools were built and occupied by 1954. This photograph of the first one completed was noted on the back: "Saturday—May 10, 1952, South Ward Grade School, Constructed in 1951, Occupied January, 1952." The other two schools were called East Ward and North Ward. Their names were later changed to Sunset, Morningside, and Green Acres. In 1965, a fourth elementary school, Hillcrest, was opened.

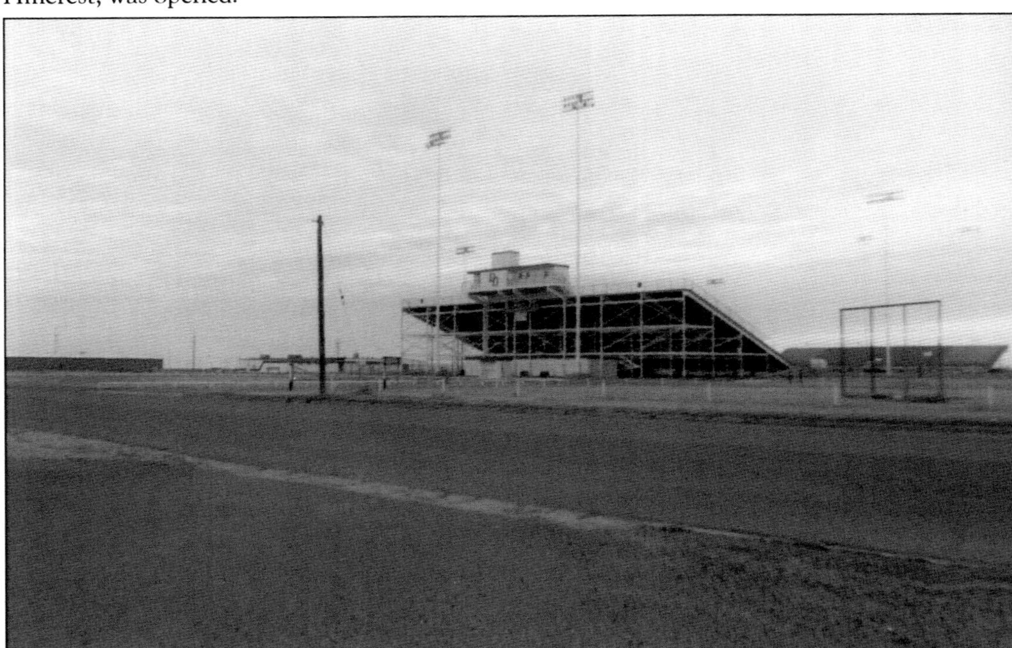

A new football stadium for the Dumas Demons was part of a $1.2-million bond approved by voters in 1965. Construction was finished the next summer. In August, Demon fans were invited to an open house to look over the stadium, field house, press box, and concession stands. Athletes and fans alike enjoy and take pride in the stadium.

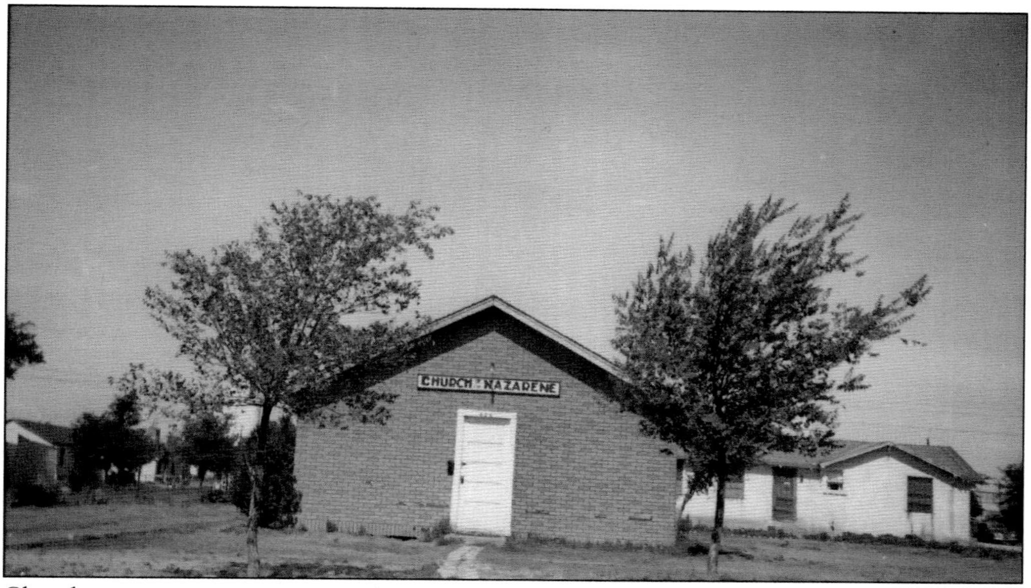

Churches are an important part of Dumas's history. They make immeasurable contributions to the well-being of the citizens of the community. Most had humble beginnings like that of the Church of the Nazarene. Organized in 1940, it met in this small building, called "the chicken coop" by members. When a parsonage was needed, building materials were hard to find. An old barrack was purchased, torn apart, and the lumber used. It is on the right in this photograph.

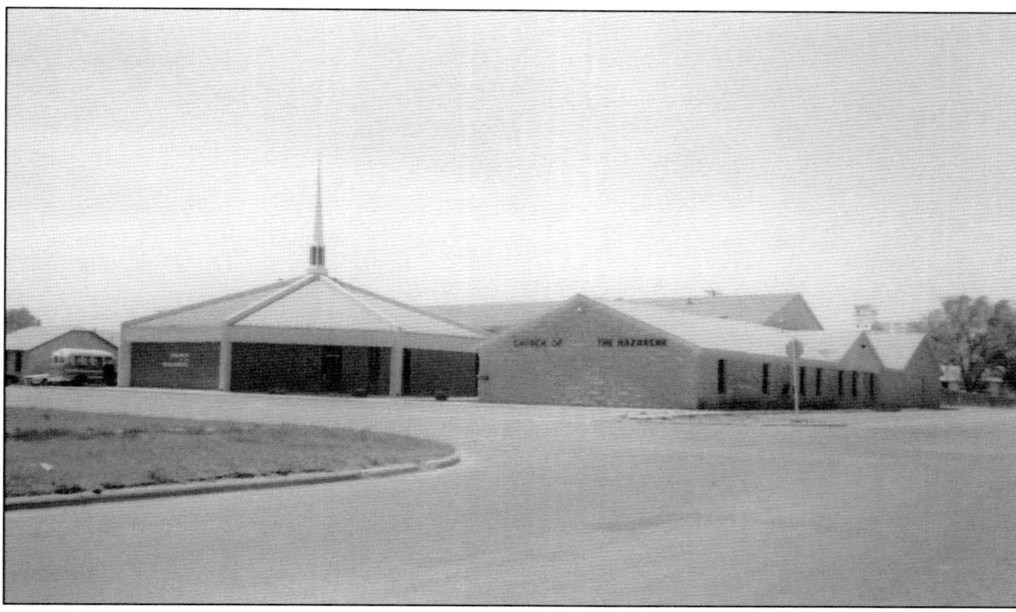
As membership increased, the building was outgrown. A bigger church was built at the same location in the 1950s. Membership continued to grow, and other additions were made over the years. Below is the spacious sanctuary completed in 1981. With a few changes in details, Church of the Nazarene's story would read like that of several other churches in Dumas.

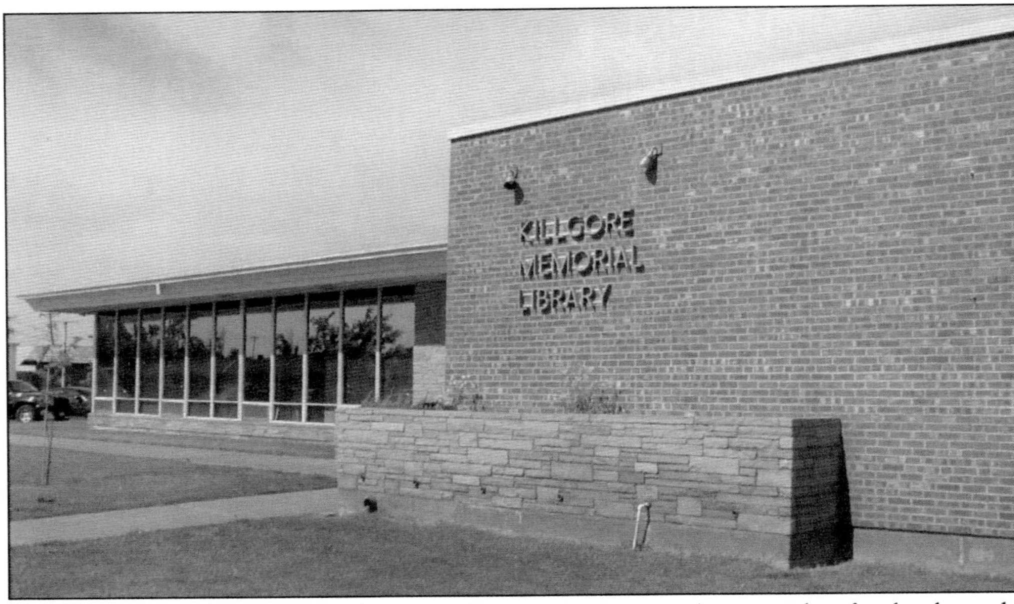

In 1936, the first library opened in a small room in the courthouse with a few books and a volunteer librarian. In 1960, a foundation established by Charles L. and Florence L. Killgore granted $100,000 to the library for a new building. The county provided land, and a campaign raised funds for furnishings. The library has branches in the other county communities, Sunray and Cactus. (Courtesy Killgore Memorial Library.)

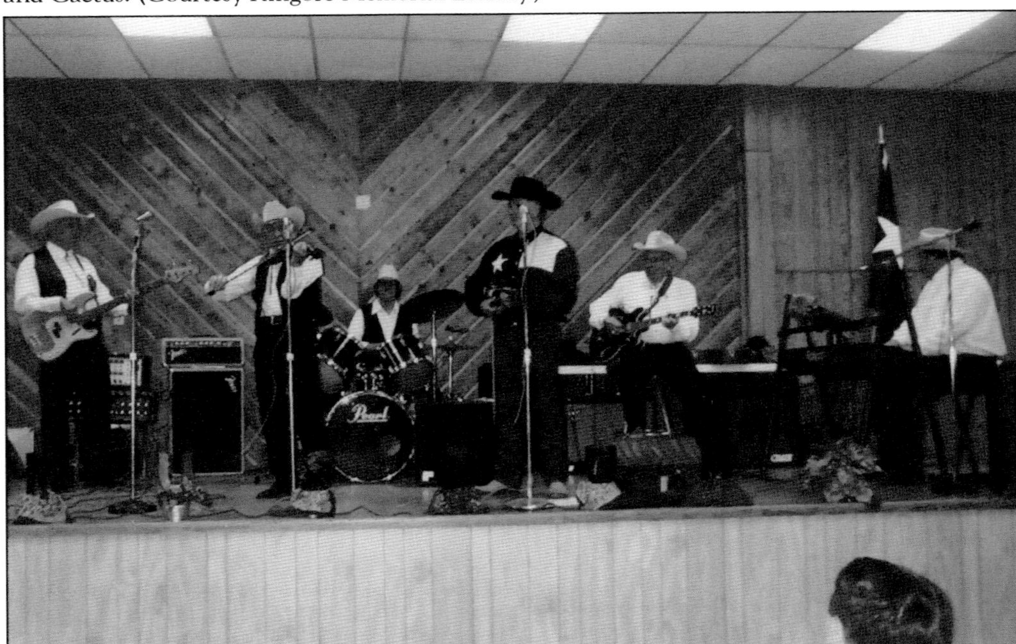

Buck Buchanan, J. W. Morton Jr., Charlie Sheldon, and Cy Burnett went to county commissioners for funds to build an all-purpose community building. Turned down, they persisted, and the project was completed for the fair in September 1964. The building is used for everything from livestock shows to this program given by Rooster Morris to benefit the museum. (Courtesy Vera Morris.)

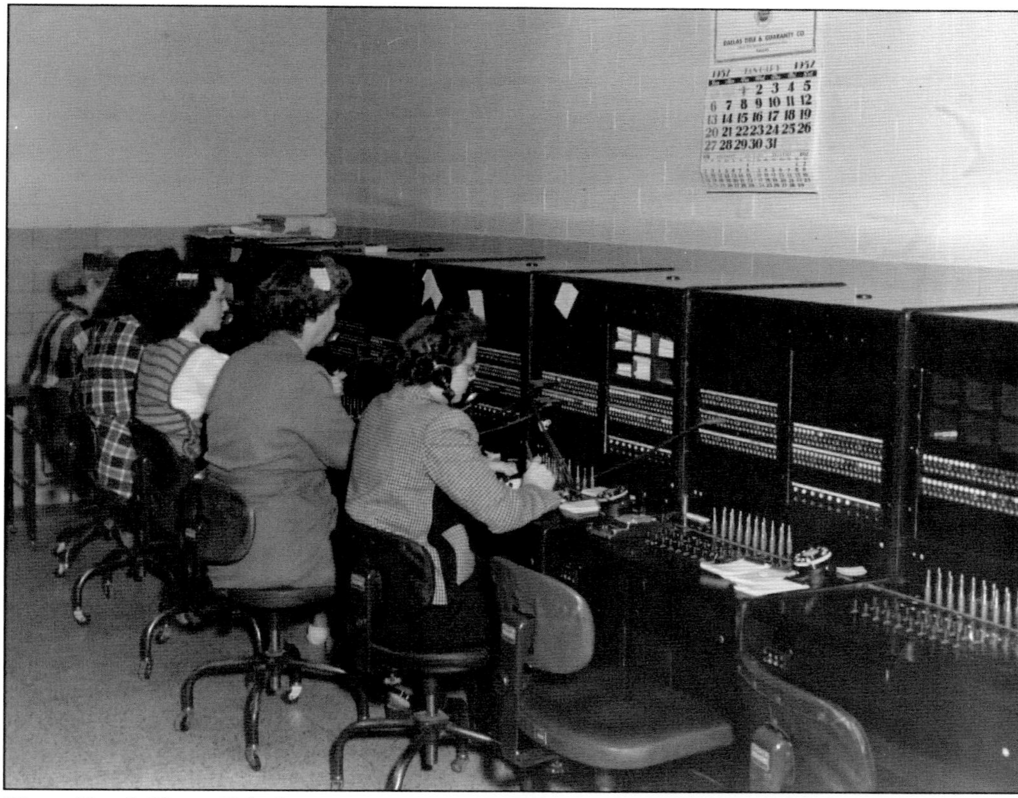

These North Plains Telephone Company operators were working at the switchboards in 1957. The system was automated in about 1982, and local operators were laid off. Operators were stationed in a centralized location. North Plains sold to Transcontinental Telephone in 1967; they were subsequently bought out by Continental Telephone. The current owner is Windstream.

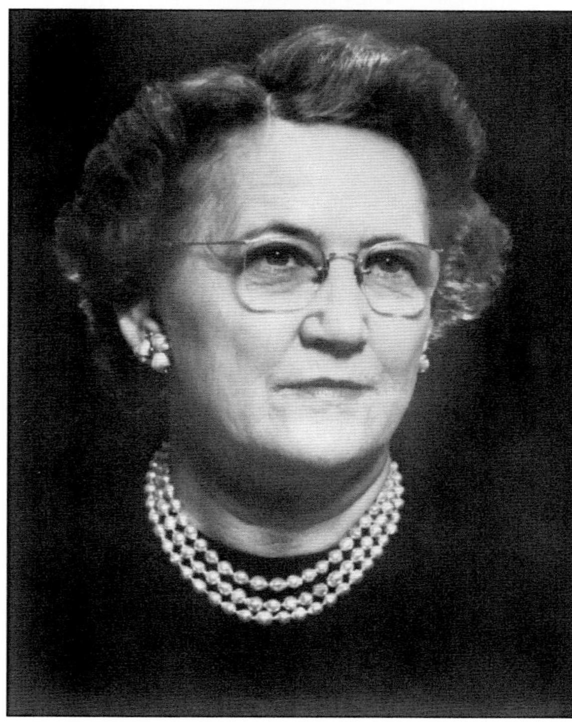

Gladys Nisbitt started in the banking business as an assistant cashier and advanced to the position of director. She and her husband, James Nisbitt, bought a controlling interest in the First State Bank of Dumas in 1938. She became vice president four years later. After her husband's death in 1951, she was president until 1969. Gladys was active in the community and helped pioneer the Girl Scout program in Dumas.

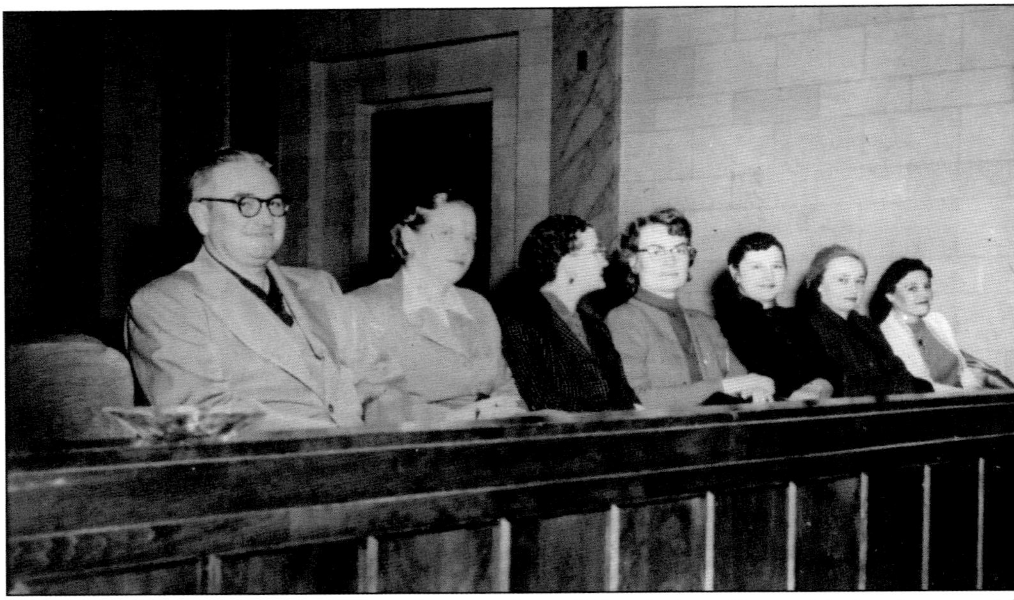

In 1955, history was made with the selection of an all-female jury. Pictured is Jess Larson with jurors Nell Jones, Cloie Phillips, Louise Tindle, Mary White, Margaret Pool, and Juanita Morrison. Tindle stated that a homeless woman, with some type of mental illness, was the defendant. A local physician testified she would be better off institutionalized. The jury agreed, and she was committed to a Wichita Falls facility.

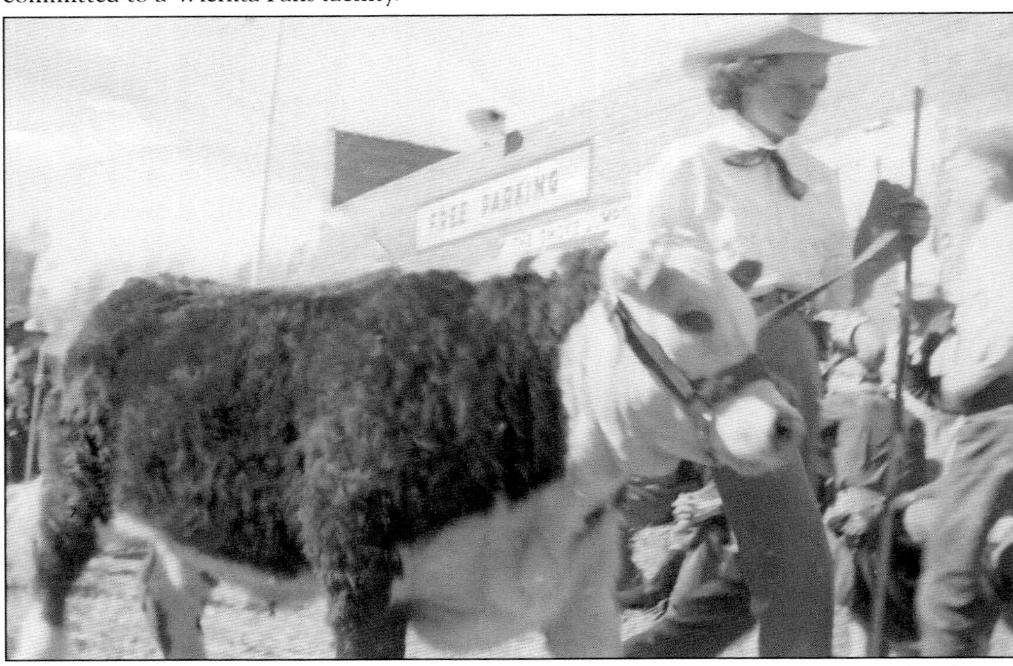

Another bit of history took place a little earlier. Sylvia Sheldon grew up working with calves on the Derrick ranch. At 15, she raised a calf to enter in the Moore County 4-H Livestock show. But rules stated girls could not enter. Her brother showed her calf. Rules changed in 1951. Sylvia was the first girl to show a calf in the annual livestock show. (Courtesy Bert Clifton.)

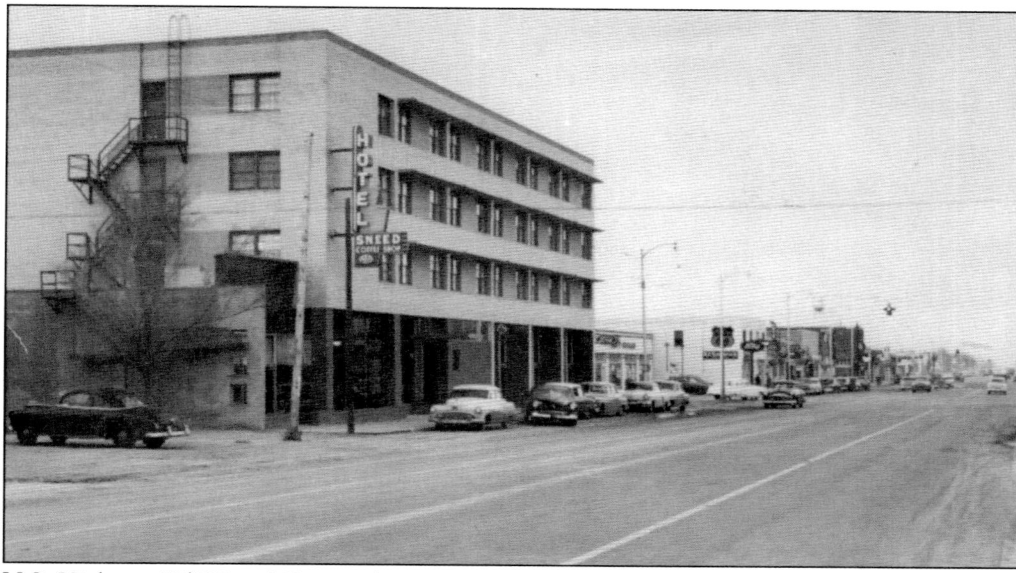

U.S. Highway 87/287 and Dumas Avenue are one and the same in Dumas. When cars became available after World War II, the highway brought more and more tourists. Sneed Hotel was built in the early 1950s to accommodate them. Later it became Flying A Hotel. When the business failed in the early 1970s, the building was donated to the county for an annex. It was vacated and demolished in about 2000.

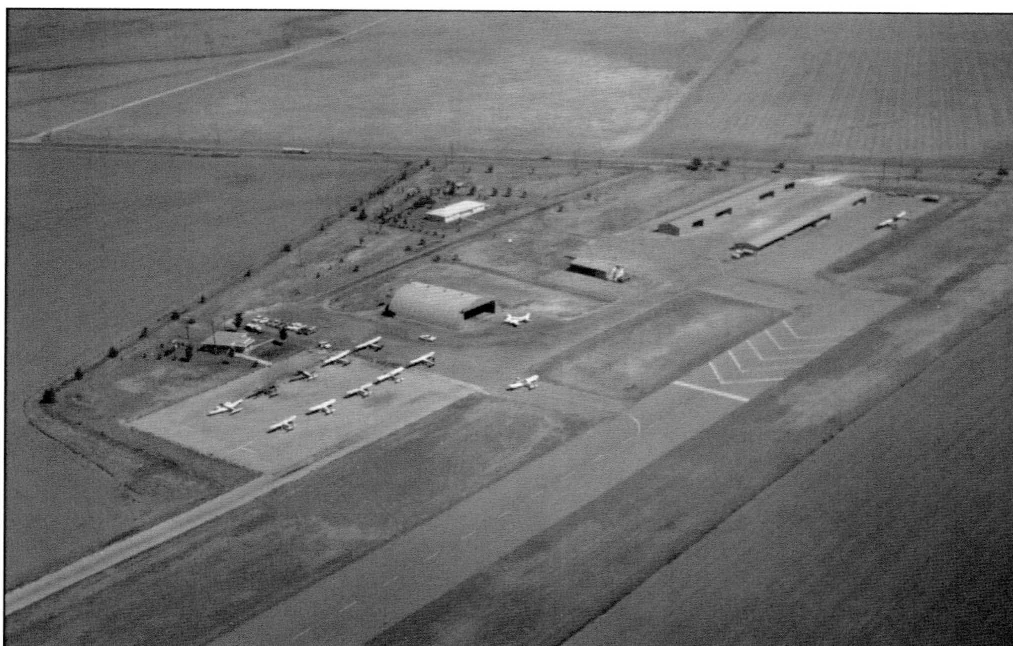

The small privately owned airport along the south edge of Dumas was closed sometime in the late 1940s. In the early 1950s, the county built this airport west of town. A number of additions and improvements have been made to the Moore County Airport. This photograph was made after one of those projects. The petroleum industry is responsible for much of today's traffic at the airport.

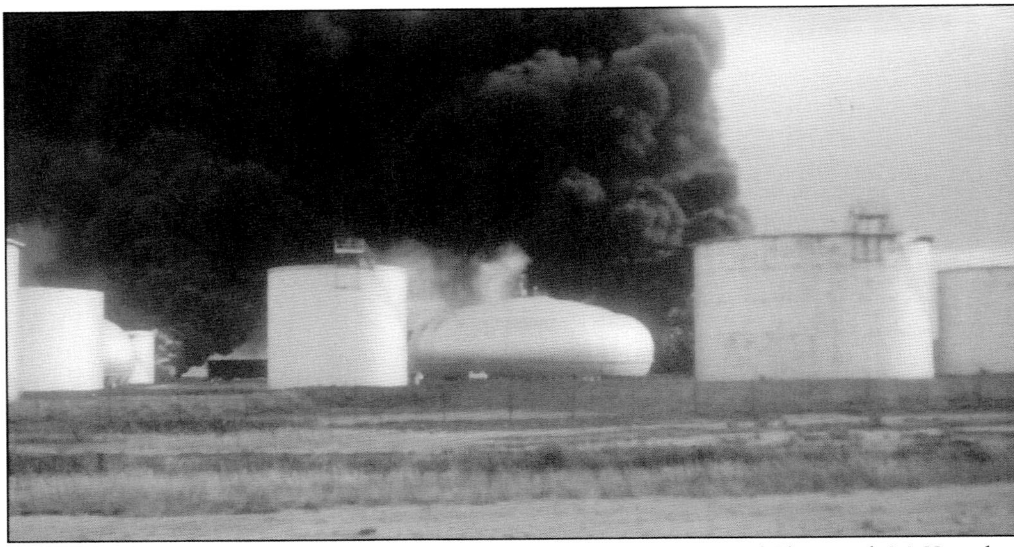

On Sunday morning, July 19, 1956, normal operations at the Diamond Shamrock McKee plant were suddenly and tragically disrupted. A 15,000-barrel tank, one of many in the tank farm, was on fire. Firemen and plant workers rushed to the scene. Shortly after, a horrific explosion occurred. Nineteen were killed and many others injured. (Courtesy Martha Crabb.)

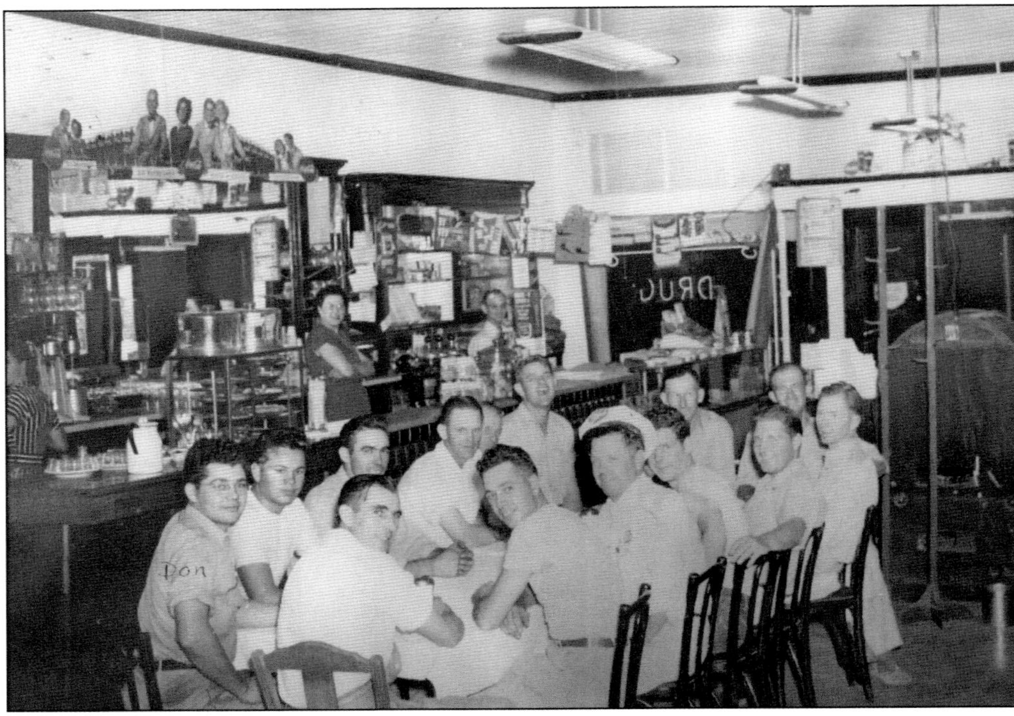

Don Thompson was active in the volunteer fire department beginning in the late 1940s or early 1950s. A group of the volunteers are enjoying a cup of coffee in C. R. Morris Drug. Thompson is identified in this photograph by his name written on his shirt. He was one of the casualties of the Diamond Shamrock fire. The worst industrial accident in Moore County's history is remembered each year with a memorial service on the courthouse square. (Courtesy Freda Keeney.)

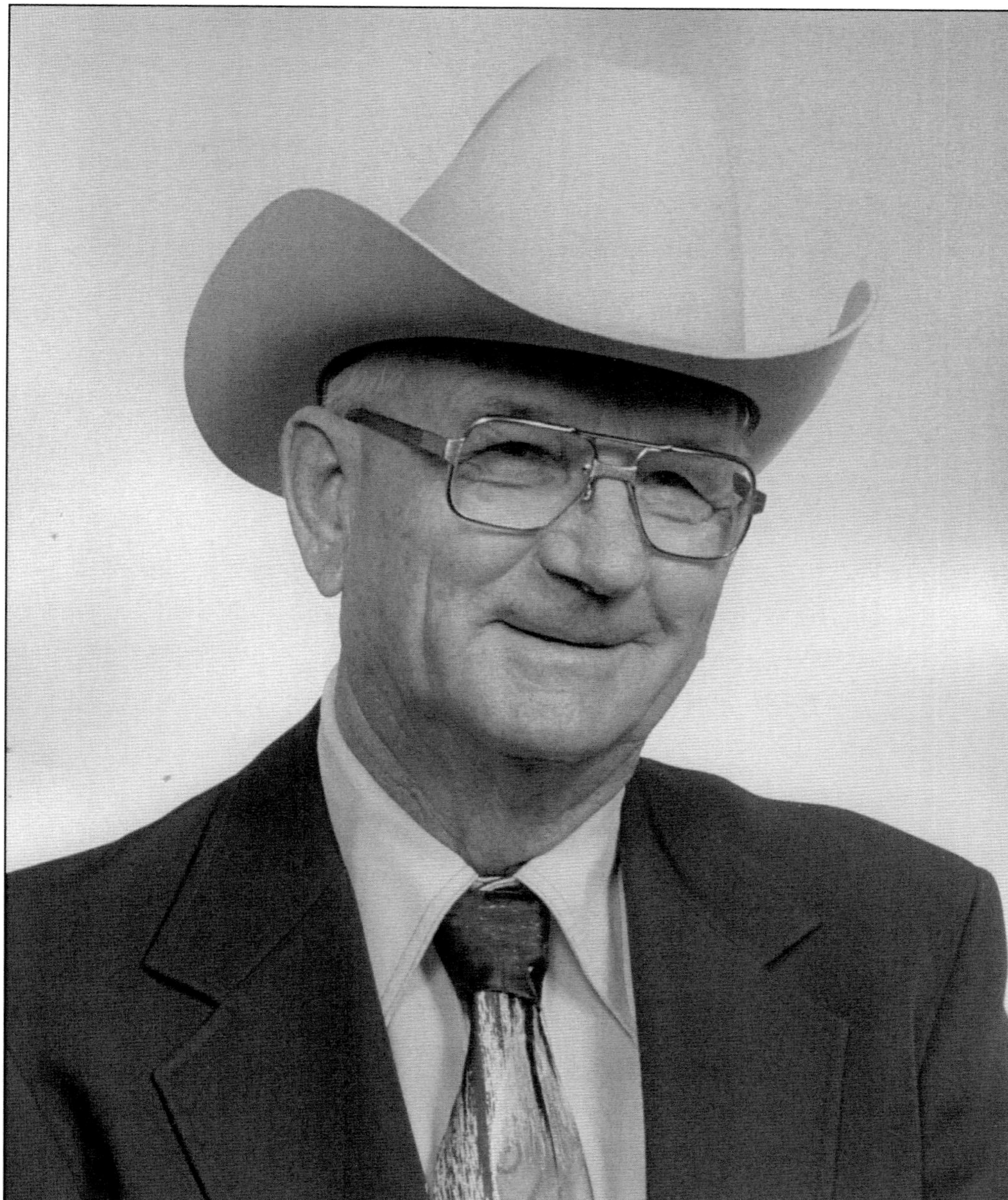

J. W. "Buck" Buchanan grew up in Hansford and Hutchinson Counties. He went to work as a cowboy at a young age. He worked for a time as manager of Borger's chamber of commerce. Many farmers had signed agreements with petroleum companies that prohibited using natural gas on their property for their own use. It was impractical to obtain gas from other sources to operate irrigation engines. Farmers were concerned that it could happen to their water rights. They formed a water district, located the office in Dumas, and hired Buchanan for the job. After three years on that job, he was elected state representative in 1958. He introduced a bill to allow petroleum companies to sell gas to the farmers without being rated as a utility company. It passed. Irrigation was made affordable and became common. It gave farmers the means to overcome some of the effects of drought.

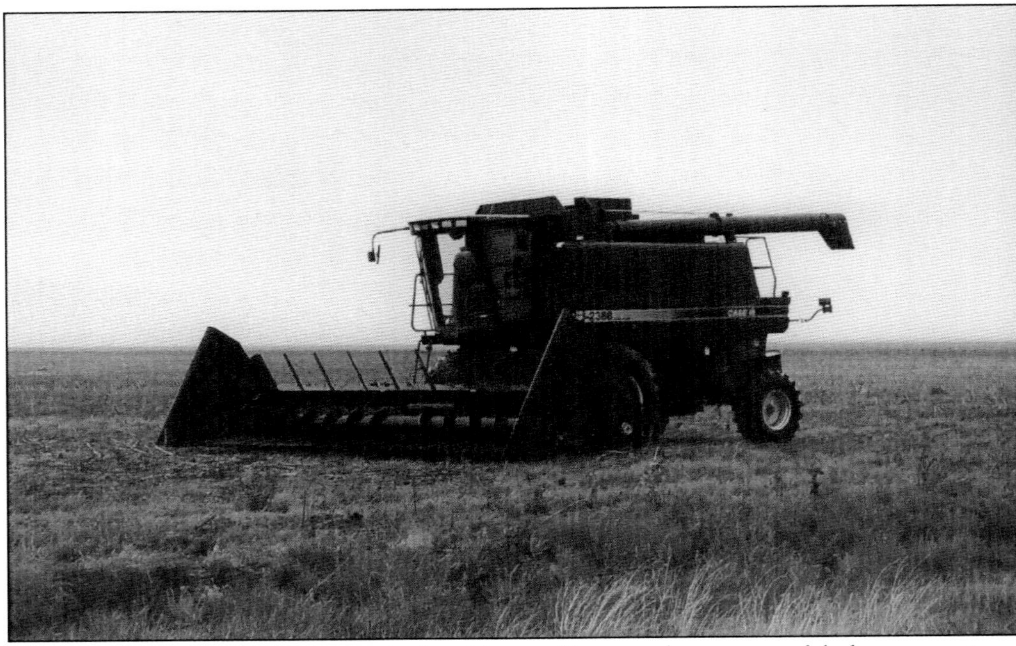

Combines have changed greatly in the last 60 years. Bigger and more powerful, they are equipped with computers to provide information as to how many acres and how many bushels have been cut and even the moisture in the grain. With its radio, power steering, and air-conditioning, one farmer stated running his combine was as comfortable as a smooth ride in his Cadillac. (Courtesy Dale Pearson.)

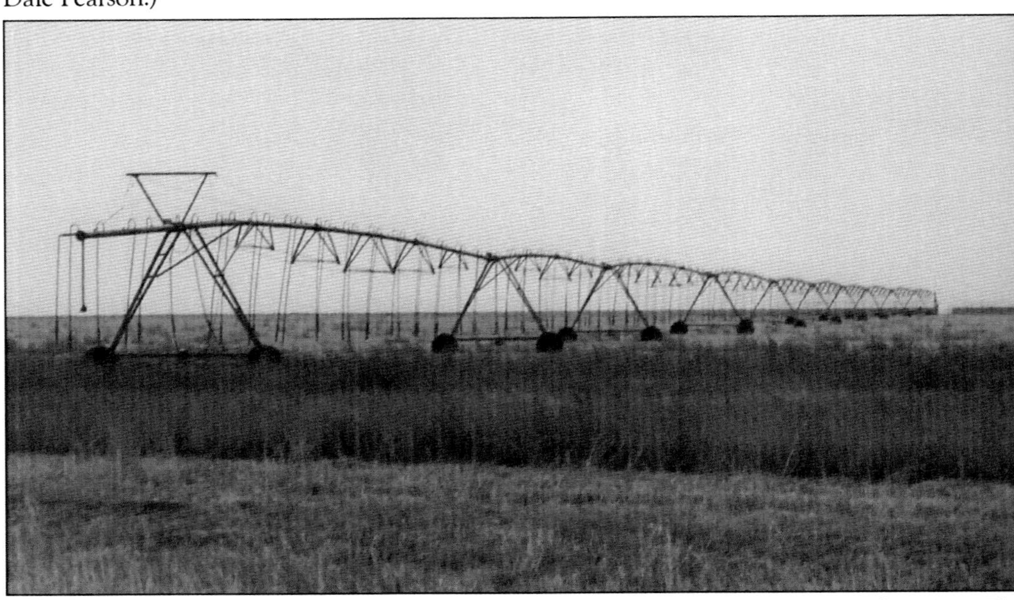

The first irrigation sprinkler systems in Moore County were installed in the early 1970s. The biggest advantage in sprinklers is the savings in water. Water often wound up in bar ditches when irrigating was done by rows. Today timers turn the water on and off, which relieves the farmer from midnight runs to change the water. Sprinkler systems can be up to a mile long. (Courtesy Dale Pearson.)

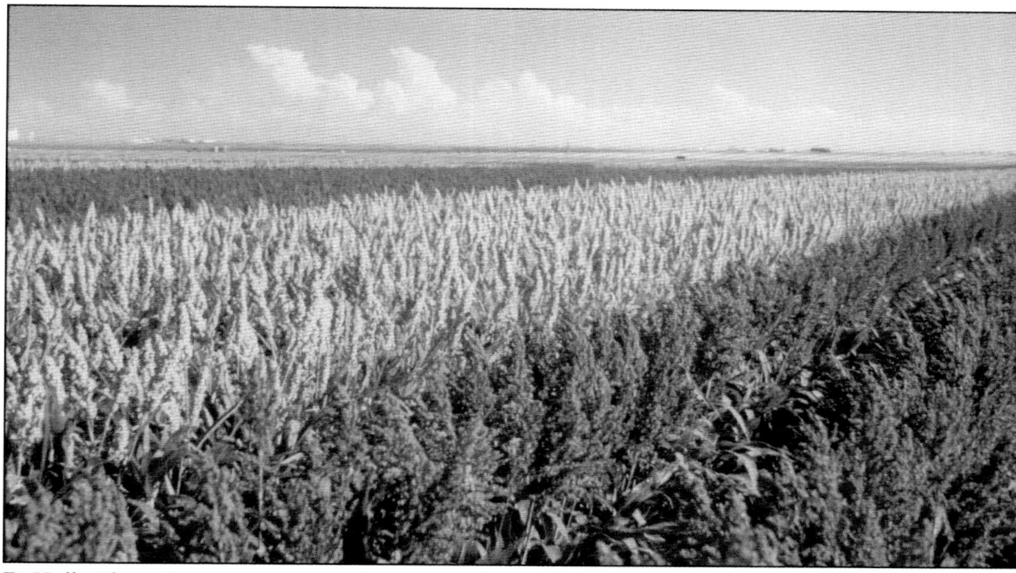

DeKalb-Pfizer Genetics came to Dumas in 1964. The company built a plant west of town and contracted with farmers to grow hybrid grain and forage sorghum for seed. From 300 to 400 seasonal workers were hired during summers to remove unwanted plants from the field. Male, the light-colored plants, and female, the dark, are arranged in a pattern for maximum pollination. Monsanto now owns the business. (Courtesy Darrel Reynolds.)

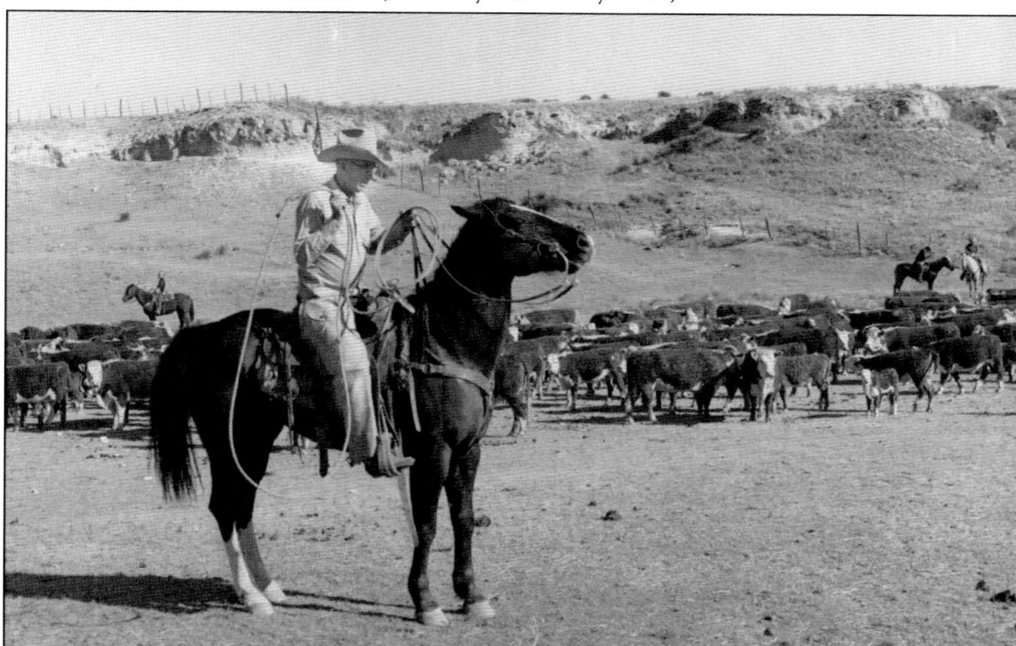

Rancher Arthur Arvel "Chuck" Perky ran cattle on four sections southeast of Dumas. He kept about 200 cows. When calves reached a certain age, he sold them. Here Perky, in the foreground, daughter and son-in-law Lola and Jess Starkey, and a neighbor, Johnny Cavitt, are getting the calves ready to ship. As was customary on ranches, Cavitt and Perky often traded work. (Courtesy Lola Starkey.)

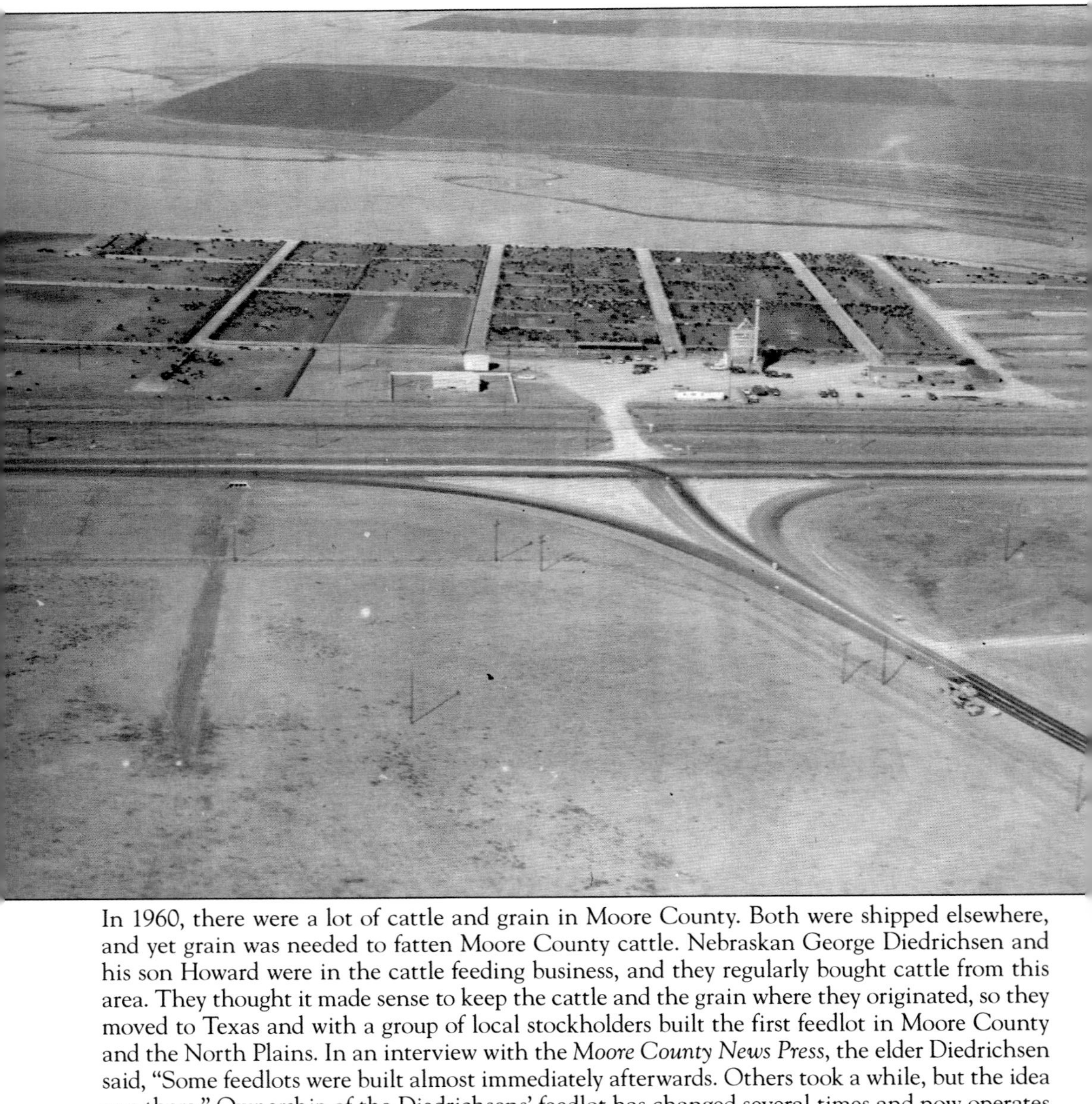

In 1960, there were a lot of cattle and grain in Moore County. Both were shipped elsewhere, and yet grain was needed to fatten Moore County cattle. Nebraskan George Diedrichsen and his son Howard were in the cattle feeding business, and they regularly bought cattle from this area. They thought it made sense to keep the cattle and the grain where they originated, so they moved to Texas and with a group of local stockholders built the first feedlot in Moore County and the North Plains. In an interview with the *Moore County News Press*, the elder Diedrichsen said, "Some feedlots were built almost immediately afterwards. Others took a while, but the idea was there." Ownership of the Diedrichsens' feedlot has changed several times and now operates under the name of Dumas Feeders. Originally built to handle 5,000 cattle, it now feeds an average of 22,000.

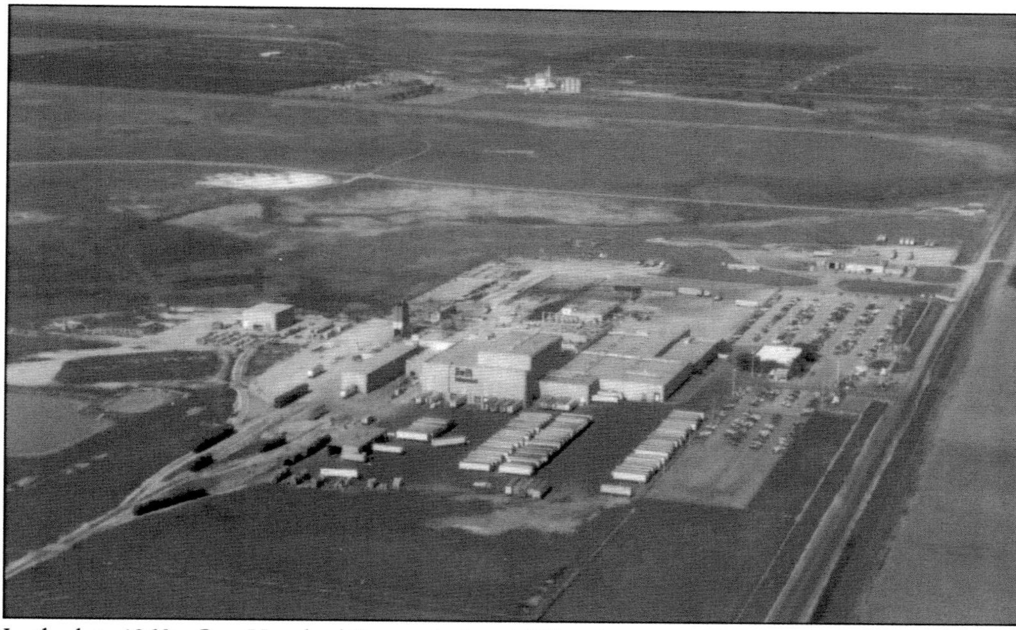

In the late 1960s, One Hundred Dumas Industrial Development, an organization to attract new industry to the area, and the Moore County Chamber of Commerce worked together to acquire 720 acres at Cactus on which to develop Schroeter Industrial Park. When American Zinc announced its closing in 1971, the groups went to work to bring a beef packing plant to the industrial park. In September that year, American Beef announced they would build. Construction was completed, approximately 600 workers hired, and production started. After approximately a year, American Beef declared bankruptcy. The plant was closed in January 1975. In September 1975, Swift Meat Packers opened the plant again. The plant has changed ownership several times since then and now operates under the name of JBS Swift.

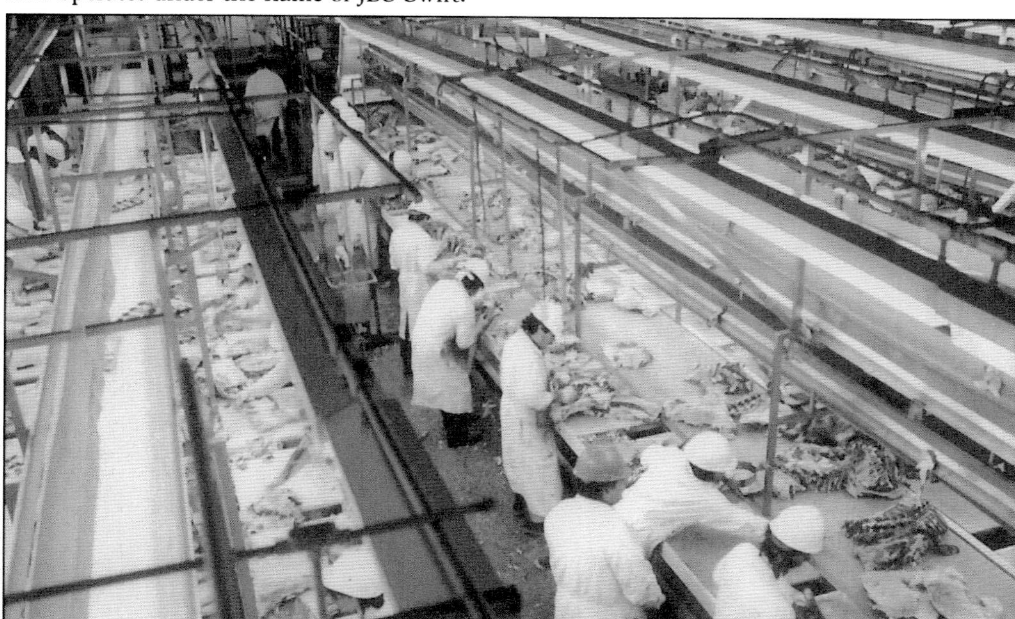

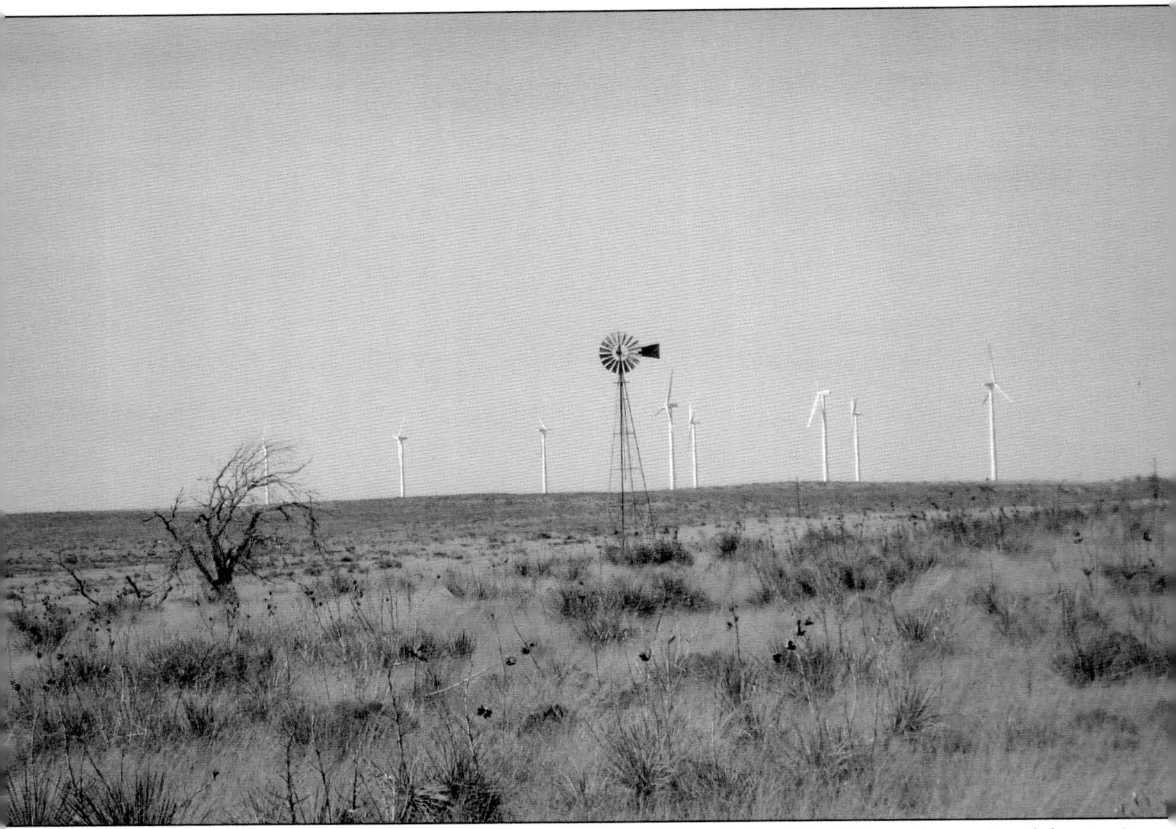

Steady growth has been the story of Dumas since 1950. Motels, bank buildings, doctors' and dentists' offices, and many new homes have been built. The hospital and schools have been expanded, and Amarillo Junior College has a Dumas campus. More than 20 churches are scattered throughout the city. A golf course, a community center and a YMCA have been built, along with parks and baseball fields. A large museum building was constructed, and a little later, an art center was built adjoining the museum. An excellent divided highway between Dumas and Amarillo makes trips there easier. On the farm, equipment became larger and much more efficient, and irrigation methods changed. Growth and change were ordinary during the last 60 years. The skyline just south of town has recently changed with these wind machines. Change keeps coming.

Seven

COMMUNITY

There used to be a sign at the edge of town that read, "Dumas, Texas: Home of 13,000 Friendly People And a Few Old Soreheads"

The population number was never updated, and the sign was only there for a few years. Just like any other community in the world, there was a bit of truth in that sign. But over time, it has been proven that even the old soreheads can be counted on when a need arises.

The same generosity that made possible new band uniforms in the 1930s and a new YMCA building in the 1970s responded to museum and senior citizens building campaigns in the early 21st century. The United Way campaign regularly exceeds its goals, and organizations not included in their program can also depend on backing. In addition to financial support, countless volunteer hours are given to the various organizations. From being a candy striper at the hospital to delivering Meals on Wheels, volunteers are there.

There is a large group of helping organizations in Dumas, and the following list is only a sampling: Red Cross, Salvation Army, Rotary Club, Noon Lions Club, Pilots Club, Business and Professional Women's Club, Masons, American Legion, Veterans of Foreign War, the Fraternal Order of Eagles, Dumas Area Crisis Pregnancy Center, Safe Place, and CASA 69.

The Moore County Citizens' Council, one of the first in the state in a small city, was organized in 2005. Its mission is to harness the power of Moore County citizens through education, training, and volunteer service to respond to the needs of victims in any emergency. When a tornado hit Cactus in the spring of 2007, organizations and individuals were on the scene immediately to help.

While the people of Dumas are generous, compassionate, and hardworking, they take time for fun, too. Playing golf or bridge or taking part in the YMCA activities are some of the year-round options. The most anticipated event of the entire year is Dogie Days, a four-day event, when fun is the only theme.

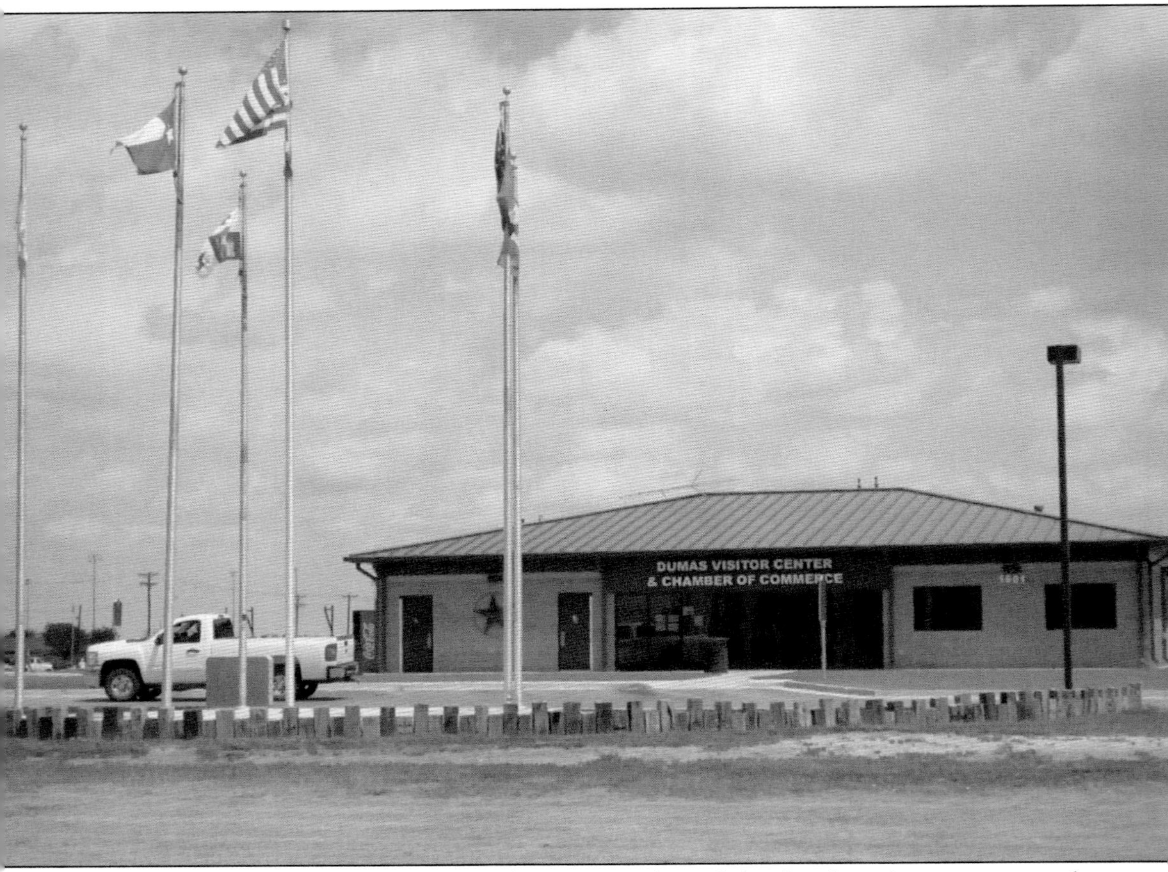

In 1927, Bob Powell and several other businessmen formed the chamber of commerce in order to get a highway and a railroad through Dumas, which they did. The chamber lasted only a few years. Other attempts, such as the Dumas Civic Club in 1937, also proved unsuccessful. The present chamber was organized in 1946 and has since actively promoted the city and county. Their success can be measured by the growth and prosperity across the area that continues to the present. A Women's Division is active in all the affairs of the chamber. An annual banquet honors citizens who make significant contributions to the community. (Courtesy Gayle Stowers.)

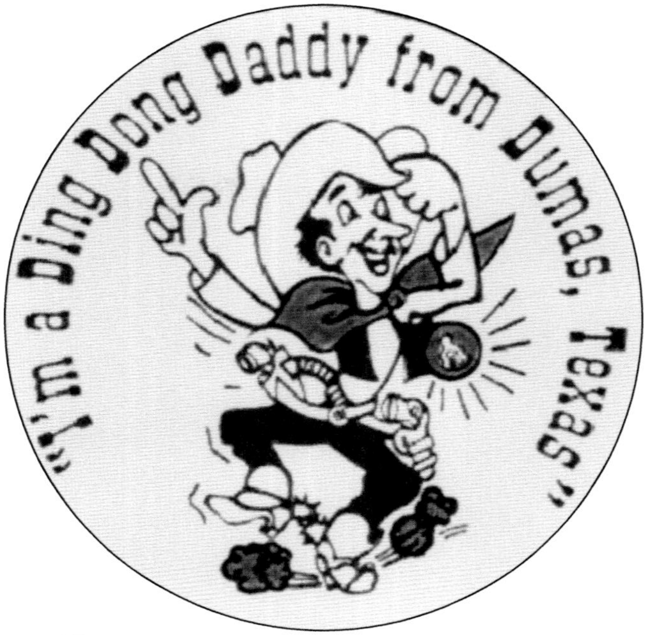

In its heyday, the song "Ding Dong Daddy from Dumas," by Phil Baxter, was played on radios around the world. Ken Duke chose the song as a theme song for the radio station KDDD, and he also commissioned an artist to create a character figure to bear the name Ding Dong Daddy. It became KDDD's logo. Moore County Chamber of Commerce adopted the logo a few years later. At some point along the way, a Ding Dong Dolly was created to go along with the Ding Dong Daddy. Plastic pins of the two characters are scattered across the country as visitors leave with the souvenirs, and Dumas folks carry them to faraway places. (Both, courtesy Moore County Chamber of Commerce.)

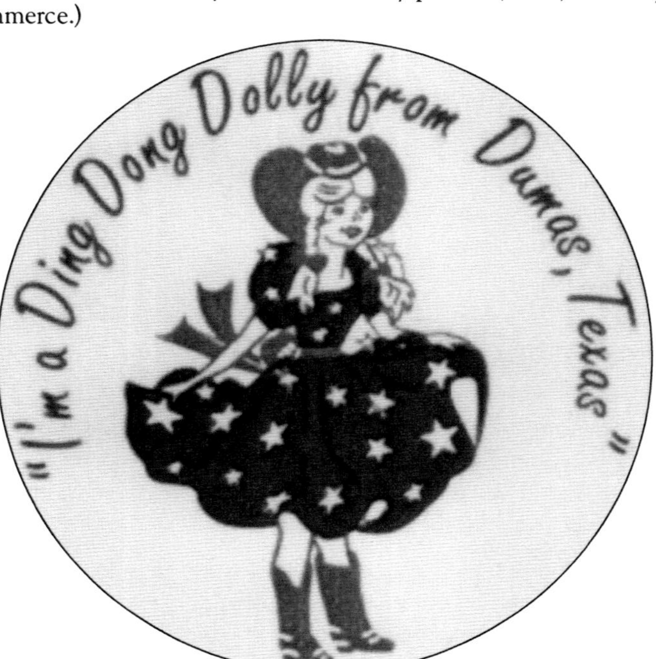

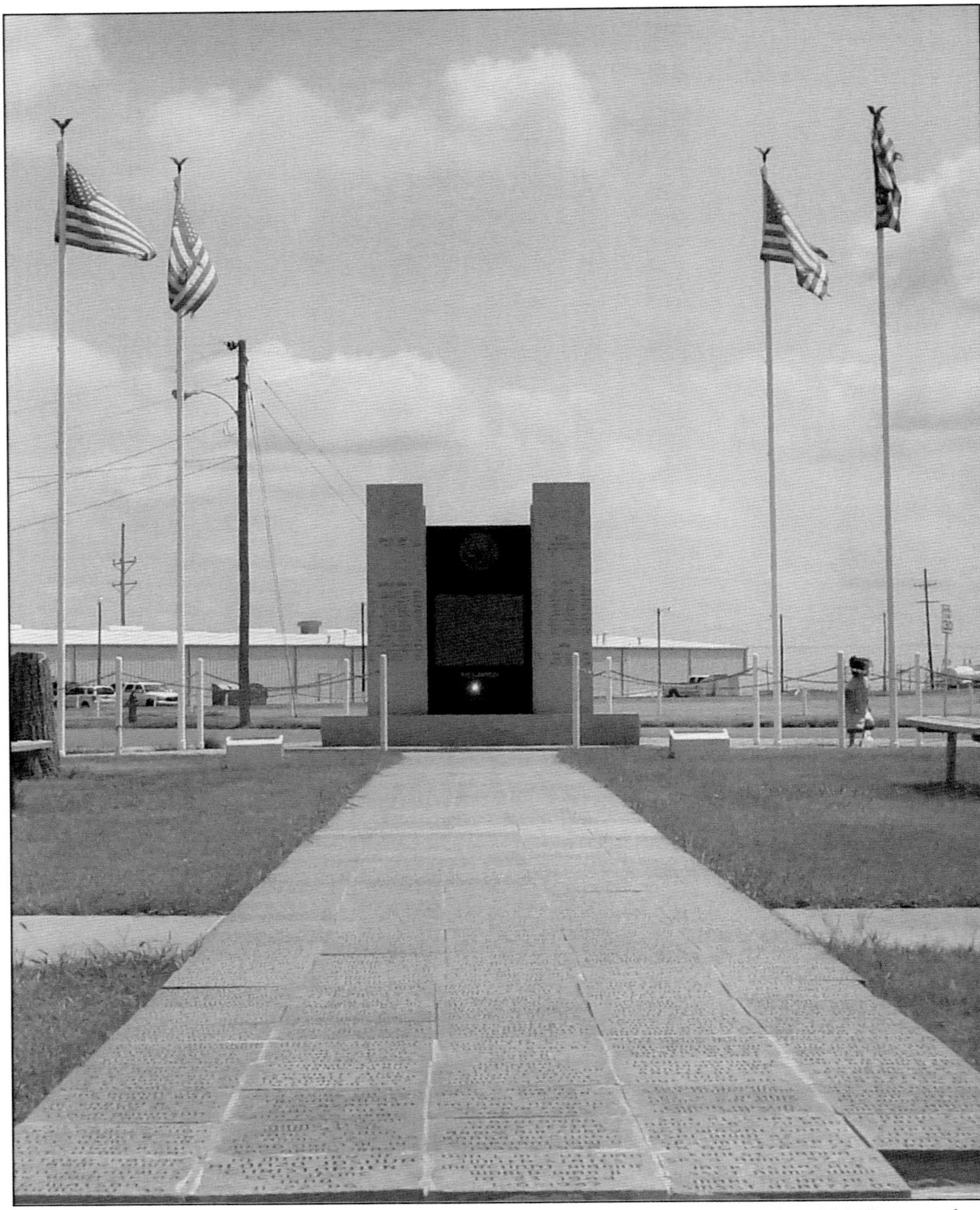

Post 9022 of the Veterans of Foreign Wars dedicated this monument on May 31, 1993. Engraved on the monument are the names of Moore County men who gave their lives in the armed services—1 in World War I, 15 in World War II, 11 in Korea, 10 in Vietnam, and 3 in Iraq. The walkway leading to the monument is made up of approximately 250 bricks, which were sold to erect the monument and to pay for etching other names. The monument is in the southeast corner of McDade Park. About 126 members are active in Post 9022. (Courtesy Gayle Stowers.)

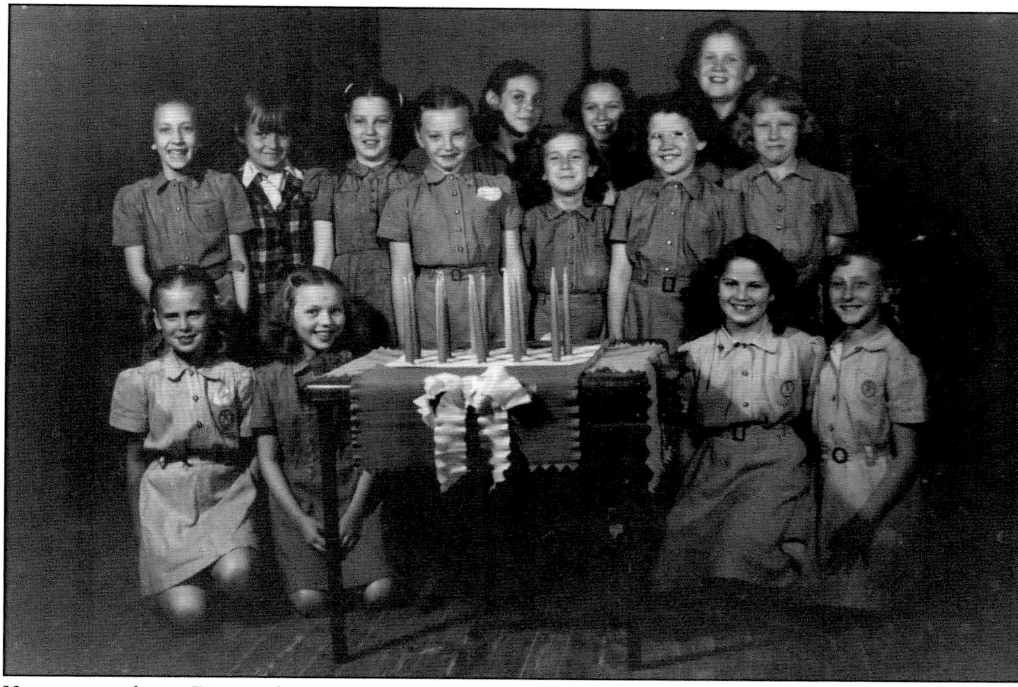

Young people in Dumas have a variety of recreational activities to choose from. The Dumas Scouting programs were organized in the early 1930s. Today between 240 and 250 girls and boys are learning the basics of good citizenship and experiencing the personal growth offered in Scouting. With a membership of approximately 2,900, the YMCA offers a variety of sports and activities, with soccer, basketball, volleyball, and swimming being the most popular. Competitive baseball was played in Dumas as early as 1910, and there are nearly 600 boys and girls involved in Little League programs each year and 80 to 85 in the Babe Ruth League. The Moore County Youth Football program involves about 250 young players.

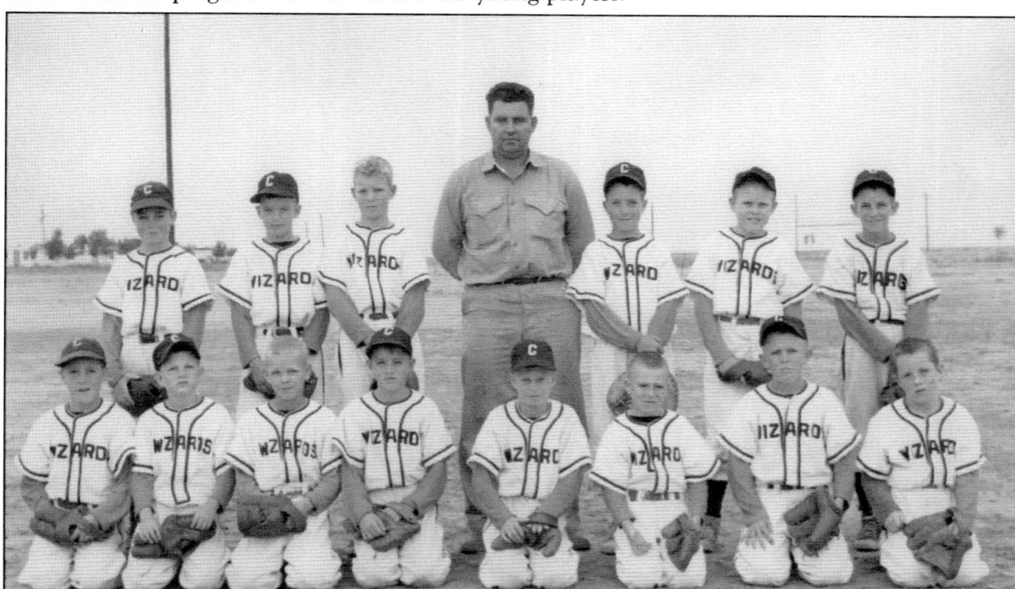

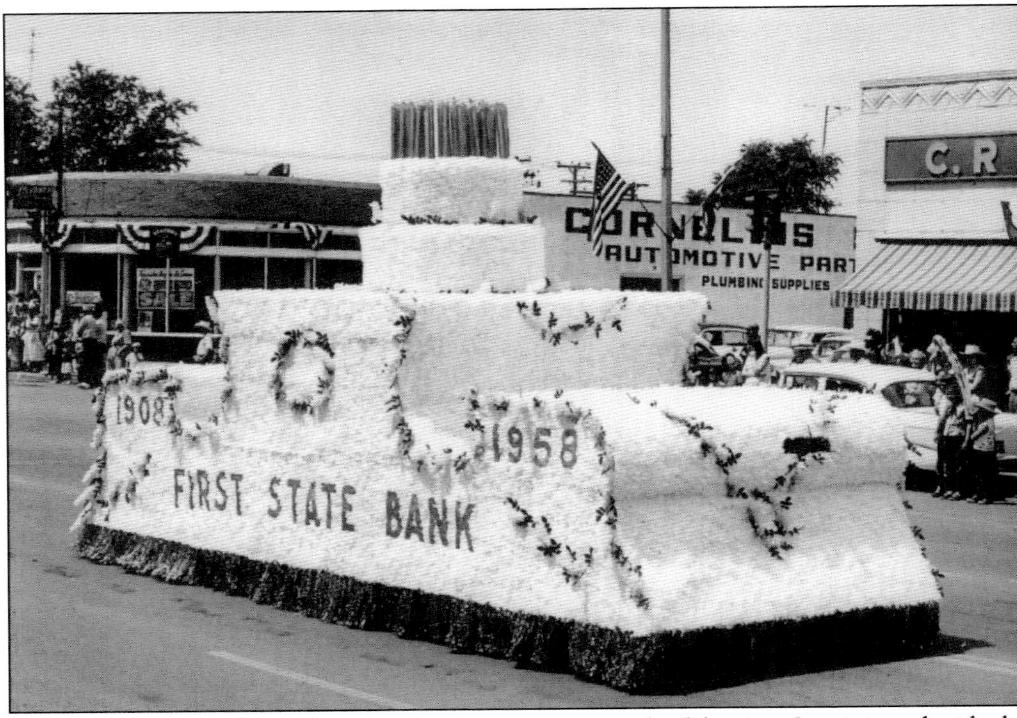

Dogie Days, held the second weekend in June, is an annual celebration. It originated with the annual Old Settlers Reunion picnic held on the courthouse square. In 1946, Lions Club took over the celebration, gave it a new name, had the first barbecue, and contracted a midway for games and concession stands. Today's celebration features a parade, barbecue, and carnival.

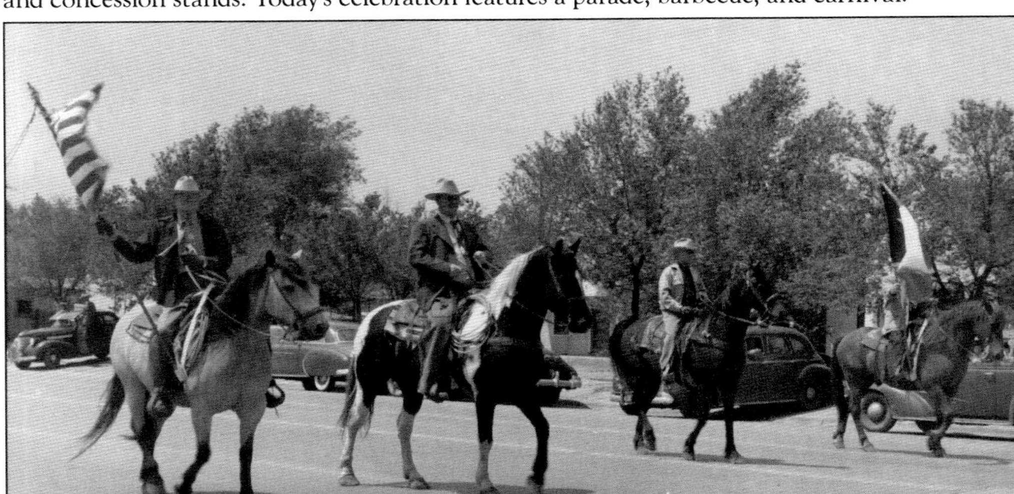

Heading up the parade are four Moore County pioneers. They were all children when they came to Moore County between the years 1894 and 1905. On the left is Lew Haile, a county commissioner for 42 years, longer than any other commissioner in the state. The others from left to right are Tom Record, Charlie Bennett, and R. L. "Boss" Crump, sheriff from 1924 to 1928.

Because of ever increasing crowds, the Lions Club moved the barbecue to McDade Park in 1977. Beef is prepared days ahead, marinated with a secret combination of seasonings, wrapped, and refrigerated until the day before the barbecue. It is placed into an open pit and a fire made with stacks of wood. After about 14 hours, it is ready to serve. The beans are cooked in these huge pots being tended Lions. (Courtesy Herb Harter.)

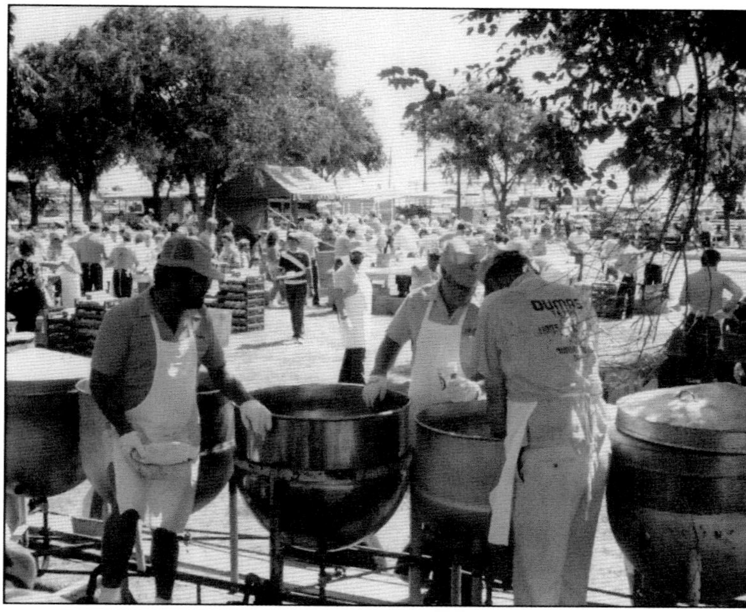

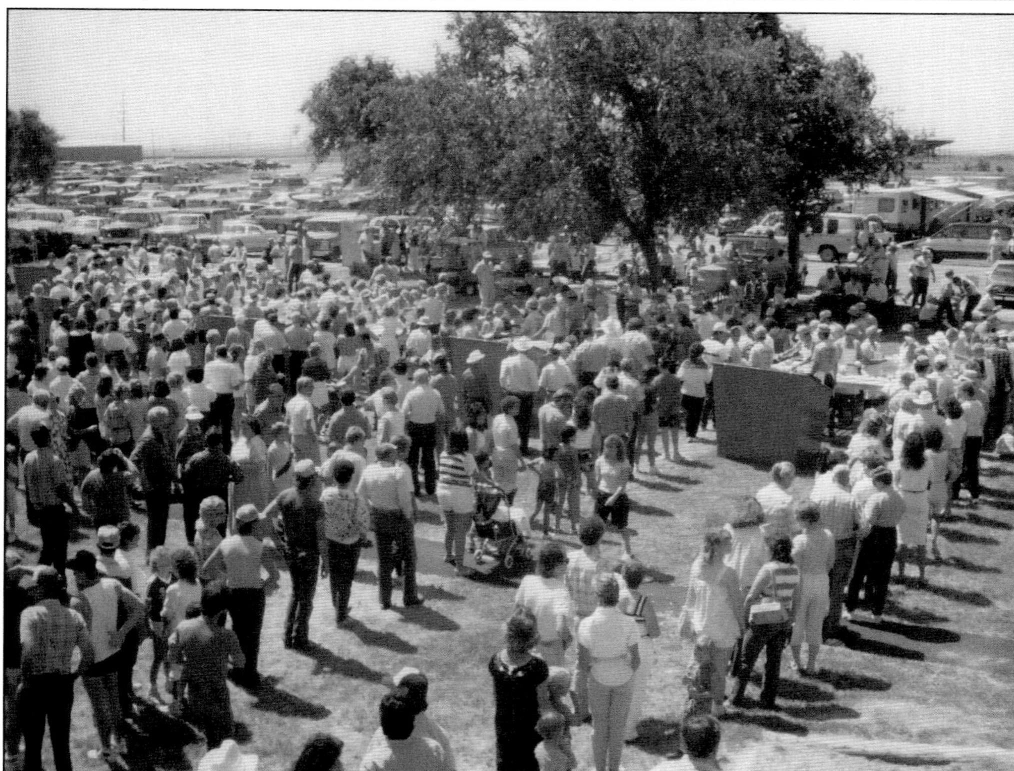

While Lions Club members are making the final preparations, long lines of people begin to form a little after 11:00 a.m. to wait for their plates of barbecue with beans, pickles, onions, bread, and peaches. Average attendance runs from 6,000 to 7,000 persons. Proceeds from all Dogie Days activities go to the many charitable causes the Lions Club supports. (Courtesy Herb Harter.)

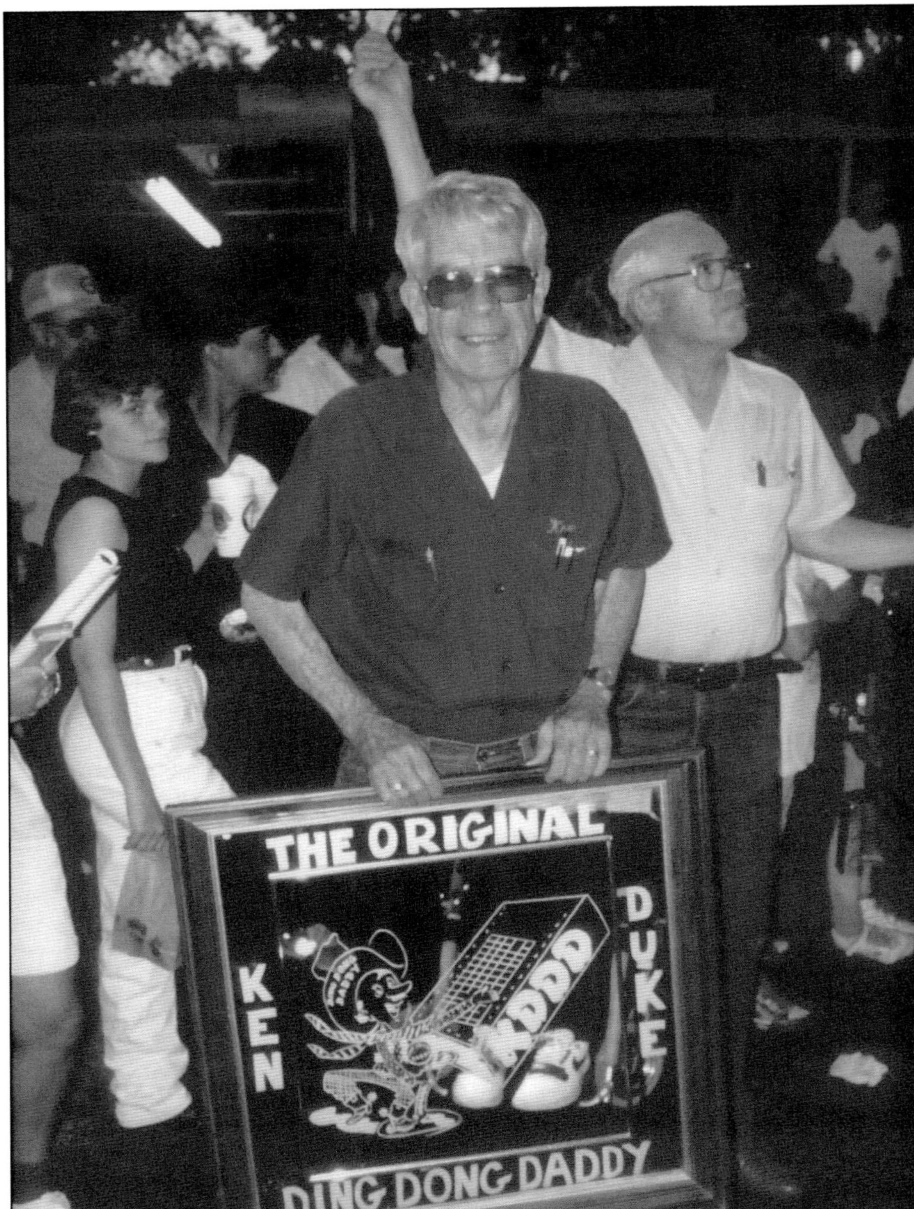

It is unlikely there has ever been a more dedicated fan of Dumas and the Dumas Demons than Ken Duke of KDDD radio. His enthusiasm was evident in the colorful commentaries he made during the hundreds of games he announced. He served on the boards of 100 DID, Inc. (Dumas Industrial Development), Memorial Hospital, the chamber of commerce, and the Noon Lions Club. He was honored for his many contributions to the community at a Dogie Days celebration. Shortly before his death, he was interviewed by Jan Thomas of WOAI radio station, San Antonio, and Bert Clifton, director of the Moore County Historical Museum. Thomas was researching the background of the song "Ding Dong Daddy from Dumas." Knowing Duke's attachment to the song and image, Thomas asked, "Do you like being called the original Ding Dong Daddy?" He replied, "I think if anyone deserves it, maybe I do." (Courtesy Herb Harter.)

Eight

Preserving Our Heritage

The Moore County Art Association, Inc., had its beginning in the late 1940s in Mil Boyd's kitchen, where she and other artists gathered to discuss their projects. It was chartered in 1954. In the mid-1970s, the association, with about 80 members, needed a place to show their work. They asked for the ballroom in the old hotel building that had been donated to the county for an annex. Their work was displayed there during the summer of 1975. The name Tumbleweed Gallery was chosen for their temporary showroom.

The art association agreed that another group, interested in a historical museum, could bring historical artifacts to display along with their art. Approximately 2,000 visitors were registered during the summer.

The historical group pursued the idea of a museum and was granted use of the room in the annex for a permanent location. Artists gradually moved their work out, and work on the museum began. The Moore County Historical Museum was organized, officers elected, artifacts collected, and displays built. The grand opening was held in July 1976 and was housed in that location until 2001, when construction of the new building at 1820 South Dumas Avenue was complete. Upon the move, the board gave the museum a new name: Window on the Plains Museum.

Individual contributions are invaluable in preserving Dumas's history. Noel McDade left a journal to the museum that covered most of his adult life. Ezell Fox, Jay B. Funk, Streatfield Cox, and others left their photograph collections. Jessie Glynn Burnett's photograph collection is in the museum. She left a sizable endowment to the museum that initiated a fund-raising campaign for a new building.

Ineze Crabb, a founding member of the art association, and her husband, Jim, donated land for the association's first building. In November 1987, a bazaar was held in the Crabb Art Center. In 2004, that building was sold and a new one built adjoining the museum. It is named simply the Art Center.

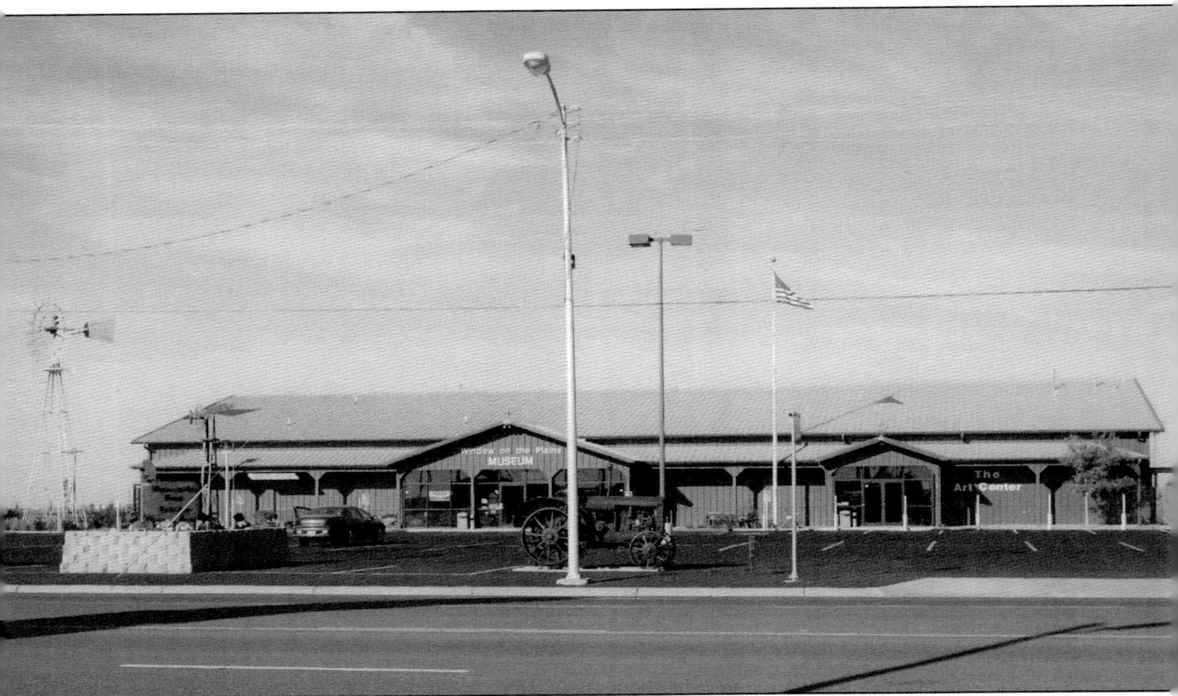

The museum and art center are located on nearly 10 acres of land on the busy U.S. Highway 87/287. Since the new museum building was occupied, a 60-by-120-foot addition has been completed for displaying agricultural and industrial artifacts. Antique farm machinery, a pump jack, and a huge industrial engine are some of the displays that have been built outside. A walking trail winds through those displays for easy and convenient viewing by visitors. Fifty volunteers assist Terri George, director, in daily operations. There is an average of 5,000 visitors annually. Of those visitors, nearly 1,000 are students. Skits and tours are prepared for them. They regularly have exhibits featuring artists from around the area. (Courtesy Carolyn Stallwitz.)

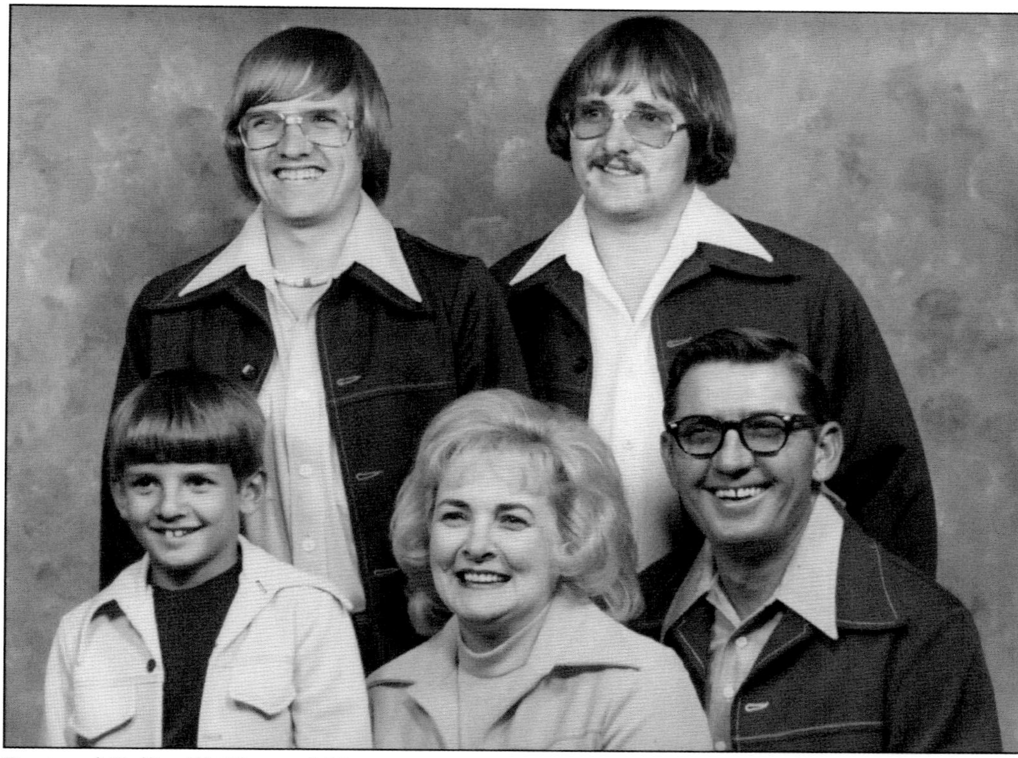

Patti and Collier Phillips and 50 others were involved in founding the historical museum. Collier was elected president of the board, and Patti became the first director. The entire Phillips family was involved in getting the museum started. The boys helped build displays, pick up artifacts, and do other chores. From left to right are Bobby, Billy, Patti, Jim, and Collier. (Photograph by Olan Mills, courtesy Jim Phillips and Patti Phillips-Dennis.)

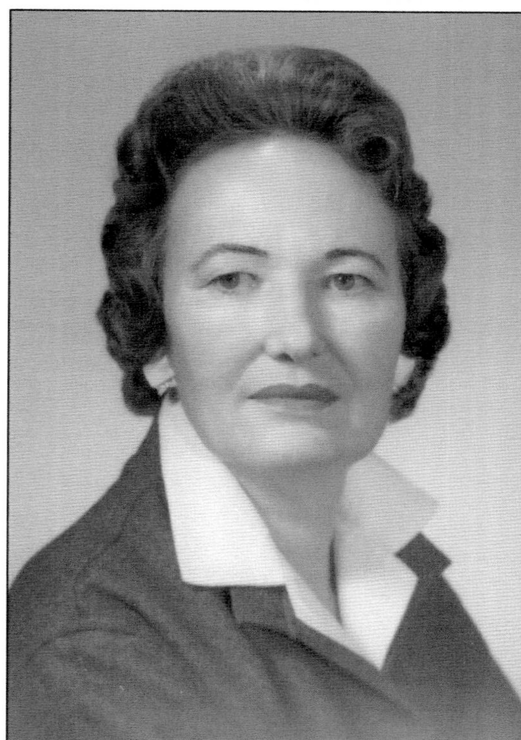

Mil Boyd was a talented artist, art judge, and art teacher. The Moore County Art Association had its beginning in her kitchen, and she was also instrumental in getting the museum started. She was involved in other civic projects, but her passion was art and sharing her knowledge of it with others. The studio in the art center is named for Mil Boyd.

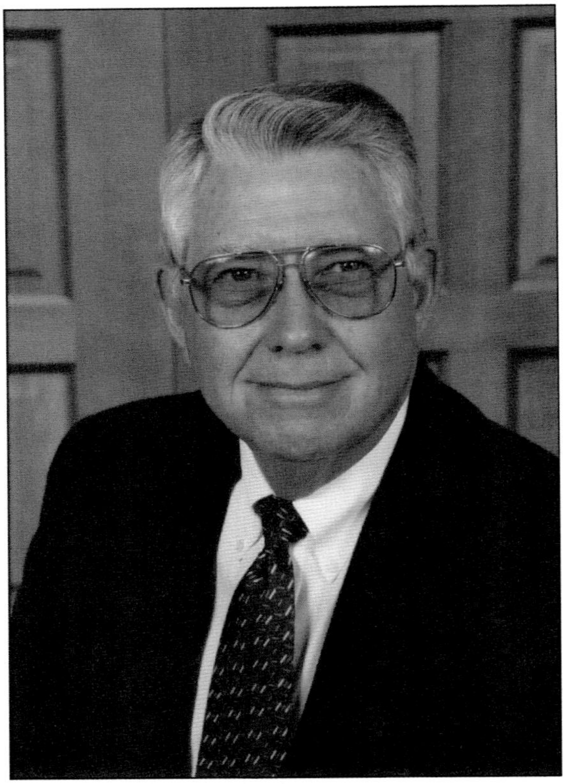

The museum has no advocate more faithful than Wayne Edwards. He served on the first board of directors in 1976, and he is on the present board—with no break in his service. He is unequalled as a fund-raiser. His skill and expertise were put to good use during the fund-raising campaign for the new building. (Courtesy Fern Edwards.)

Another founder, Woods Coffee Jr., remained dedicated to preserving history throughout his lifetime. He was enthusiastic about getting the museum started and served on its first board. He also served on the Moore County Historical Commission and helped to obtain several historical markers. His writings about his life in the area are on file at the museum.

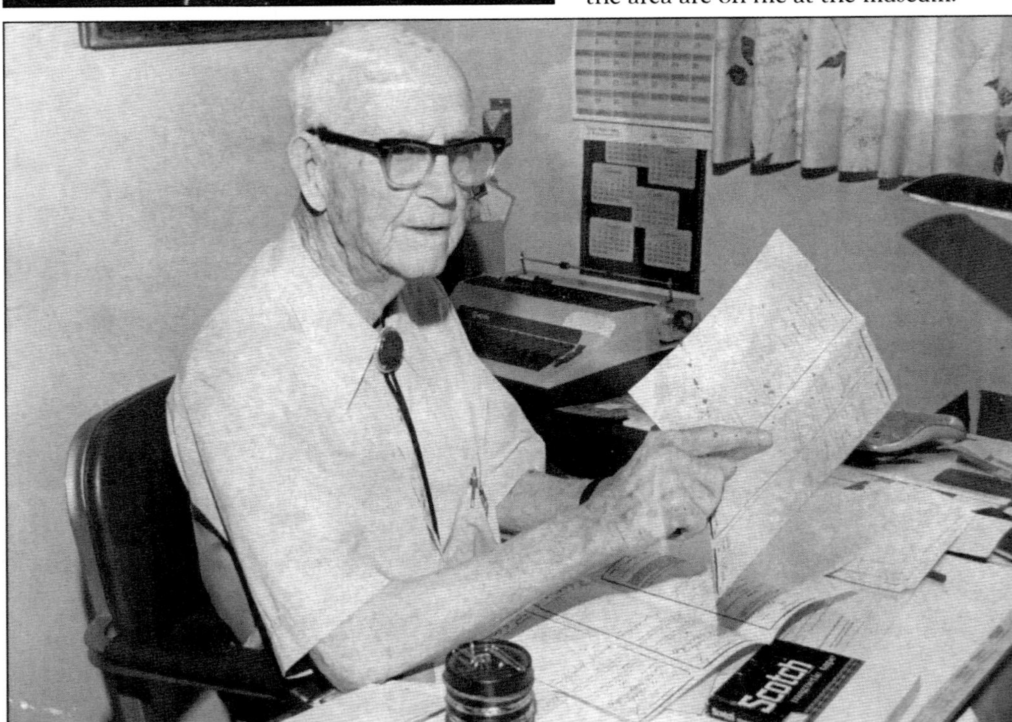

Bert Clifton (right) went to work for the museum in 1981. She was assistant director until 1988, when she became director and curator. She retired 10 years later, but that did not end her interest. Recently she was recognized for 10 years as a volunteer in the museum. Oiling saddles is one of the chores she recently tackled. Helping her is summer intern Anna Reznik. (Courtesy Gayle Stowers.)

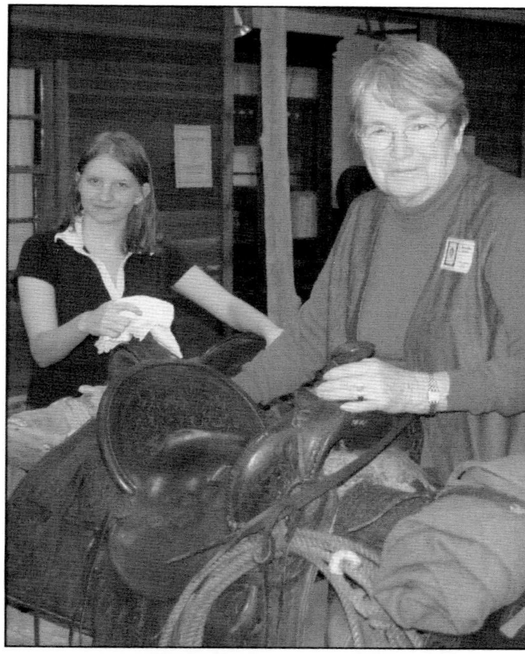

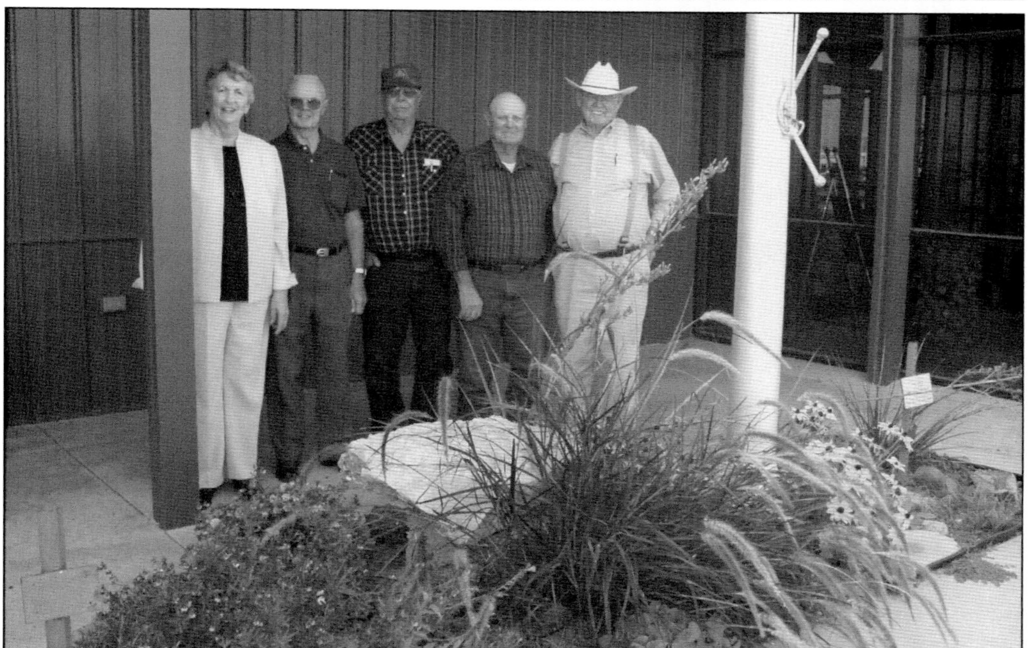

Moore County Historical Commission's purpose is to recognize and preserve historically important sites. Historical markers are scattered throughout the county. Another project involves filming interviews with longtime Moore County citizens. Films are donated to the museum. From left to right, current members are Louise George, Dr. Arthur "Rusty" Davidson, Harold Dean Morton, Eddie Stallwitz, and R. O. McMurry. Not pictured are Jay Stewart, Lynn Cartrite, and Howard Bose. (Courtesy Gayle Stowers.)

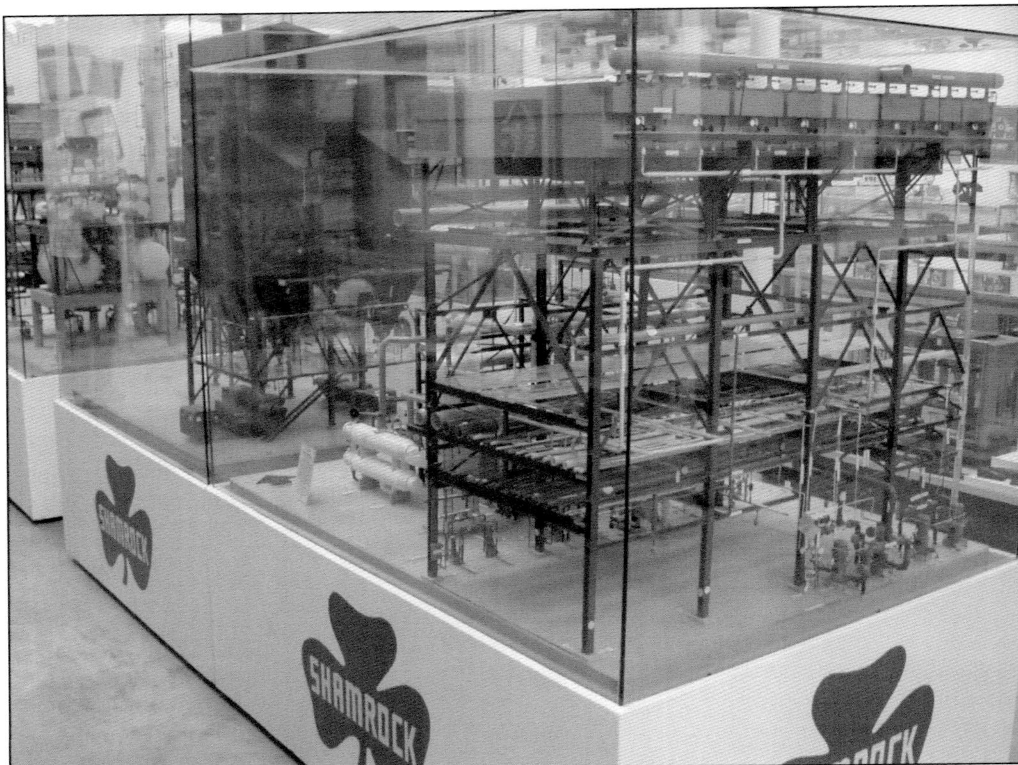

In the room dedicated to artifacts from industry and agriculture is this scale model of the Diamond Shamrock McKee plant. There are scale models of several other plants and dozens of artifacts from other Dumas industries. The agricultural display features a collection of barbed wire and a number of small implements used on the farm. (Courtesy Gayle Stowers.)

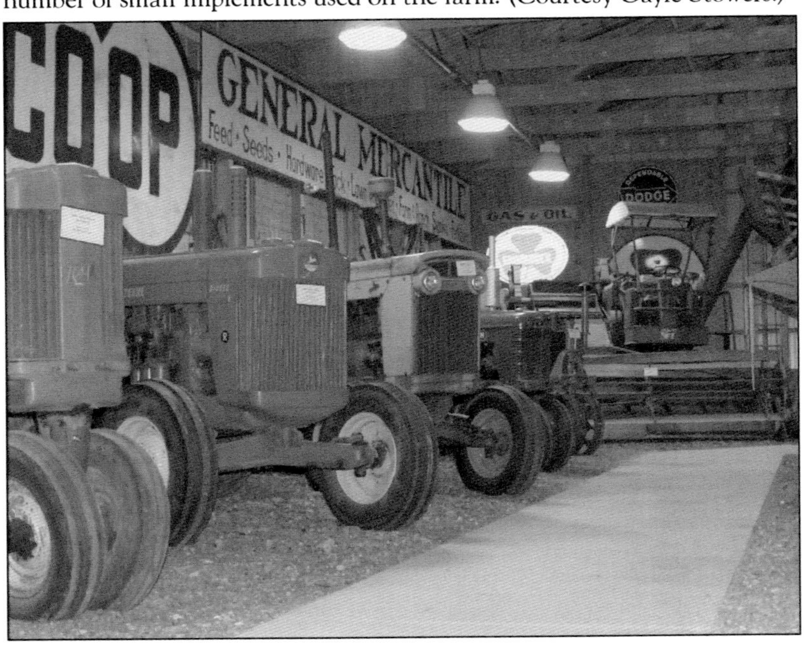

This row of antique tractors is in the addition behind the main building. To the right of the tractors is a McCormick Deering D31 combine of the 1930s. There are a number of other antique tractors, combines, trucks, and pieces of farm equipment, in addition to a huge collection of tools. (Courtesy Gayle Stowers.)

A. L. Anderson bought the blacksmith shop in 1912 and operated it until his death in 1934. His son Frank took over, added a machine shop, and ran it until the mid-1940s. This entire display was taken from the shop. The weathered lumber used in the display was donated by Harold Dean Morton. (Courtesy Gayle Stowers.)

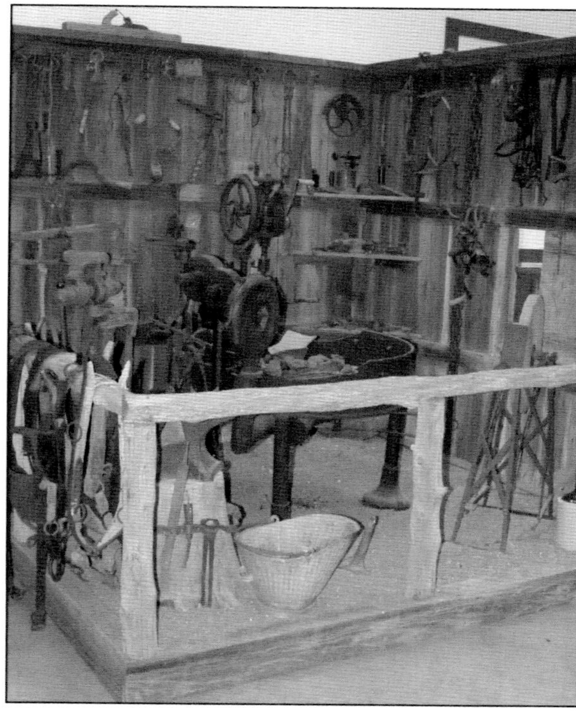

Volunteers tore down old barns and other buildings to collect weathered lumber to build a street scene as it might have appeared in the early 1900s. Vic Lewis designed the plans and was master carpenter. Jerry Pflug, Kurt Stallwitz, Eddie Stallwitz, Marvin Clifton, Delton Emmett, and Doug Beck spent hundreds of hours on the project. No value can be placed on their contribution. (Courtesy Gayle Stowers.)

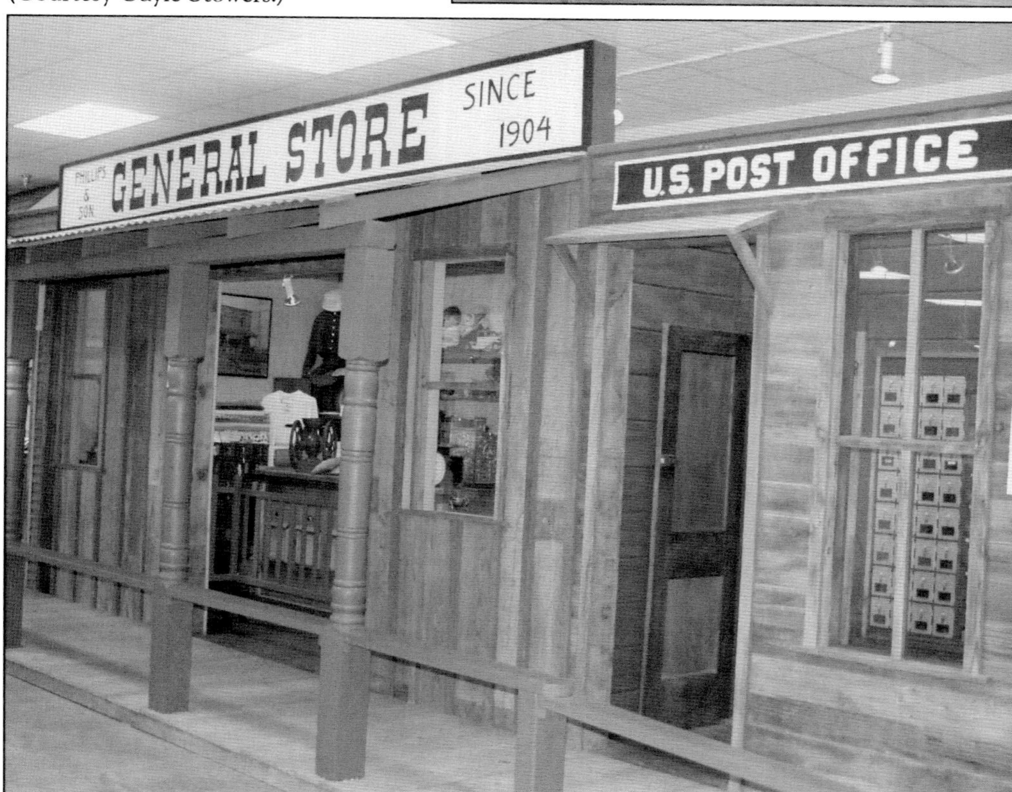

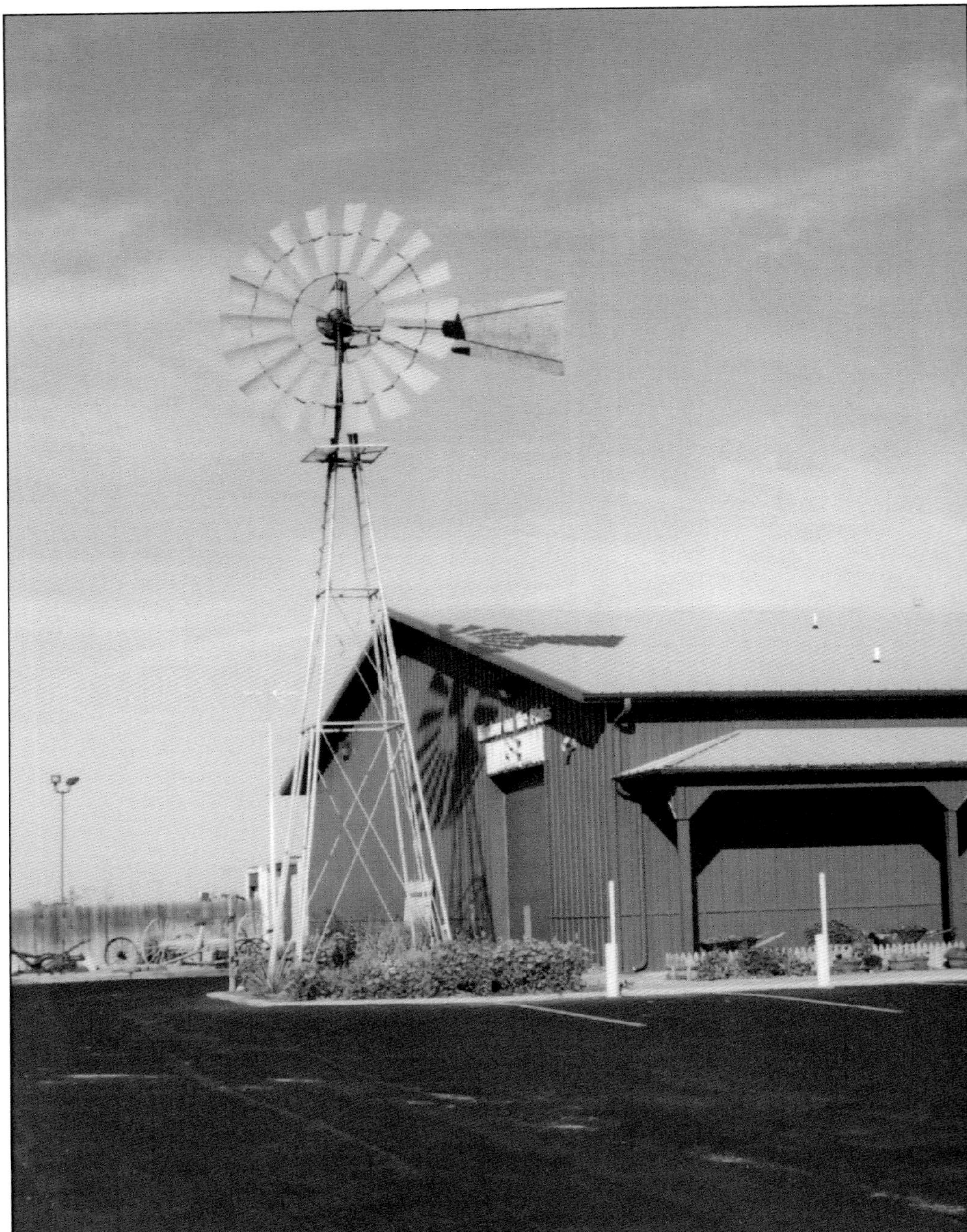

Window on the Plains Museum is a valuable asset to the people of Dumas, Texas. Protection and display of artifacts is the primary mission of the museum, but its service to the community goes further. Special tours are planned for school students, but tours are provided for other groups as well. Upon request, a program will be presented at a school, nursing home, or meetings of other organizations. There are two open house events during the year, one in late summer and another at Christmas. For a small fee, clubs or businesses can use the conference room. Volunteers make it all possible.

Bibliography

First Baptist Church of Dumas. *A History of First Baptist Church, 1894–1994*. Dallas, TX: Taylor Publishing, 1994.

Funk, Jay B. and James C. Jarrett. *Moore County, Memories That Count*. Canyon, TX: Staked Plains Press, 1986.

Jones, Ruth Ann. *Pioneer Partners, Thomas and Molly Bugbee*. Amarillo, TX: Copperleaf Press, 1996.

Moore County Centennial Committee. *100 Moore Years*. Baltimore, MD: Gateway Press, 1992.

Moore County Historical Commission. *Moore Sunrises . . . Sunsets*. Dallas, TX: Taylor Publishing Company, 1985.

Rathjen, Frederick W. *The Texas Panhandle Frontier*. Lubbock, TX: Texas Tech University Press, 1973.

Robertson, Pauline Durrett, and R. L. Robertson. *Cowman's Country*. Amarillo, TX: Paramount Publishing, 1981.

———. *Panhandle Pilgrimage*. Amarillo, TX: Paramount Publishing, 1976.

Thomas, Myrna Tryon. *The Windswept Land: A History of Moore County, Texas*. Dumas, TX: self-published, 1967.

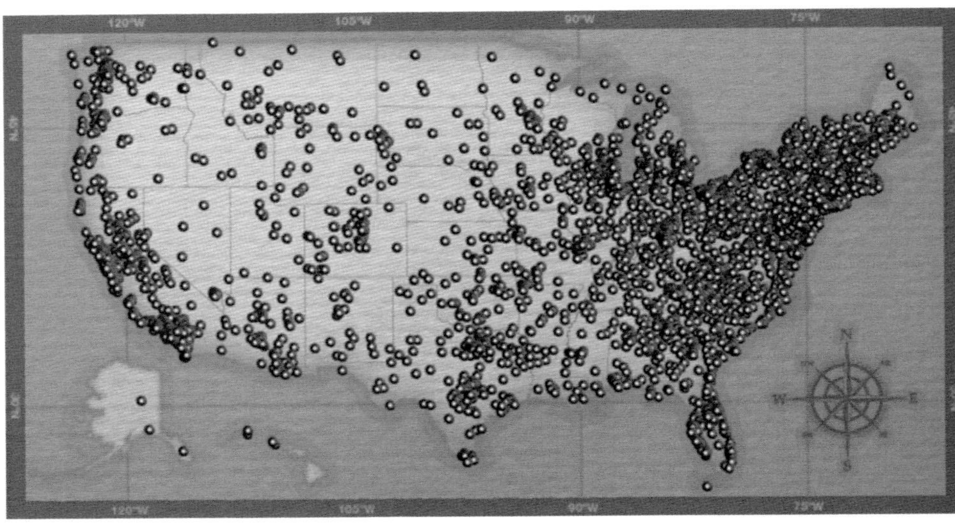